TEDDY BALDOCK

THE PRIDE OF POPLAR

The story of Britain's Youngest Ever
Boxing World Champion

TEDDY BALDOCK

THE PRIDE OF POPLAR

The story of Britain's Youngest Ever
Boxing World Champion

Brian Belton

Historical Editor Martin Sax

Contents

	FOREWORD	11
	INTRODUCTION	13
1	BORN TO BOX	19
2	FROM STREET FIGHTER TO JOCKEY	27
3	BALDOCK THE PRO	31
4	NOBLE HUMILITY	41
5	MUMTAZ MAHAL AND FIFTEEN THREES	49
6	THE UNBEATABLE STRAIGHT LEFT	67
7	BANTAM BALDOCK	79
8	TO AMERICA	85
9	STRONG AS A BLEEDIN' LION	117
10	THE WORLD CHAMPIONSHIP COMES TO POPLAR	127
11	BALDOCK IN DEMAND	137
12	THE CROWD EXPECTED A SHOW	153
13	THE CHAMPIONSHIP OF THE EAST END	167
14	FIGHTING, FIGHTING, FIGHTING	183
15	FOR THE LOVE OF MAISIE	195
16	PANAMA AL AT LAST	199
17	THE GOLDEN ROAD HAD TURNED TO DUST	207
18	LIFE OUTSIDE THE RING	213
	TEDDY BALDOCK CAREER TIMELINE	229
	BIBLIOGRAPHY	276
	EPILOGUE	279

Dedication:
To My Father
Jim Belton
No ordinary man.

Acknowledgements:
Martin Sax (Teddy Baldock's grandson), without whom the memory of
Teddy Baldock would have continued to fade and whose dedicated work
made this book possible.
All those who have shared their memories and knowledge for the sake of a
fighter's legacy.

FOREWORD

By Duke McKenzie, Three Times World Boxing Champion at Different Weights, Trainer and Commentator

I will never forget the day I won a world title for the first time. It was 5 October 1988 and I was due to fight the Champion, Rolando Bohol of the Philippines, in front of my fans at Wembley for the IBF flyweight title. I was 25, and had been a professional boxer for six years. Two years earlier, I had beaten Charlie Magri to become the European Champion. That result really made people sit up and take notice of me, but the fight against Bohol was when it was all on the line.

It always killed me to make flyweight; at 5ft 7in; I was a big guy for 8st, and I had been impossible to live with for weeks. Colin Smith, my trainer, had got me into the best possible shape, and my manager Mickey Duff insisted I was ready. But I can just remember being petrified that I might get knocked out, even though I had never lost.

I just didn't want to be embarrassed in front of all those people. Bohol was a southpaw, but that didn't bother me. My brothers Clinton and Dudley were both southpaws so I was used to the style and everything he could do. But, honest to God, I didn't think I could win until about the ninth round. I remember Colin telling me to look in the other corner, and I could see Bohol was blowing and that his head was down.

It was then I knew I could be the champion, and after that he fell apart and I stopped him in the 11th round. My brothers jumped in the ring, and they were hugging me. I was on Dudley's shoulders, and there were tears – not so much of joy, but relief, relief that it was over and that I'd done it; I was Champion of the World.

It wasn't until later, when the interviews were being done and I was talking to Harry Carpenter on BBC Television and John Rawling for BBC Radio, that my emotional state began to change. I was unwinding. It was over, and I could start to be me again.

Perhaps in my career I had better fights, maybe better performances, but winning that first title was so special. And I believe it would have been exactly the same for Teddy Baldock, except that he was just 19 when he became the World Bantamweight Champion in 1927. He won his title at the Royal Albert Hall in London, in front of his own people, and he became a hero of his time, when boxing was massively popular. He must have enjoyed the adulation, and become something of a sporting icon. Yet he was burned out by the time he was 24 and would ultimately finish his life sleeping rough on the streets of London or living in hostels for down-and-outs. It is a sad story and, in its way, a human tragedy.

I never made a fortune from boxing, so fair-weather friends were never going to get rich on my back, and I had strong people around me who made sure that I looked after myself and kept my feet on the ground. I was never much of a drinker, and family has always been everything to me. But that doesn't mean to say I have not seen the sort of temptations that might lead a young boxer to squander his money and damage his health.

Boxers are probably among the most emotionally vulnerable athletes on the planet. They experience highs and lows from the day and hour that they decide to take up the profession. Constantly making weight, going without food and fluids, is torture in itself. And at the same time, you are supposed to be trying to live like a normal everyday guy. And that is now. Back in the 1920s, they really knew very little about nutrition and the science of training.

Being a former champion, I know where Teddy Baldock came from. Just another young kid who had a massive following, who tasted fame but died penniless. Maybe he couldn't differentiate between friends and hangers-on. Perhaps he was ultimately too generous for his own good. But he would be forgotten without works such as this, and that would be the saddest fate of all for a man who once ruled the world.

INTRODUCTION

By Martin Sax

My grandfather, Teddy Baldock, was and still is (at 19 years and 347 days old) Great Britain's youngest ever boxing World Champion and the only British boxer to win a world title during the 1920s. His fight for the vacant World Bantamweight Championship, which took place at the Albert Hall on 5 May 1927, was the first contest for a world title fought in Britain since the 'Mighty Atom', Jimmy Wilde, defeated Young Zulu Kid at the Holborn Stadium, London, for the World Flyweight crown on 18 December 1916. This made Baldock a landmark sportsman and for a time a national hero. Yet sadly, and almost inexplicably, his name and achievements are hardly heard about in boxing circles today and he is practically unrecognised in British sporting history.

I never met my grandfather, I was just two years old when he died in 1971 and by that stage he was already living rough on the streets or in 'common lodging houses' around London. His marriage to my grandmother was long since over and he had not been in contact with my mother, Teddy's daughter, for many years.

I first knew of his boxing past when I was about 15 years of age, after my mother had been up in the attic and found some old scrapbooks that my grandmother had kept. My mother remembered there had once been a large chest full of photographs, press cuttings, programmes, trophies, etc. but unfortunately she could not remember what happened to it all. Perhaps it had been given away or sold. Who knows? But by just looking at what was left I was instantly hooked. The grandfather I had never met immediately became a hero in my mind.

Unfortunately, my mother, Pam, a wonderful lady, had only sad memories of the father who had walked out of her life when she was just a young girl. She really didn't know much about his achievements in the ring and the iconic status he once held.

It was after I left school that I started finding out more about my grandfather, the man who had thrilled packed boxing arenas for almost a decade. It started with a visit to the *Boxing News* offices in London when I was invited by the then editor, the late Harry Mullen, to view a portfolio of over 70 photos they possessed of my grandfather; it was a fantastic find and I will always be grateful to the *Boxing News* staff for giving me the opportunity to see them.

I spent many months in the British Newspaper Library at Colindale, North London, reading through every copy of *Boxing* from 1921 to 1931 and also the main newspapers of that era, having every article copied in order to make a scrapbook to chart my grandfather's boxing career. I placed adverts in boxing magazines and overall used every method I could think of to gain information about Teddy Baldock.

My research over the last 20 years has been a fulfilling journey, during which I have acquired film footage; photographs and original programmes, including my grandfather's world-title fight with Archie Bell. I have met the families of sparring partners, opponents and past champions with whom my grandfather had been associated. I even received a letter from the late Reggie Kray stating that he and Ron had been great fans of my grandfather, telling how they had given him two shillings and sixpence out of their five-pound winnings from their pro-fight debut at Mile End Arena as they knew he was an old fighter who had fallen on hard times.

Since creating the Teddy Baldock website, I have had emails from sons and grandsons of people my grandfather fought. I must now have the biggest collection of memorabilia on Teddy Baldock, which I hope will remain in the family for posterity. However, I can't help but think that all this might not have been necessary had his life taken a different path after he retired from boxing.

This book is the culmination of what I have discovered over the years about a grandfather I never knew, and my mother now tells me, 'You know more about my dad now than I ever did.' It tells a story of his rise from the roots of boxing in London's East End to the very heights of what the sport could provide more than 80 years ago, and his journey from that dizzying pinnacle into the mists of obscurity and ring mythology.

It is the story of a man who was blinkered to the pitfalls of success – an ordinary man who did extraordinary things. It is the tale of an almost super-human talent undermined by all-too-human flaws. The mistakes were his to make and make them he did. But, even so, he was helped along this self-destructive path by those 'hangers-on', endemic to boxing, who masquerade as friends. Without them things might have been different, but we'll never know.

In spite of his failings outside the ring, his achievements within it mark him out as someone special. I will always be proud to say that in an age when it really meant something my grandfather was Champion of the World.

Teddy Baldock – The Pride of Poplar.

The Story of Britain's Youngest Ever Boxing World Champion

AUTHOR'S NOTE ON RESEARCH STYLE

I have drawn on material produced over close to 90 years to inform the pages that follow. Many records of boxing results that have been developed in the contemporary period are unavoidably incomplete; Teddy Baldock himself had many more fights than those about which records survive. At the same time, some records produced in the 1920s are often not as reliable as their modern counterparts. Records of fights could be 'bespoke', made to fit political, financial or social exigencies. Although it would be unfair to say this was common, there has been anecdotal material over the years enough to override any argument that such practices did not occur. Wartime destruction, changing interests and 'ownership' of boxing and genuine mistakes and oversights have also had a cost, in terms of attaining perfect accuracy. I have also included Teddy Baldock's own chronicled recollections, drawn from a range of media and whenever possible kept his memories intact, both out of respect for the man but also to stay true to the spirit of narrative research and 'hearing the true voice', albeit sometimes 'flawed'.

As such there are some details included in this book that modern records might disagree with or not include. Where possible (and mostly) I have conformed with current material, but I have also included referrals to contests made within time frames closer to the pre-Second World War period that today cannot be found in some of the contemporary literature. For example, in 1950 'Boxing News' referred to a particular fighter claiming two victories over a 'champion' by 1925 although existing records show that the 'champion' didn't win his first title until 1928 and provide no evidence that the two fighters met at all. However, I have embraced the referral to the two fights as true because the lack of collaboration in modern records is as likely to mean that the records are imperfect as it is that the fights didn't happen. That said, I have engineered the insinuation that the contests were against a then current champion in line with modern historical consensus.

Overall, I have tried not to let pedantry spoil the story being told – avoiding detailing diversions and disagreements between particular records and accounts drawn from 100 years of history – while maintaining the effort to make that story as accurate and as respectful of Teddy Baldock and his time as possible.

The truth about biographical research with its roots over a century old is that it will never be premised on guaranteed certainty and is always going to be more or less an exercise in compromise, certainly if it is to be more a story of a life lived and the frailties incumbent in that, than a mere list of sanitised events.

1

BORN TO BOX

While I was researching this book, more than once it was suggested to me that what I was writing might be thought of as Britain's *Cinderella Man*. However, the biography of 'Lightning Fists' Teddy Baldock, the 'Pride of Poplar', bears little resemblance to the life of James J. Braddock (who, fighting Lou Barba, was on the same bill as Teddy on 12 November 1926, when the East London lad fought and beat Tommy Lorenzo at the Pioneer Athletic Club in New York). Teddy was a different, and in some ways a much more complex, personality, and the conclusion of his tale is far removed from the happy ending of the 2005 Ron Howard film. But, while there is also a possibility that Baldock's life might be seen as a typical boxing rags to riches and back to rags proverb, Teddy did not helplessly fall after a meteoric rise as seems to be taken as the archetypal account of so many pugilists' lives, particularly from his era. Later, Teddy didn't seem to have thwarted dreams, the building blocks of regret, the foundation of despair. He appeared to cruise though life, almost blindly trusting in its tides to keep him afloat. Baldock was a man apparently uninhibited by whatever difficulties he encountered; he appeared to manage the vicissitudes of existence mostly by ignoring or even dismissing them, often with the mantra, 'That's life'.

Although Teddy did leave a measure of damage, disappointment and disillusionment in his wake, throughout his life, there was a sense of subtle, underlying purposefulness, rather than the drive or passion that might have directed his contemporaries or other boxers before and after him. During Baldock's time as a fighter, aims stood in the place of ambition and his hopes seemed to be premised on his not wanting to disappoint others, his trainer, his manager, boxing fans and, most of all, his father.

Having spoken now to dozens of people who knew the man and/or his reputation, read most of what was ever written and listened to and watched everything broadcast about Baldock still in existence, it seems to me, for the most part, he was a logical thinker.

Teddy admitted that he did not read much, but he was most definitely a man who could learn. He once quite eloquently said, 'Every young man must concentrate on his work, study it, learn it; get other people's views, follow their methods; compare them; improve on them if possible, and then, when one has evolved one's own style or method, be dissatisfied with it, criticise it, jump on it, make holes in it and rings around it – until finally you have evolved something which you know is worthwhile, which you know you can believe in and bank on.'

As a fighter, there is no evidence of Baldock being anything less than in complete control of his temperament; he was not prone to chaotic anger nor was he dictated to by vindictive feelings. He seemed to deal in directed aggression and had no propensity for the unbridled violence that could over-take some boxers of his time. This is likely to be why he was thought of as a 'scientific' fighter, although Teddy was not a technician as such. His style was refined but not complex. His repertoire often reads as being predict-able; the straight, hard left, the right hook, delivered with the advantage of height and reach. However, the source of his talent was practised instinct, stimulated first by his father's tuition (which dated from Teddy's toddling years) and then his blooding as a professional in his very early teens. He had innate speed and athletic ability, coupled with an aptitude to coordinate the movement of his legs, torso, arms and head. But Baldock's main weapon was the ring itself; it was his ability to engage his physical skills within the space corralled by ropes that marked him out among his peers; he made himself and his gifts at one with that milieu. In short, 'the square' became his natural habitat, his psychological home, a stage he was seemingly born to make his world.

Although for most of his life all but those closest to him knew him as Teddy, the Champion to be was registered at birth as Alfred. He was given the name 'Teddy' by matchmakers when he began to make his mark as a boxer and this was apt as he loved every aspect of the 'noble art' and as such warranted a 'baptism' into the sport.

Teddy was born Alfred Stephen Baldock in Poplar, East London, on 23 May 1907, one of Louisa Rose and Edward Henry Baldock's eight children. The area he grew up in was among the poorest districts in London and Britain. Infant mortality, poverty and disease were rife, while the majority of housing was at least crowded and mostly unfit for human habitation, with rats, bed bugs and infestation in general part of everyday life. At that time East London was a place where you either survived or died and its trials and tribulation tended to breed either extroverts or modest and humble people, often uncomfortable outside of what was deemed to be their designated 'place'. Teddy was a shy lad and later, even as World Bantamweight Champion, he hated the idea of talking about himself. What he did as a young man was, for him, simply to take things as they came and he never thought what he did was particularly spectacular.

The First World War broke out when Teddy was just seven and thus began a sustained period of aerial assaults first by Zeppelins, then the dreaded Gothas and Giant bombers, on London, and in particular the East End docks. This, by mishap or intention, included the collateral damage and destruction of homes, schools and workplaces nestled along the narrow roads and streets that surrounded the docks and railway lines which served them. To reside or work in that area meant having to live with the constant fear of attack, injury and death, and, between 1915 and 1918, nowhere else in Britain were so many families, densely packed within a few square miles of sprawling streets, so persistently exposed to enemy strikes as in the East End of London. Those who lived through those years of bombing raids, including the young Teddy Baldock and his family, long retained vivid memories of those terrifying nights. With death so random, close and unpredictable, it is hard not to conclude that, at least in part, Teddy's later 'devil may care' attitude was informed by the experience, in his formative years, of these frightful threats from above.

The Baldock family had quite a tradition of fighters and the young Teddy was raised on stories about these early stars, many concerned with their exploits beyond the sporting arena. Teddy's grandfather, Jack 'Bulldog' Baldock, as a contemporary of Tom Sayers, had been a tough and able bare-knuckle fighter. Another no-gloves relative, Jack 'Hoppy' Baldock, while not being in Bulldog's class as a bruiser, became a second of some notoriety, a priceless asset in a fighter's corner if a bout wasn't going well. Hoppy kept the Chapel House hostelry in Islington (the 1912 building still stands in Chapel market, housing 'Supercuts') and, alongside a certain Jack Harper, he had a lucrative part-time job as second to legends like Charlie Mitchell, Ted Pritchard and Jem Smith.

Baldock's father, Ted, inherited his father Bulldog's taste for a scrap. Ted was a big, muscular man and Teddy always thought his dad might have been disappointed or surprised when his offspring seemed to simply stop growing as he hit his 14th birthday. In fact, Teddy was so small as a young child that, in a world where barely nourished children were not uncommon, from early on, he was known as 'Titch'.

Baldock Sr would box at fairs, but he would also appear at the old Wonderland, a legendary boxing venue that stood on the south side of Whitechapel Road in East London. Ted didn't speak to his son much about his experiences in the fight game. It seems after his marriage to Louisa Rose a halt was (more or less) called to Ted's adventures in the ring, but Teddy did discover that his dad entered a middleweight competition at the National Sporting Club (NSC). Ted had been led to believe that the contest would not be challenging and as such he neglected to put in the usual training that might be expected before taking part in an event of that type. Consequently, he was well beaten, returning home with two black eyes as his only prize. Baldock Sr's bruises were the first Louisa Rose knew about her husband's return to the pugilistic arts and it was some time before Ted was allowed to forget this.

Everyone who came into contact with the family followed boxing and in Teddy's own words he 'had it for breakfast, dinner and supper', and he had no doubt that he had the heart of a ring warrior that pumped 'boxing blood' through his veins. He was 'putting 'em up' and posing in 'fistic fashion' in the family scullery (as what passed for a kitchen in London's East End before the Second World War was called) almost from the moment he could stand. Ted encouraged his son to mimic the boxer's action in the kitchen of the family home at 32 Byron Street, Poplar, although this started out as a bit of a pantomime, an effort to tease Teddy's mum. Ted would go down on his knees and put his hands up, while his son danced around him like a gnat. In fact, the boy fired straight lefts with such swiftness that Ted had to work hard to avoid taking a punch, much to the amusement of Mrs Baldock. For a time, his mother had objected to this but, aware of her son's lineage, she had finally acquiesced, saying, 'The breed's in him, so I suppose it must come out...if the boy's going to be a boxer he will be. All I hope is that he keeps a level head and doesn't get above himself.'

There were six brothers in the Baldock household and those that outlived Edward Jr (who died in an accident while still young) were all keen sportsmen. Teddy, in particular, looked to be 'good' at anything he turned his hand to, and that also applied to his efforts at school; he was an above average scholar. Running, jumping, swimming, boxing – Teddy wanted to be the best he could be at any sport, as he put it 'fast and good', and he understood that the only way to excel in anything was 'to do it the right way', to perfect a technique. He was completely serious about everything he attempted, and, in these sporting contexts, he appeared to assume a different personality. His apparent habitual shyness was cast aside the instant he focused on what he was doing in the sporting context, even at the most intense moments. Indeed, had Teddy not become a boxer, he would have made a fine footballer or athlete. His build, lean but strong, gave him that vital body weight/strength ratio that makes for sporting excellence that has been gifted to most sporting high achievers, from Canning Town's very own World Bantamweight Champion Pedlar Palmer or three-time Kentucky Derby winner, Isaac Burns Murphy (the 'Coloured Archer') to Lewis Hamilton and Frankie Dettori.

Teddy's elder brother (Ted, who young 'Titch' described as 'a good chap but very fat'), born two-and-a-half years before him, was a big boy but boxing was never to grab his imagination. This older sibling was always in some kind of trouble and, at that time in Poplar, it was not unusual for 'trouble' to include a fight, and it became usual for Teddy to be called on to bail his brother out of his latest scrap. A fast runner, the younger Baldock brother would soon be on the scene and, despite the exertions of the journey, he was invariably ready to step in as required. But what ensued was never the usual childhood mindless brawl.

The other kids had quickly understood that, when Titch shaped up, shutting their eyes and swinging was not going to work. Teddy's skill far exceeded the average Poplar lad's capabilities.

Teddy's reputation as a kid with remarkable ability in a scrap began to grow, and, as a consequence, his time as a street fighter came to a premature end; he literally ran out of opponents willing to face him. One of his last 'alfresco appearances' came about when his brother Ted once more arrived home having come off worse in an altercation with a lad from Yatton Street. A few days later, Teddy came face-to-face with the boy and a tremendous punch-up ensued. The Yatton Street kid went home looking pretty battered and bruised. Shocked, his mother marched him to the Baldock's house to voice her horror at what had been done to her boy. Teddy was duly brought to the front door but, rather than berating Teddy, the Yatton Street mum clouted her own lad for letting himself to be bettered by 'such a little titch'.

A technical fighter by raw instinct; made by intuition, the exigencies of his environment and culture. However, Teddy had also been coached by a good trainer, his father, who had a massive knowledge of the 'fistic' science, despite having been unable to take advantage of it himself. But, above all, the slight lad from Poplar was in love with boxing, and never ceased to want to learn more about the intricacies of the sport.

Baldock senior only had to show his boy a technique once and it set in his muscle memory for life. Later on, when he took Teddy to a Premierland matinee (another famous boxing hall in Back Church Lane just off the Commercial Road in Aldgate that boasted Ted 'Kid' Lewis as a graduate) and other local boxing venues, the lad would sit watching some of the best boxers from one of the most renowned fighting districts on earth, studying their methods and tactics. Afterwards, back at home, the youngster would practise replicating the moves he had seen, and adapt them to his own style, making appropriate modifications so as not to hinder one of his main weapons – quicksilver speed. Having found the right balance, the boy would constantly practise his newly won expertise until it became part of his repertoire.

For Baldock, this didn't take any huge genius, although he became aware that he had a knack of 'absorbing boxing'. But looking back he was not surprised by this. From the beginning he had been embedded in a boxing milieu (family and area); his father's enthusiasm, and his own response, seemed to socialise him into the crafts and art of the sport.

Baldock was certainly blessed with the gift of speed and what boxing trainers have for centuries called 'flair'; that inherent quality that exists somewhere between persona, talent, a feeling for the sport and personal aura. In terms of ring-craft, this flowers in a confidence that seems to enable an individual to know, almost without being told, where to place their feet, which way to move, when to strike and when to retreat. But, from a very early age, Teddy understood that boxing was more of a science than the mere battling trade his grandfather had practised. It was incomprehensible to him that a fighter would go into the ring expecting mental and physical punishment; boxing was about out-thinking an opponent as much as anything else while balancing the avoidance of harm with the need to overcome a rival. Later, of course, he was to understand that all sportsmen, to a certain extent, take risks in the pursuit of success, and that this might involve getting hurt, but Teddy would never understand why boxers should take more, or be expected to endure, greater threats than other athletes. This was an attitude way beyond his time. Many years later, the great Glaswegian World Lightweight Champion Jim Watt made the point that for him boxing was primarily about not getting hurt, as any fool could climb in a ring and take a battering. In top-class sport, rivals are so close in terms of their preparation and conditioning that competition often becomes not so much about being a winner but being able to lose more slowly than one's opponents.

However, the young Baldock had no ambitions to become a World Champion or to win a Lonsdale Belt; he was never a dreamer. For all his aptitude in the sporting arena, as a 12-year-old, Teddy was happy taking street bets for his bookie dad. Outside of boxing this was the only occupation he was ever to really know well.

2

FROM STREET FIGHTER TO JOCKEY

Teddy Baldock was quick to realise that for him a straight left was the ultimate punch in boxing and that no other blow in the book could realise the same potential for success. As such, he set himself the task of making sure he threw more straight lefts than anybody else, and he practised throwing these hurtful strikes until he believed he was the swiftest 'straight lefter' in the game. None of these shots could be classed as 'flips and taps'; they were solid jarring punches with the back knuckles, blows that met the targets at the full extension of the arm, summoning power all the way from his ankles.

For Teddy, the execution was simplicity itself, yet he knew many fighters who failed to perfect this first fundamental of boxing – how to deploy the straight left. He was gifted in this respect. He was however, surprised and quite pleased should an opponent's left get past his guard and land with little or no effect.

Teddy joined the boy scouts and it was this organisation that gave him the encouragement to harness and channel his boxing skills. His earliest championship was the 'East End Boys, five stone', the first of many medals and amateur trophies he would win. He became a consistent winner, but the 'unbeaten' tag didn't turn his head. He attributed this attitude to his personal confidence in his own ability, but also the feeling that he could do better. He understood that to continue winning and make progress he needed to meet better opponents, and he became even more determined to perfect his style, build his strength and learn yet more moves.

During that period, Teddy's father didn't have the long-term goal for his son to take up professional boxing. In fact, there had not been a definite choice to box rather than, for instance, to become a runner. Teddy loved to be on the move, and racing gave him tremendous joy. He did almost everything at speed. His dad would often send him on errands that began with the instruction 'run down the road', and he never had to tell the lad to hurry as all Teddy wanted to do was to show his father how quick he could be.

When Teddy's father realised his son had prospects as a boxer, he introduced him to professional boxing trainer Jim Varley. The then instructor at the Port of London Authority (PLA) Club at Custom House was a famous advocate of the orthodox style. Years later, at over 80 years of age, Jim continued to coach at the West Ham Boys' Club, at that point situated in a huge shed-like structure at the back of a pub at the Green Gate, Plaistow. Like most of the young men who Varley took under his wing, Baldock considered this elder statesman of East End boxing a wonderful old man.

More than a few worthy professionals owed a lot to Varley, including Tom Berry, who became British Light-Heavyweight Champion. Jim knew the sport inside out, and noting the relatively extensive knowledge of the young Baldock boy, while sensing the lad's enthusiasm to learn, he agreed to take Teddy on. Varley allowed his student to turn up for training as often as he pleased, which turned out to be an appreciable amount of time. Teddy sparred with Len George, a fine featherweight in the area. Len and Teddy had developed at much the same time and there was a keen rivalry between their fathers, each claiming that his son was the better fighter. However, given the considerable weight difference between the two lads, the argument would never be resolved.

As Ted seemed about to decide to allow his son to box semi-professionally, there was a change of plan. Ted was working for a bookmaker, Mr F. Weedon, who owned a few horses, and this association with the turf together with Teddy's love of speed caused the boy to be attracted to the notion of becoming a jockey. A few strings were pulled and it was arranged for the promising boxer to take a place at Epsom as an apprentice at Weedon's stable.

Ted had probably realised that his son had finished growing, and maybe thought he had more potential for making a mark on the track than in the ring. However, Ted didn't make a habit of discussing his son's future with the boy himself. According to Baldock, it was a case of Ted saying 'You'll do that' and he did it.

At Epsom, Teddy took to the horses like a natural and grabbed a mount at every opportunity; he began to think, 'This is indeed the life for me – I *must* be a jockey.' However, one afternoon, a favoured boy at the stable called the new lad 'out on the cobbles', informing Teddy that he was 'going to sort you out'.

Like many young riders, Teddy's challenger turned out to be an able boxer. But he must have been more than a little surprised as Baldock took up the gauntlet. The challenger's nose was bleeding after Teddy's initial punch and, within a minute, following a short right to the chin, Teddy saw his opponent on his back.

The shouts of encouragement from the other stable boys brought the head stable-lad running, and he shook Baldock by the shoulder, demanding to know what was going on.

'He was sorting me out,' Teddy replied.

The incident signalled the end of young Baldock's career in the saddle and he caught the next train back to London to inform his parents that he had been sacked. He had been at Epsom less than two weeks.

Ted's response was decisive: 'All right. If you want to fight, you can fight!'

However, according to Teddy, his father said this as though it had always been his ambition that his son should enter the clergy! But there was a sat-isfied gleam in his dad's eye, even though he made it appear to his wife that Teddy was being made to fight as punishment for losing his first job. Baldock was always to wonder if his dad had really fooled his mother. She had seven other children, so Teddy understood that he could only expect an eighth of her protection. The young fighter shrugged his shoulders and thought, 'Well, I could always go looking for a horse if I felt like riding one.'

The call for professional boxing in Teddy's home district was plentiful. In addition to the three evenings a week at Premierland, the Public Baths at such places as Canning Town, Bow and Barking were used regularly by smaller promoters, and it wasn't hard for Baldock to get a match with a local boy at his own weight or a few pounds heavier. When Teddy started boxing 15-round contests at Premierland, he could earn £50 and £60 a time; quite a tidy sum in those days.

Although not amounting to much in terms of poundage, Teddy was relatively tall (5ft 6½in) with an extraordinary long reach relative to his build. Most of his opponents were a couple of inches shorter than him, and when he stabbed out his well rehearsed straight left it hit its target before his rivals could manoeuvre close enough to him to land a blow.

3

BALDOCK THE PRO

1921

Baldock's first professional fight took place at the Public Baths, East Street, Barking, on 14 March 1921, two months before his 14th birthday. Promoter Ray England put Teddy on first with Young (Harry) Makepeace, from Custom House, and the two young fighters made a good start to the programme, with half-a-dozen stirring rounds. But Baldock was too fast for Makepeace, winning a comfortable decision. Teddy got 7s 6d (37½p) for that first fight which he gave to his mum, and, throughout his career, he would always send her something for herself out of whatever purse he earned.

Topping the bill that night was Mark Swan, from Plaistow, facing Aldgate's Alf Craig. Swan worked under Jim Varley at the PLA Club in Custom House. Following his own fight, Teddy dressed and sat at the ringside to watch Swan win on points.

After this debut, Baldock defeated a number of up-and-coming East Londoners, which necessitated finding him opponents from other parts of London in order to maintain the quality of challengers. Teddy fought many of his early contests in a hall attached to St Michael's Church, Poplar, which seated about 600 spectators. Teddy's father and a close friend of his, George Carrington, became interested in this place and they staged small shows there. George was a goalkeeper with Clapton Orient and he used weightlifting as part of his training regime (which was quite innovative at that time). Ted and George had a training gym in a converted loft over a banana drying shed in Dewsbury Street, Poplar. The green fruit was stored below straight from the ships that moored in the nearby docks to ripen in the heated shed.

This made the gym overhead a pleasant place to train during the winter months.

Teddy was one of many famous boxers who started at St Michael's Hall including Bert Harris, who as Al Foreman won the British lightweight title, and Jimmy Corp, from St George's, Stepney, who won a Belt at The Ring, the famous venue in Blackfriars. The Ring, built in 1783, was originally called the Surrey Chapel. The rather odd-shaped building was bought by former British Light-weight Champion Dick Burge in 1910, who, with his wife Bella, staged regular boxing events there. It was billed as 'London's Premier Arena' and it certainly lived up to that title, staging bouts with such well-known fighters as Len Johnson, Jack Drummond, Alf Mancini, Jack Hood and the famed Ted 'Kid' Lewis.

The Ring boxing arena was destroyed in an air raid in 1940 and now only an echo of that historic boxing location in South London exists in the form of The Ring public house, just across from the site where the arena used to stand. The pub's walls are adorned with posters and pictures of the many boxers who once fought at The Ring, and until recently the hostelry had a working gym upstairs from the bar.

While not quite in the same class as The Ring, St Michael's played host to some fine East End pugilists such as Arthur Abbott (St George's), Young Johnny Brown (Spitalfields), Billy Boulger, Len George, Tom Cherry and dozens of others.

1922

Baldock recalled that his father sent him to see Nat Sellar, who looked after several boys, to find out if the trainer had anyone who could give Teddy a good contest. Sellar had the able Jimmy Corp in his camp, but also a lad by the name of Johnny O'Brien. Sellar told the young Baldock, 'He's a bit heavier than you'. But Baldock told the trainer 'Don't matter' and dashed home to tell his father that he had sorted out a fight for himself.

On 16 February 1922, Teddy fought a good fight with O'Brien at St Michael's Hall, winning the verdict over six rounds. The prize was a bicycle, and he immediately put himself in competition with everything on wheels in his neighbourhood.

Baldock would rise early to do his roadwork while the streets of East London were still deserted. He wanted to avoid the possibility that, typical of cockney banter, people might laugh at him and ask if he thought he was going to be a boxer, or who he was running away from. It seems Teddy was a terribly shy young man. So, if he saw someone he knew coming down the road, he would duck up a side street and rapidly make for the next corner in order to avoid being teased. On his route, there was a square around which buses would turn to begin their return journey. Teddy would wait for a bus and then race it to the first scheduled stop, and even if the driver took up the challenge Teddy was always the winner; he was hooked on speed. He found that a swift left hand coming from a fast-moving body completely bewildered his rivals, giving them no time to think between the punches. It's probably not too had for many of us to imagine the buzz that might be consequent of that experience.

When his dad's Dewsbury Street gym wasn't available, Baldock would train at Liverpool Street Fire Station. This was a well-equipped place and Teddy felt privileged to be allowed to train there. Like many others in East London, the firefighters were always ready to lend a helping hand.

Teddy filled his time between boxing by collecting bets for his father in the mornings, then meeting him in a public convenience half-an-hour before the first race to hand over the slips and the 'readies' (this was a time before 'off-course' gambling had been legalised). One day, a client gave Teddy 10 bob (50p) to lay on the *Star* noon double (a two-horse tip in a national newspaper), and he put the money in a separate pocket, promptly forgetting all about it. Of course, the bet was a massive winner so young Baldock was in trouble. His dad accused him of deliberately 'sticking' the bet (holding on to the stake and not actually laying the bet). Feeling poorly judged, Teddy lost his temper and decided to leave home. He packed up a few things, including his boxing kit, and left with the idea that he would earn a living from boxing and manage himself.

Needing somewhere to sleep, Teddy turned to a man who kept a barber's shop and who had always been friendly to the young fighter. The barber gave the young man a job as a lather boy and allowed him to lodge with his family. But he only stayed a few days before his mother found out where he was, and, following minimal persuasion, he moved back home.

By this time, Ted had made up his mind that his son could be a good professional fighter, and realised he would need a reliable manager; someone 'in the know', within the professional boxing networks.

Joe Morris was matchmaker at Premierland, which was owned by Victor Berliner and his partner, Manny Lyttlestone. The building had originally belonged to Faircloughs meat contractors, but was converted into an ideal fight arena that just suited the 'fistically inclined' East End clientele. Premierland staged three shows each week, sometimes four, and more often than not it attracted such a crowd that many had to be turned away from a full house.

Morris got to know about Baldock through Mike Honeyman, the former British Featherweight Champion, who Morris was managing. Mike lived in the dockside district of Silvertown and trained in a small shed in his back garden. One day, Mike walked into the gym run by Teddy's dad and Carrington and decided to train there.

A fine boxer, Honeyman only lacked a power punch to add to his speed, accuracy and possibly the best left hand in the business according to Baldock. Teddy was unable to take his eyes off Honeyman when he climbed into the gym ring, as he had never seen anything quite like this man and wondered how he had lost his title.

Honeyman had won the vacant British title and Lonsdale Belt by beating Billy Marchant over 20 rounds in January 1920. Then Tancy Lee, who had relinquished the Championship, decided to come out of retirement. Lee (from Leith in Scotland) was an extraordinary boxer, who became Scotland's first European title holder on 19 October 1914 when he stopped Percy Jones of Wales in the 14th round in London. When Lee defeated the legendary Jimmy Wilde the following January, it was also recognised by the International Boxing Union (IBU, which would become the EBU) as a world title fight, but Lee was never to gain universal recognition as a World Champion. Given that Glamorganshire's Wilde is still seen by many as the greatest flyweight of all time, this seems harsh. At his heaviest, Wilde only weighed 8st 10lb, but he scored

101 knockouts in his career and the great Gene Tunney said that the Welshman was the best fighter he had ever seen. Wilde won the world flyweight title, knocking out Joe Symonds in the 11th round of their fight in 1916, and he held on to that crown until he was himself knocked out by Pancho Villa in 1923.

In his 'comeback' fight, Lee was stopped in the 19th round by Honeyman. That gave Mike two notches on his Lonsdale Belt, and he only wanted one more win to make it his own property.

Next, Honeyman met Joe Fox, of Leeds. Fox had already won a bantam belt outright and now saw himself taking a second. Honeyman had weakened himself in making the weight, and at the end of 20 rounds the verdict went against him.

Mike was 27 when Baldock met him for the first time, after watching Teddy train, he gave the lad a few tips, correcting faults the young boxer didn't think he had, but the he had enough sense to take note of the observations of the experienced pugilist. As time went on, Baldock found that he was modelling his style on Honeyman's, while remembering his mentor's instructions to cultivate his right hand and not sacrifice it for increasing the speed of his left.

Honeyman took Teddy to see Dan Sullivan, who was then promoting at The Ring at Blackfriars, hoping to give Baldock some decent paydays. On introducing the young fighter, Sullivan said, 'I'll back this boy to fight anyone up to 8st.'

Honeyman advised give him a break Dan, and you won't regret it.'

But Sullivan was known as a shrewd, wise character in the game and he took one look at Teddy, and told Mike, 'I'm too old for such kidding. Bring him back when he's older and bigger.' One can't help but wonder if Sullivan ever regretted that response.

Morris came along to watch Teddy at one of the small shows at St Michael's Church Hall, and afterwards had a chat with his dad. A little while later, the Premierland matchmaker visited the banana loft. Mike had told Baldock just to do his stuff as usual, and Morris appeared to be impressed. Before leaving, he asked when Teddy's next fight was scheduled.

In due course, Ted told his son, 'You're going to have someone else in charge of you. Report to Joe Morris down at Premierland tomorrow morning and do as you're told.'

Although Teddy had visited Premierland a few times with his father, his experience had been limited to afternoon shows, as Ted was very strict about his son getting early nights, not that the youngster needed to be forced to bed; he believed that plenty of sleep was necessary for an athlete. He was so keen to be good at sport that he didn't think anything else was worth staying up late for.

Morris took over the management of Baldock while he was also managing Honeyman and of course Teddy got plenty of work at Premierland. The fledgling fighter regarded Morris highly and named him as 'the straightest man I ever knew in the boxing game'. He never took more than 17½ per cent of his purse money, even after Baldock became world champion.

From the time Teddy turned professional until the day he walked away from the ring, he never received any of his purse money in bulk. It was all banked for him and he drew a bit for pocket money each week. When the time came to hang up his gloves, he had something of a nest egg, which was much more than most fighters of that era ended up with although it would turn out to be much less than he expected.

Baldock's first fight at Premierland was an eight-rounder against his old pal Johnny O'Brien. He wasn't keen on meeting O'Brien for a second time, as he knew another fine fight would probably mean a third meeting: 'I didn't specially want to meet him again, but you know what it is when two boys put up a bit of a show. Everybody wants to see them do it again, and, if it comes off the second time, they can't dodge one another if they try'.

Over eight rounds, Teddy won the contest. He was just a month past his 15th birthday, but no one saw eight rounds as being too much for such a young fighter. Indeed, such competitions were in no way exceptional, as the professional rings in every big city in Britain would have staged many a contest between young men in their mid-teens, some of whom would have as many as 300 fights before their careers were over. Purses would range from a few shillings to several tens of pounds and fighters were motivated by everything from desperate poverty to burning ambition. In the early 1920s, professional boxing was part entertainment, part gladiatorial sport, and the amateur set-up was nothing like the system we have today. It had only been 40 years since Mr R. Frost–Smith arranged a meeting at the offices of *The Referee* (in London) on 21 January 1880, looking to organise a governing body for amateur boxing. The meeting produced the idea of establishing the Amateur Boxing Association (ABA) but this would have little impact on the likes of Teddy Baldock.

As was the case in the amateur game, the structures that supported and surrounded professional boxing were not as they are today. While it would be unfair to call the organisation 'lax', there was the NSC and later the British Board of Boxing Control (British Boxing Board of Control – formed in 1929), but it was hard to tell the difference between that body and the NSC (which in practice controlled the British Boxing Board of Control as it was made up of mostly NSC members) and, according to Teddy, 'no one paid it any attention anyway'. However, the controls of boxing were not the disciplined process they became in the modern era; for instance there was no weigh-in at Premierland, unless it was a so-called 'money match' and even then no one could ensure the accuracy (or consistency) of the scales.

The day after the second Baldock/O'Brien fight, one newspaper told the world, 'A couple of midgets gave an excellent display. It's a pity some of the bigger men cannot give even as good an exhibition as these two youngsters.'

There were three other 15-year-olds on the bill that afternoon, another eight-round and two six-round bouts, providing spectators with 65 rounds for a tanner (6d, 2½p) standing, one and three (1s 3d, about 6p) in the balcony, half-a-dollar (2s 6d, 12½p) and three and six (3s 6d, 17½p) ringside. According to Baldock, 'You could expect real scrapping for that money, and if you didn't get it you hollered until you did.'

1923 – A STRING OF VICTORIES

In 1923, Baldock met with Johnny O'Brien for a third time. Ted's bookmaking employer was also a member of the NSC, and, when the stable lads held their annual tournament at the Club, he got Teddy on the bill. But, when they told Baldock he would be meeting O'Brien again over eight rounds, he quite rightly asked, 'What for?'

The show was staged in aid of St Dunstan's (the charity that supports blind ex-servicemen and women) and as usual a packed audience came to see the stable boys having a go at one another. There was plenty of keen rivalry between them, and they fought like demons. The bouts were made up of three three-minute rounds, but most of them only went a round before one of the lads stopped the other. The lowest weight was four stone and the heaviest about 8st.

Steve Donoghue (10 times champion jockey on the flat between 1914 and 1923), the great Australian rider Bernard 'Brownie' Carslake (champion jockey in Austria-Hungary and Russia, who once claimed he existed on 'a cup of tea and hope' and who, in addition to his seven Classic victories, won the Ascot Gold Cup on Foxlaw, the Doncaster Cup on Epigram, the Salford Borough Handicap on Diadem and the Portland Handicap riding Irish Elegance) and other turf celebrities were there, and Moss Deyong conducted the auction. Deyong, who was of Dutch descent, refereed for many years, officiating all over Britain and Europe, including the heavyweight contest between Primo Carnera and Paulino Uzcudun in Barcelona in 1930, and in 1935 in Manchester he was the third man in the ring for Benny Lynch's World Flyweight Championship win against Jackie Brown. Moss was also a successful auctioneer at boxing shows, raising in excess of £100,000 (a massive sum in his lifetime) for a range of charities. That night, he collected £20 for a box of Corona Coronas (highly rated Cuban cigars), and a pair of riding boots, worn by the famous Fred Archer (the most successful sportsman in horse racing in the Victorian era), were auctioned, sold, put up again and so on, and finally went to Carslake.

Baldock, once more, got the measure of O'Brien; the referee stopped the fight in the third round. He was also to stop his next opponent, Hoxton's Young Stoneham. This bout took place on 13 February 1923 at the Central Finsbury Radical Club (which from the late 19th century had offered 'free lectures' to the public). The fight had been scheduled as an eight-rounder but it finished midway through the fourth, when Stoneham's seconds threw in the towel.

Next up for Teddy was a trip to Scotland. A Poplar man ran a show in Edinburgh for the Scottish branch of the British Legion in the Industrial Hall, and the bill was made up of practically all Londoners. The boxers were a big party and Teddy had a good time, although he thought it was a long way to go for a fight. The group included Tom Berry, Jim Rideout, Fred Newberry, Tom Cherry, Jimmy Corp, Billy Housego, Billy Pinn and Arthur Webb (Baldock defeated Webb on points over 10 rounds). The Scottish capital provided a poor house, which was hardly surprising as there wasn't a Scotsman on the programme.

The best contest was provided by Wally Pickard and Joe Bowker (who had been acknowledged as the finest of British bantamweights before Baldock was born), who performed their famous 'boxing burlesque', causing great mirth among the little collection of spectators. Baldock had seen them do this before, but nevertheless found their show highly amusing.

Baldock's next fight, facing Deptford scrapper Arthur Webb for a second time, was on 24 April 1923, just four days before West Ham United, the East London football team that Teddy was to support all his life, played in the first Wembley Cup Final against Bolton Wanderers. An estimated 250,000 people turned up for the event and for a time it looked as if the match would be abandoned because of the crush. But the game was played and the Trotters won 2–0 after the wings, the main channels of the Hammers attack, were made practically unplayable by the effects of crowd incursions and the police horses churning up the flanks of the pitch.

Teddy once more outpointed Webb, a strong fighter who never failed to put up a good display, over 10 rounds at Hoxton Baths in a benefit for Canning Town's Tom (Pedlar) Palmer, the Old Box of Tricks as he was known. He had been acknowledged as the World Bantam Champion in 1895 and was still contesting the title a decade later. Palmer, who had an acute awareness of the whereabouts of the referee, always handy when attempting to bend the Marques of Queensbury rules a little, told Baldock that the craftiest boxer he ever met had been Digger Stanley, another World Bantam Champion.

Baldock gave away a stone to a lad named Young Riley at Premierland on a Sunday afternoon in October. His opponent came in at 8st and they fought for 10 rounds. It was quite a battle, but once again Baldock's speed was his greatest asset and he beat Riley on points.

When Teddy turned 16 he was able to box on evening programmes, and his first dusk encounter took place on a Thursday-evening bill at Premierland, meeting Kid Roberts, from Bethnal Green. Baldock had a comfortable victory over Roberts in three rounds. He punched too hard for the Bethnal Green boy, and the towel floated in to stop him taking further punishment.

It was a very special occasion, as arch rivals Ted (Kid) Lewis and Fred Archer were matched over 20 rounds at 11 stone. This clash had been the cause of a great deal of excitement for months throughout the East End.

Lewis was the British Welterweight Champion, but he was continually being challenged by Archer, however, according to the Kid, Fred wasn't in his class. This angered the Archer camp, and eventually Lewis was persuaded to meet their man at catchweight. It was rumoured that £200 a-side had been put up, and the purse was said to be a massive £1,000.

The referee, the famed Dick Smith, was especially appointed for the fight. However, Dick's arithmetic was hardly tested as Lewis won by a street.

It was around this time that the legendary horse owner Aga Khan III was racing his record-breaking two-year-old, Mumtaz Mahal (a phenomenally fast thoroughbred that was a consistently powerful contender over six furlongs). Given the connections between horse racing and boxing and Baldock's own flirtation with the 'sport of kings' it is perhaps not surprising that Teddy was nicknamed after the filly, appearing on the Premierland bill as 'The Mumtaz Mahal of the Ring'. But the name didn't catch on around Poplar, and people usually greeted Teddy with a 'Wotcha, Alf', just as they had always done.

Fights became plentiful and Baldock did the best he could to win them all. Johnny Faithfull was knocked out in the second round in front of the Surrey man's hometown crowd at Addlestone. His brother Percy travelled from 'Capon County' to the East End with vengeance in mind but was beaten by Teddy over 10 rounds at Premierland.

A win over Joe Goddard, of Brixton, who was stopped in three rounds at Hoxton Baths, finished off Teddy's year. Goddard had been a substitute, and the promoter offered him £3 for the fight, or 10 shillings (50p) a round. He opted to be paid by the round, and as it ended in the third he only made himself 30 shillings (£1.50p). Baldock was fast becoming a name to be reckoned with.

4

NOBLE HUMILITY

1924

Victory over Arthur Cowley, when the St George's man was forced to retire in the second round, was followed by a first-round knockout of Young Bowler. The bout lasted just 63 seconds, and Baldock was nearly as surprised as Bowler. Teddy shot a left at his rival and he received the same in kind, but Baldock crossed him with the right, which caught his man flush on the chin, and he was out like a light.

That win earned Baldock a deal of editorial attention in *Boxing*, the first time his name had been mentioned in this esteemed journal. It described how Baldock had shaped 'like a second Jimmy Wilde', and forecast that he might develop into an even greater fighter, given the fact that he carried a definite KO punch.

Mike Honeyman had been in Baldock's corner, as he was many times during this period. Teddy was always learning something from Honeyman, and because they shared a stable they often found themselves on the same programme, which was usually a good thing for Baldock as it was another opportunity to extend his boxing education watching his mentor in action.

Young Bill Lewis, from Bethnal Green, who subsequently became the Southern Area bantam titleholder, was the first really classy boxer Baldock faced. The fight was a 10-rounder at Premierland. Teddy won, but he was obliged to work hard for his victory as Lewis was an energetic and determined fighter, and never let up until the final bell rang.

Baldock met his next opponent at the NSC. This was his first Monday night proper there. Every boy in those days wanted to fight at the NSC, and, although

Teddy was pleased at the prospect, it became just another venue once he got inside the place. Baldock knew it was considered an honour to box there, but, for Teddy, 'there wasn't much in it, and the pay wasn't any better.'

The fight, on 24 March 1924, pitted Baldock against George Kid Socks (real name Harry Stockings) who was later to fight for the British Flyweight Championship. Socks was a fine boxer, and Teddy learned a lot from him. He could match the Poplar lad for speed, but his 'dig' held no real threat. Baldock found it hard to hit him flush, although he did get in one stiff left that put the Kid on the canvas. But Socks got to his feet before the referee began to count to come back at Baldock. He made for an awkward foe, and when the final bell rang Teddy returned to his corner convinced that he had been beaten for the first time. However, the referee made it a draw, however Baldock's supporters responded by claiming that their boy had been robbed. But Teddy felt sorry for Socks, seeing that his opponent had taught him that you could be fast and efficient without being flashy. Baldock never saw himself as a flamboyant performer, but that evening, having been impressed by the noble humility of Socks, he made up his mind that in terms of his ring persona he would never try to be showy.

The fight with Socks was followed by another meeting with Young Bill Lewis at Premierland. Baldock chalked up another points victory in his first 15-round contest. Teddy would not take part in a fight made at less than 15 rounds again until he went to the US two years later. At first they were two-minute rounds, as Joe Morris turned down all offers for his boy to go 15 'threes'. Baldock had passed his 18th birthday before his manager would allow him to take on that additional minute for each round, and nor would he allow Teddy to go beyond 15 rounds, even though, in those days, title fights and top-liners at the biggest halls were all 20-round affairs.

Harry Jacobs, who was promoting at the Albert Hall, offered Morris £1,000 for Baldock to take on the British Flyweight Champion, Elky Clark, over 20 three-minute rounds, but Joe took no time at all to refuse, telling Jacobs, 'I'm nursing this kid along and I'm content with the small money he gets in the East End until he's fully matured. It won't be long, however, before he'll be topping the bill on your programmes.'

Mike Honeyman was pleased with Teddy's results against Lewis and Socks. He had suggested to the boy's father that he should stay with him for a while and improve his defence and footwork. As such, Baldock went over to Silvertown and trained with Honeyman in the garden shed that was equipped with a small ring.

Baldock had picked up a lot from his father and Jim Varley and under the tutelage of Honeyman he honed his skills further. As a consequence he started to stop more of his opponents inside the distance. But there were those who would endure to the bitter end, especially when Baldock was obliged (for the sake of a match) to give weight away, or when he met one of a breed of tough fighters of the time who it seemed could not be stopped, no matter what was thrown at them. However, Teddy usually managed to get things over and done with in a significantly shorter time than the scheduled 15 two-minute rounds.

Baldock began to focus on developing his delivery of a left hook to the body, making his target the often unprotected spot under the ribs on the opposite side to the heart. A well-aimed bomb there, with plenty of drive behind it, normally caused the rival's guard to fall, and at that point a swift right hook to the apex of the chin practically guaranteed an opponent would find themselves crashing to the canvas. If they did get up, most of the fight would have been knocked out of them.

However, for every move in boxing a counter exists; there is one manoeuvre that will almost be calculated to take advantages of the space left by another, including Baldock's combination left hook to the body and right hook to the chin that he was to use time after time. This was until he met a fighter who lured him into the move, but blocked the path to the body with his elbow, resulting in serious consequences. Teddy broke his left hand and it was this recurring injury that would eventually bring the curtain down on his boxing career. Baldock was later to relate a bit of ring philosophy based on this lesson: 'No matter how clever you think you are, there's always a time when you meet someone just a shade cleverer.' As Joe Frazier once had it: 'Life doesn't run away from nobody. Life runs at people.'

Teddy never had faith in the then popular double punch with a straight left lead. For him, one was enough, especially if it was a good hard dig. He believed that a second blow could not carry any meaningful weight, as necessity dictated it would be delivered from too close a distance. According to Baldock, boxers who deployed a double left-hand lead to the face would be better advised to make sure they got a strong single strike on target. He also found that a firm, hurtful left lead would not be crossed. An opponent might have planned to cross him with a right, but his swift, powerful and accurate left would soon put an adversary out of his stride or off balance, stopping any resulting counter. He believed fighters who consistently got crossed when leading with their left were failing to back up their punches with sufficient force.

Jim Varley taught Baldock to always watch the other man's eyes, telling him, 'If you watch his eyes you can read his thoughts. If he smiles after you've smacked him in the kisser, you can bet he's hurt. When he laughs it's kid stakes to the public, and that's the time to follow up smartly and give him some more.'

Mike Honeyman and Baldock, pupil and teacher, often journeyed to fight shows together and they travelled up to Leeds in each other's company one Sunday to compete at the NSC in the afternoon. Over the course of the journey, they discussed Teddy's opponent, a local lad by the name of Dod Oldfield, a Gypsy bantamweight (this was Oldfield's fifth recorded fight – he would go on to record 111 contests, including 54 victories). The 'Romany Rock' was as tough as any fighter Baldock had met to date and Honeyman was adamant that his protégé would have to watch the Birkenhead boy carefully in the opening rounds. The bout, on 20 July 1924, went the distance and Teddy got the verdict, but as he was to confirm it was a 'sizzler' of a fight, so much so that a return was organised at Premierland 18 days later.

Teddy's second meeting with Dod Oldfield was another battle of speed and aggression that went the distance, but once more Baldock won on points. Joe Morris told his boy that he and Oldfield had given the finest performance of the evening. This was praise indeed as the black Mancunian middleweight Len Johnson and Aussie Frankie Burns had topped the bill. Teddy had every reason to feel satisfied.

The next time out at Premierland, Baldock stopped Maesteg's Kid Hughes in seven. The Welshman was a lot shorter than Teddy and, at 7st 8lb, a pound lighter. Baldock's long reach made it hard for Hughes to land a punch of any consequence, and after being put down for four counts of 'nine' in the sixth round he gamely came out for the seventh. However, after he took a further beating his corner threw in the towel.

Another Manchester fighter, Vic Wakefield, was the next obstacle for Baldock; he was stopped in the 10th, the referee intervening after Vic had been dropped for a lengthy count. From the start he crowded the East Ender, who was forced to keep moving in order to stay out of trouble. But Teddy managed to get the left working, and the right finished his rival off.

Baldock's final bout of 1924 pitted him against the clever Birmingham fly-weight Harry Hill. This contest saw the Cockney boy came close to losing his undefeated record. Hill was an astute scrapper, and in the opening round he caught Baldock with a left swing that landed flush on his chin, sending him to the canvas. Teddy, more surprised than injured, rose just as the gong signalled the end of the round. This gave Baldock time to recover, but he quickly discovered that Hill was a match for his intellect and seemed to have one or two more moves in his arsenal than the Poplar lad.

The fact that Baldock took the fight to the Brummie from the second won him the decision. Hill countered most of Teddy's efforts with extremely accurate punching, but, inexplicably, after the fourth round, his right stopped working. He may have sustained some damage, but after this stage Baldock pushed forward more intently. However, Hill's left struck out like a viper, but his rapidity was not underwritten with power and he could not stop Teddy's progress.

Baldock's catalogue of victories earned him much popular acclaim around Poplar and the surrounding East End of London. Seemingly everybody knew his face and his business; sometimes he thought others knew more about his affairs than he did. It wasn't unusual for him to be stopped by a complete stranger to be told, 'I see you're on at Premierland next Thursday,' and it would be news to Teddy. He would often reply something like, 'Oh, yes. How'd you know?' to be told the details of the bout were on bill posters around the district.

This situation did not trouble Baldock as he was training every day and as such was always prepared to fight; in that period, he never once failed to make weight. Names and reputations were of no account to Teddy, although his opponents were getting better and better. But all this did was confirmation to Baldock that he was improving. His dad might mention that someone he was matched with was a good body puncher, or could throw a hard right, just to ensure against any carelessness, but Teddy was a fast learner, and he had picked up a whole range of evasive strategies; he was becoming a dab hand at getting himself out of tight corners.

In 1924, Jack Lakey took over as Baldock's trainer. Lakey impressed Teddy's father, having sound knowledge about the required conditioning of fighters; he was to remain Baldock's trainer for the rest of the boxer's career.

Although Teddy didn't rate Lakey as the best trainer in the world, he found it hard to compare him with others as he never had another trainer, but he felt that Jack suited his style and temperament, and believed that he brought out the best in him in terms of fitness.

In his early thirties, a good-natured, thoughtful and composed man, Lakey had a seafaring background, and like many sailors his travels had been his education. He was a capable masseur, and knew how to help a fighter make weight. He kept a book that only he could understand, full of figures and details relating to every time Baldock stood on the scales. Jack would note the ounces as they were added or taken off and for most of his career Teddy never had a problem scaling within the required poundage.

However, it was in the training-camp environment that Lakey came into his own; he was a positive companion, who, with a never-ending run of stories, ready wit and an ability to pull out a clever retort to whatever was said to him, kept everyone laughing and in good spirits. He was never known to resort to any type of threat or bullying and dealt with Teddy's work without a harsh word or needing to raise his voice to anything coming close to a shout. It was rare for him to use bad language and while he was involved in training he neither smoked nor drank. But he was also a hard taskmaster with high expectations in terms of his fighter's commitment. Nobody's mug, the few who had seen Lakey raised to anger had let others know he was not a person to be trifled with. A good-looking man, without an ounce of spare flesh on his muscular frame, Jack possessed a powerful punch of his own and even in later life his reactions shamed younger men.

Lakey understood Baldock's every caprice and want; he instinctively grasped how to respond to the boxer if ever he was tense during a training regime. Jack also had the intelligence to motivate his charge to work harder but, maybe more importantly with Teddy, how to make him lay off when he was on the edge of over-training.

There were, of course, times when Baldock could be difficult – most boxers, like most people, are prone to some type of malaise or another – but Lakey was a patient man, and, whether Teddy trained in Poplar or at one of the renowned training camps of the time, Jack always brought the boxer to the scales at the peak of physical condition and with his mind focused on the task. As Teddy said, working with Lakey and Morris, 'I couldn't go wrong.'

5

MUMTAZ MAHAL AND FIFTEEN THREES

1925

Teddy's reputation for speed had spread and Tom Berry, who was getting ready for his title contest against Sid Pape, and Ted (Kid) Lewis (generally thought to be the first fighter to use a mouthpiece; he certainly was the first fighter of note to use one), who was preparing for a return match with the Frenchman Francis Charles (at the Palais des Sports, Paris), invited Baldock to take part what was to be Teddy's first training camp at Billericay, Essex, with the aim of helping these top fighters develop their ring speed. Baldock was able to buzz round Berry like a tick, but with Ted Kid (born Gershon Mendeloff) he was totally disoriented. He had two rounds with Lewis, but knew hardly anything about the second. In training, Lewis was untouchable and Teddy was always to remember going on the road with him.

The 'Aldgate Sphinx' (as Lewis was called by the boxing press) would not blink about walking 10 miles at such an astounding pace that Baldock had to run fast to keep up with him. The twice World Welterweight Champion would go up hills quicker than he came down them (so predating the innovation of 'Fartlek' training by the best part of a decade). Berry was not too far off Lewis in terms of his performance on the road, but the Poplar light-heavyweight had long legs that helped him keep close to Lewis.

Lewis was to put in an amazing performance to beat Francis Charles. It was exhibition stuff, Lewis looking every inch a class act.

Berry was of that breed of fine boxers who made next to nothing from the sport. When he eventually won the light-heavyweight crown, beating Sid Pape in March 1925, it was close to worthless from his point of view; he got a Lonsdale Belt but that couldn't feed his nine children. Like so many winners of the illustrious trophy, Tom would be obliged to flog his belt that would ultimately, for the price of few week's keep for a family like Berry's, be bound to be little more than a rich man's bauble, hanging over a grand fireplace or exhibited in some ostentatious study.

Baldock was to recall that Berry took him to the NSC to see his championship fight as a reward for helping him out with his training. However, Teddy was refused entry (probably because of his age) so Tom asked him to wait in the car, telling him that he'd be as quick as he could. Baldock waited a long time as it took Berry the full 20-round distance to win on points.

In the first quarter of 1925, Teddy met Fred Hinton from Forest Gate twice, both fights ending with stoppages in favour of Baldock, whose left hand was too much for Hinton (who would record 58 contests in his career).

Between his fights with Hinton, Baldock had two encounters with Willie Evans, from Port Talbot. In the first bout, Teddy stopped the Welshman in five rounds, finishing the contest with a right hook to the chin. Willie did a bit better the next time he met Baldock, getting to the 12th before succumbing.

While training, on his morning run, Teddy would sometimes pass the Millwall fighter Ernie Jarvis coming in the opposite direction. They would often exchange a 'Hi-yer' as they passed. One day they grinned at each other as they crossed, and Ernie said, 'Be seeing yer,' which meant that they had been matched for 15 rounds at Premierland on a Thursday evening.

Jarvis was just as keen to make a name in boxing as Baldock was, and a bout between Poplar and Millwall was a local derby of the highest order. Each of the fighters had a huge following, and they had both been generating impressive results.

The Stepney Marsh man probably had a better record than Baldock, having fought a better class of opponent over a longer period of time. Ernie had beaten Kid Socks, Frankie Kestrell and Harry Hill (in four rounds) among others, and had recently gone the distance with flyweight Len Harvey (who had moved to London from Plymouth).

More square in terms of build and shorter than Baldock, Jarvis was also a good technician, so Teddy understood that he would need to move more swiftly than he had in previous contests. Ernie liked to get inside, where he was more than effective with both hands, but Baldock had the reach, and was to make the best of that advantage. Occasionally, Ernie would duck under Teddy's lead and tear in a clutch of rapid blows to the body, but Baldock didn't allow his opponent to dwell too long on his torso, dancing away to evade his lunges.

In the eighth round, Teddy gambled a right, clipping Jarvis firmly on the chin. Later, Baldock was to speculate that if he had been a little more experienced he might have known that Ernie was badly hurt, and that a second solid stab around the same area might have finished the fight.

Active footwork together with fast leading saw Baldock pile up the points, but as the fight continued his admiration for Jarvis grew; holding his composure under extreme pressure, Ernie's demeanour remained focused as he dragged concentration from the depths of the stupor that threatened to engulf him. Even when Baldock backed him into a corner, darting about in front of him, looking to tempt him into exposing an opening for a right, Jarvis calmly rubbed his feet in the resin, ducked a left and escaped in an instant.

Ultimately, the verdict was given to Baldock, and it wasn't close. Jack Goodwin, the referee, had no hesitation in declaring Teddy the winner, with the support of the huge crowd, despite the fact that many of them were Jarvis supporters.

Following the contest, Ernie told Baldock he was soon leaving to try his luck in the US, and Teddy replied, 'I'd like to go there. It's a place where I reckon you've got to go if you want to be a champion.'

Jarvis smiled and said, 'Well, see you over there then.'

They would indeed share an American dream, and Baldock was correct in his assessment of the rewards that might be gleaned on the other side of the Atlantic.

In Baldock's era, the NSC, which once held great sway in the sport, was a governing body in name only. Increasing competition from enterprising promoters such as C.B. Cochran and Major Arnold Wilson had weakened the authority of this once great institution. It had enough difficulty when trying to impose its authority on contests for the British Championship and so its voice went unheard when it tried to establish the often-rightful claims of British boxers for world title bouts. By 1925, the world boxing capital was New York and its empire was the vast, sprawling, fight-hungry American 'bucklands'. There was enormous income to be generated via a range of huge venues, primarily on the East Coast, but also throughout the United States, hosting mass audiences and attracting enormous general public and media interest. Europe, chiefly Britain, certainly produced worthy world titleholders but it was only in the US where champions were *made*. America could turn a champion boxer into an icon, a folk hero of epic proportions; the overwhelming majority of greatest legends of the game, its immortals, were and still are Americans either by birth or adoption. The New York State Athletic Commission (NYSAC) was America's version of a world governing body and it frequently nominated challengers for the various World Champions, irrespective of the views and opinions of the Europeans. Not surprisingly, these challengers were usually American fighters and their nomination was often engineered by just a couple of managers and a promoter. On the few occasions that the NSC managed to trumpet the claim of a British challenger, their declarations would be ignored by the NYSAC. The best way for a British fighter to assert his right for a crack at a world title was to go to America and to beat the Americans in their own backyard. It seemed that no amount of shouting, however loud, from the British side of the Atlantic would have the same effect.

The defeat of Ernie Jarvis had enhanced Baldock's reputation, but it was clear that he would need to meet a different class of opponent if he was going to make progress. He had met Jarvis two days before his 18th birthday, and later he remembered going into the Dewsbury Street gym one morning to find Joe Morris talking to Jack Lakey about his future.

His manager told the trainer, 'Now Alf is over 18, I reckon he can go 15 threes. So you'll have to get him used to the extra minute.'

Turning to Baldock, Joe said, 'I want you to start training for three-minute rounds from now on, but I've got a couple of fights booked up over twos which you have to take first.'

Morris told Teddy that the first of these contests would be against Johnny Haydn, who had put up a good fight with Elky Clark, the British Flyweight Champion, at Premierland a year earlier, and had also stopped Young Johnny

Brown in the same ring. For Morris, a Baldock win over Haydn would get the attention of the newspapers, something that was crucial in the 1920s. If a fighter could get the boxing writers interested, it had a direct effect on the quality of opponents he could be matched with and on attendances at venues, both of which would increase the purse; the size of a boxer's last prize (given that he walked away a winner) more or less dictated that the next fight would match or better that amount.

Baldock met Haydn on a Sunday afternoon, with Jack (Kid) Berg fighting on the same bill (the 'Whitechapel Windmill' defeated Billy Shepherd from Sheffield over 13 rounds).

Haydn did not have Baldock's lengthy reach, which meant he had to get close enough to Teddy to score heavily. This gave Teddy a significant advantage, and he was able to jab Johnny with a long left, while receiving little in the way of a counter-attack. However, Haydn kept driving into Baldock, who used all the evasive strategies he had devised or been tutored in, and ducked and dived out of his opponent's path until it seemed as though the Welshman couldn't land a punch.

In the third round, Baldock introduced his right hand to Haydn. Halfway through the seventh round, Teddy crossed his opponent with a right, which brought him to a complete halt. Before Johnny was able to throw up a guard, Baldock let loose a second pulsating drive at Haydn's exposed chin; like a wet sack he fell where he stood. In stopping the fight, the referee almost certainly saved a knockout result. Baldock had finished his fight with Haydn two rounds sooner than the Flyweight Champion had managed and, as Morris had foreseen, the boxing writers homed in, calling the victory a 'classic win', acclaim which put a smile on Teddy's face.

A few weeks later, on the first day of the Brighton Races, Mike Honeyman and Baldock were fighting at the Dome: Teddy had a 15-round contest with Johnny Murton, one of the well-known Plymouth boxing brothers, and Honeyman was up against Chelsea's Billy Bird, whose full-time occupation was as a bus conductor.

The show was something of an East London get-together, promoted by Messrs Dorras and Hymans, with referees Sam Russell, Moss Deyong and

Joe Wilson, and Joe Morris as matchmaker, which was the principal reason why Honeyman and Baldock were on the programme. Top of the bill was Alf Barber, a native of Brighton, and Plymouth's Frankie Ash, a smart and experienced flyweight.

On the journey to Brighton, Honeyman made it clear that his wife would be unhappy if he got home late and was put out when his manager let him know he would be in the last contest of the day. Honeyman told Baldock, while giving Morris angry looks, 'Then you'll have to win your fight quickly, young Alf, and I'll make certain of catching my train even if I have to take a dive.'

Teddy quipped, 'Brighton's the right place for diving.' But no one was amused.

Baldock was on first with Johnny Murton, and the opening round was spent with the two fighters measuring each other up, a dance of assessment that any fight-goer will know well. But remembering Honeyman's matrimonial situation, in the second, Baldock pulled out a sharp right that put the lights out for Murton. He was unconscious before he reached the canvas and his head struck the boards with a sickening bump; it was some minutes before he came round.

The time Teddy had gained was taken back by Barber and Ash going the full 15 three-minute rounds. The Brighton man won on points, but then a featherweight novice competition was added to the bill. When Honeyman entered the ring late on, he was in a dark mood and as the leather started flying he soon forgot about the idea of taking a dive; resentment exuded from his very pores and it was all directed at the man in front of him. However, in the second round, Mike's blind rage made him careless of his own protection and Bird floored him, but the bell came to the Londoner's rescue. There had obviously been some damage done, so it wouldn't have been out of the question for Honeyman to call it a day in his corner, but the former British Champion possessed too much personal pride; this, added to the fact that he had been obliged to take a count, made him more determined to win.

Mike fought back fiercely against his younger rival and used all the tricks he knew to avoid further punishment. Gradually he was worn down by Bird's deliberate punching and, by the seventh round, after Honeyman had twice been floored for long counts, his seconds threw in the towel. (In fact, their was no rule dictating that the towel being thrown into the ring necessarily ends a fight, as only the referee can stop a fight and linen being slung could be interpreted as contravention of the laws. However, this informal symbol – once it was the sponge of surrender – has its foundations in the ritual fighting of the dim and distant past and as such carries with it an unlicensed authority.)

In the end, far from an early night, the East London party just about made their train.

Premierland in those days seemed to enjoy seeing a Welshman in the ring, and Baldock appeared to get his fair share of adversaries making the, what was then, considerable trip from the Principality to Commercial Road to test his metal. Just over two weeks after the Brighton show, Teddy was matched with Frankie Kestrell, who in Wales was considered to be the natural heir to Jimmy Wilde. Like most Welsh boxers, Frankie entered the ring sporting red shorts.

Most knowledgeable spectators would have supposed that Kestrell, whose left-hand work was renowned, would have proved a severe test for Baldock, but the East Londoner had little trouble snapping back the Welshman's head with his speedy left jab, while bobbing out of range of anything Frankie came up with in return. Baldock repeatedly made his opponent miss, twisting and turning to avoid Kestrell's rights that were, in vain, seeking his mid-section.

Close to the end of the second round, Baldock attempted his favourite move, the left to the body and the right to the chin; it came off first time. Kestrell went down for six, with only the bell coming to his rescue. But coming out for the third he had not recovered and, after Teddy landed a couple more hurtful punches, he was practically out on his feet and, mercifully, his seconds tossed in the towel.

The win brought Baldock more press attention than he had thus far experienced, and awarded him a record of 100 undefeated contests. Although this was a vast over-estimate, by that time, Teddy had a fair few fights under his belt, having started at a very young age. But he had never kept a record or a scrapbook; he really didn't have the ego for such a pursuit. He just boxed out of love for the game, encouraged by his friends and family. His success was of course an added incentive and he was later to say if he had been beaten early on he might have given up on boxing and looked to other athletic pursuits. However, overall, Baldock was as close as one might come to a born boxer in terms of physical skill and psychological makeup.

Frankie Ash was Teddy's first opponent over 15 threes. A classy flyweight, Ash had been in boxing for a decade, and had recently fought in the US against some quality flyweights. He met both Frankie Mason, an American Champion, who had beaten him, and Johnny Buff, who he defeated. In 1921, Buff had won a Bantamweight World Title defeating Jackie Sharkey on points at Madison Square Gardens.

This was a 'newspaper decision'; in the early 20th century in North America these kind of decisions were usually made following an official 'no decision', often under the 'Frawley Law', which regarded matches as exhibitions and did not allow points decisions to be granted. A 'no decision' could also be enforced when the rules being used for the fight dictated or by pre-arrangement between the fighters involved. A 'no decision' was usually given when both boxers were still standing at the end of a bout, in which there had been no knockout and no official decision that either fighter had won could be reached. However, Americans have never liked 'ties', so groups of ringside journalists would agree a result that would be printed in the newspapers they worked for. But officially, a 'no decision' contest meant that neither boxer had lost or won (a draw).

Ash went on to contest 15 rounds with Pancho Villa, the 8st World Champion, but he lost a narrow points decision. This was followed by another 15 rounds with the World Champion-to-be Izzy Schwartz, where Ash got a more than creditable draw.

Baldock felt he had contrived how to defeat Ash after watching him in Brighton, but Teddy had been instructed not to take any chances and he understood that the meeting with Ash was the sternest test of his career to that point; he had still to acclimatise to the extra minute on each round as well as concentrating on getting the better of a dangerous opponent.

For the first time in his life Baldock saw his name at the top of Premierland's posters, and he was amused when he saw the title 'Mumtaz Mahal' added after the word 'Poplar'.

When Baldock Sr and Jack Lakey accompanied Teddy to Back Church Lane that Thursday evening, no one was more surprised than the young fighter to see people crowding to get into the venue. As the show commenced, the place was full to capacity, while hundreds contented themselves with standing outside to await results relayed by word of mouth.

Not everyone who got into Premierland managed to find a pew, but all sorts of chairs, seats, benches and stools were improvised from an array of boxes while others brought perches with them. People were sitting on windowsills, and others climbed up the walls to the rafters for a bird's-eye view of events.

There were certainly those among the multitude that wanted to see the Cockney boy beaten; as was nearly always the case, a lot of 'informal' betting was going on and the odds for an Ash victory were healthy.

It was clear Ash was intent on sapping his opponent's stamina with attacks to the body. Baldock parried each assault with his left; but he found Ash to be 'extremely tough'. The East Londoner repeatedly landed telling blows that jerked back his opponent's head, but for the most part Frankie initially appeared to be undaunted and as soon as he made Baldock miss he was inside, working away with both hands below the ribs.

Most neutrals would have given the first five rounds to Baldock. But it was at this stage that Jack Goodwin, Ash's trainer for the fight, advised him to work on pinning Teddy in a corner or on the ropes. Taking on this counsel, Frankie persistently charged Baldock, harrying him into these traps by the pure force of his advance. Ash did well in the second five-round stint, but, although he had taken a lot of punishment, Teddy was in no way distressed, and, ducking around on the ropes, the Londoner managed to avoid a lot of his pursuer's punches. Another factor in Teddy's favour was that Ash would often hit with the inside of the glove, which he was warned about by the referee Sam Russell on more than one occasion.

Baldock was taking advantage of his opponent's tactic by grabbing hold of Ash as he came in, pulling him on to a punch, before pushing him away. However, all this was not going to be enough. Teddy was finding the extra minute at the end of each round a difficult extra exertion.

In the 10th, Teddy dredged the bedrock of his resolve to find the means to knock his man out. He landed a few crisp rights to Ash's jaw, one almost dropping him, but the Plymouth lad remained on his feet, although he was begin-

ning to feel exhaustion dragging down his limbs and he was slowing significantly.

In the final five rounds, Baldock was able to sustain his defence and launch
some telling attacks. And, although he too was drained, by the bell at the end
of the fight he got the decision.

Following the contest, Teddy was presented with an engraved silver cup by
his supporters. For some reason, he decided not to read the inscription until
he got home, but the cup was stolen from his dressing room that same evening
and as such he was never to find out what the message had said.

A short while after, Baldock was matched with the exceedingly strong Sheffield flyweight Tiny Smith. Smith (somewhat predictably given his nickname)
was shorter than Teddy and his reach was nowhere near that of the rangy
Poplar man, but he battled with determination, all the time looking to get in at
close quarters where he certainly had the better of things, and he made it clear
he had travelled South prepared for a fight.

But Baldock's well-taught and absorbed ring sense, together with his grace-
ful footwork, were enough to get him out of trouble as the Yorkshire lad
crowded him to the ropes or attempted to pin him into a corner. Teddy knew it
could prove fatal to allow Smith to get close enough to use his short but powerful arms, so, for the 15 rounds, he combined defence with attack, keeping
Tiny at bay while scoring from long range. But this was a hard bout for Teddy.
Smith was a fine boxer, cultivated in a town built on steel that created tough
fighters, and Baldock, along with many others, believed that Smith deserved
to win a title.

The clear public demand to see Baldock, as evidenced by the turnout at Premierland for his top-of-the-bill fights with Frankie Ash and Tiny Smith, convinced Joe Morris and Teddy's father that their lad was on the path to a title
fight, and a concerted publicity campaign was initiated.

Morris threw out a challenge via the sporting press declaring that Baldock
would meet anyone hitting close to the 8st mark in a range of athletic contests
that included a mile run, a boxing match of 10 rounds, high and long jump, a
100-yard swim, skipping for half an hour, punching a ball for the same period
and half-a-mile scull, with £50 put up for Baldock to win five out of the eight

events. These kinds of challenges were not unusual for the time and demonstrate how much sport was merged in the public mind with entertainment. However, there were no takers, much to Teddy's disappointment, as he had done a fair amount of special training for all the 'events'. His high-jump best was 5ft 6in, which was pretty good, given that was almost his own height, but he thought that Morris should have included cycling, because he considered himself a bit of a speed-king on a bike.

Although he had established himself as a winner, Baldock seemed unable to overcome his apparent shyness, and appeared to dislike being surrounded by people in the dressing room, all spouting different versions of how he had won a fight. He often speculated that those who observed his fights, being on the outside of the ring, might have had a better view of what he did than he had, but there were other times when he thought these onlookers had got his fights confused with other contests and were attributing the feats of his fellow boxers to him.

In fact, being told how good a boxer he was embarrassed Baldock as he was quite aware that occasionally he had been close to losing and that at points he had felt he could just succumb when there seemed to be no resources, mental, physical or spiritual, left to call on.

As often as he could, Teddy would return to his dressing room after a fight, change quickly and go directly home. Sometimes, if there were other quality fighters on the bill, he would take a place at the ringside and watch the contests, but he often found himself the centre of attention, in which case, he would even miss an historic main bout and make for the relative sanctuary of Byron Street.

The day after a fight, Baldock would try to get away. Skipping any post-fight training, he would try to put some distance between himself and Poplar. During the summer he would take himself to see a county cricket match, and in the winter lose himself in a football crowd, West Ham if they were at home, or another outdoor sport. If the weather was too bad, he would go to a billiards match or the cinema.

Periodically, reporters would even haunt the Baldock home, looking for an interview, but they were hardly ever successful, as his mum would feign ignorance of his whereabouts. His dad and Joe Morris were unhappy that he so consistently avoided any publicity, but Teddy felt it was what he had to do. In his view, Ted and Joe mostly had their own way, but he thought that if he continued to win he had the right to some privacy, at least on the day following a fight. And, despite his reclusiveness, Morris was not having any problems organising fights for his boy; he was now pretty well guaranteed a capacity crowd at Premierland if Baldock featured on the bill. However, the time was coming when he would need to move on from East End venues and Albert Hall promoter Harry Jacobs was interested in staging an event that included Baldock.

Believing that he had been unfortunate not to get at least a draw against Baldock, Frankie Ash was keen for a return fight, and his manager was insistent that any rematch would be at 8st and over 20 rounds. However, Morris was adamant that Teddy would not go more than 15 rounds and would fight at 8st 2lb. This was because he thought Baldock's potential for a title shot was at flyweight, and defeat at 8st would damage his chances of making this happen.

While this wrangling was going on, Teddy was matched with Jim Haddon, a talented Birmingham flyweight. Once more the Poplar puncher had the reach and height advantage, but there was a nagging doubt about how well his young, slight body was conditioned to withstand sustained punishment from close quarters, as he had not been tested in the top class of body beaters. This meant he had to concentrate on keeping opponents like Haddon literally at arm's length.

Most capable boxers would have known how to undermine Baldock, and Haddon was quickly laying into his mid-section and succeeded in breaking through a few times. He showed himself to be a dangerous customer for Baldock, and, by the time he stood up to go out for the second round, Teddy had decided to try a right to see if he could stop the Midlander.

The first one Haddon ducked inside and Teddy's effort went harmlessly round his opponent's neck, but the next attempt caught him flush on the chin and he went down in an instant. In that second, the bell rang and the reprieved Haddon leaped to his feet and made for his corner. He staggered and almost stumbled to the floor on his way, but he seemed to gather his senses together, grasping on to the ropes as he slumped on to his stool.

Teddy took this as a clear indication that Haddon was hurt and his right became a devastating weapon from the third round on, consigning his adversary to the canvas on a number of occasions. Following each visit to the boards, Haddon came charging back, attempting to fool Baldock that no real damage had been done; however, by the fifth round he was all in and the referee stepped in to stop the fight.

Billy Shaw was the next to try Baldock just over three weeks later. The Leeds boxer had fought a stirring battle with Young Johnny Brown at Premierland, and had defeated Tiny Smith, so he was considered stern enough opposition.

As was normal for bills that included Baldock, Premierland had a full house, although some might have considered they didn't get much in the way of value for money that night. Teddy started off against Shaw with some swift lefts to the face, then stepped in with a left to the body, and, as his opponent's guard fell, he sent over a sweet right that caused Shaw to tumble to the canvas. He rose at six, but was dazed and not really aware what was going on around him. Baldock sensed this and decided to finish his opponent, stepping in with the right. But every time Teddy hit home and dropped Shaw to the floor, he would rise with Lazarus like inevitability. In the end it was the referee who called a halt to the battering. The whole exercise had lasted two minutes!

At this stage in his career, Baldock became even more conscious of the need, with both right and left punches, to strike hard, straight and accurately, making contact with the back knuckles. He was to reflect on how much he owed to those who taught him his trade early on and their insistence that he continued to practise his punching technique until the most effective and damaging method became something that could be carried out without thought, as an instinctive reaction. Every successful boxer will find the best way for them to hit; there are general standards but individual delivery is unique, and Teddy's father's tuition in the back kitchen of the Baldocks' Byron Street home was never forgotten. With his baby fists shod in tiny gloves, strapped on to his wrists with rubber bands, Teddy had been taught how to deliver these blows, achieving the correct balance to force the whole of his body weight behind them.

Like all boxers, from time to time, Baldock's shots went adrift – after all he was up against worthy opponents, men who had trained hard to make him miss – but he certainly hit his target much more than most. Teddy applied his mind in order to connect with the right punches at the right moment, timing his man as he came in so that he met his blows with double the force. He learned to turn his feet in the direction of his punches, in order to hit correctly and find openings for his long shots in the split second they were exposed.

Ernie Veitch, from Leamington (near Barnsley), posed Baldock's next challenge, in what would be his last match at Premierland for a while. It took Teddy just seven rounds to finish the Northerner. Following this fight, Joe Morris gave up his role as matchmaker at Premierland, and confined himself to arranging matches for his own fighters, which had grown in number; he now also had responsibility for Johnny Curley, Alf Simmons, Billy Bird and Billy Boulger (who was to take on the job of Baldock's sparring partner).

TEDDY THE CONQUEROR

Eventually, Joe Morris reached an agreement with Harry Jacobs, and Baldock's final fight of 1925 pitted him against the Frenchman Antoine Merlo over 15 rounds at the Royal Albert Hall. The contest was one of a number of main events, which included Alf Mancini against Laurie Raiteri, Harry Corbett fighting Jack Dando, and a bout between the Scottish welterweight Johnny Brown and the French Welterweight Champion, Emile Romerio.

Merlo was a class act. He had gone 17 rounds with Elky Clark, the British flyweight titleholder, and had claimed two victories over François (Titi) Moracchini, the man who met Clark for the European flyweight title in 1926 and who would be the French Bantamweight Champion two years later. The match was made at 8st 3lb; Merlo came in spot on, with Baldock the lighter by three-quarters of a pound.

For this event, Teddy had trained just outside Brighton, at the Chinese Gardens at Hurstpierpoint, a hotel and tea garden. Jack Lakey was in charge of the training camp set up to prepare Baldock for his big fight. Everyone slept in one large room during the stay, so naturally there was always room for practical jokes while taking breaks from the strict regime.

The evening prior to the Merlo fight, Baldock went to the gym. He didn't switch on the light and on the way out he slipped and hit the back of his head, knocking himself out. Teddy was unconscious when his colleagues picked him up, and they rushed him into the Chinese Gardens, where Joe Morris was contacted by telephone. He immediately left London and reached Hurstpierpoint at 1 am. Although Baldock had recovered by the time he saw his manager, Morris was shocked; in fact, Teddy had never seen him so worried. However, when Joe realised his star wasn't hurt, he wanted to know why he hadn't taken more care.

Trying to calm his manager, Baldock told Morris, 'I'm all right.'

Furious, Joe hollered, 'You might be, but what about the fight?'

Baldock tried to be reassuring. 'Don't worry. There's no bones broken, and I feel good as gold.'

But this did not satisfy Morris, who called in two doctors, and after a full examination they gave Baldock a clean bill of health.

Teddy did no more training and felt no ill effects until about the halfway point of the fight, when his strength seemed to drain from him, and he found himself needing to summon up all his energy reserves. It was clear that Merlo had trained to the peak of condition and, like many continental fighters, was extremely strong. Baldock understood that, in those days, when an athlete represented France, it was considered a patriotic duty to be fit, and to be beaten by an Englishman would mean returning to France in shame.

As was his wont, Teddy started at a brisk pace, labouring with intent, rifling straight lefts to the face while Merlo did his utmost to fight his way in close. One look at his broad shoulders and muscular physique made it obvious to Baldock that allowing Merlo to get near enough to score with his half-arm blows could cause him serious damage, and so he moved around the ring at great speed, dizzying Merlo as the Bouches-du-Rhône boy attempted to follow his movements.

Baldock threw some hefty shots at Merlo's nose, but he continued to advance almost unflinchingly. One and then two powerful rights slammed on to his chin, but still he came on. Seemingly oblivious to Teddy's efforts, the Marseilles machine repeatedly charged Baldock on to the ropes, and the Londoner was obliged to tie up his opponent's fast-moving arms.

Every time the fighters went into a clinch, the referee broke them and that helped Baldock get back to his long-range shots, piling up the points in the process and avoiding being hit.

But the Frenchman's stamina and bravery were amazing. He seemed programmed to merely hunt Teddy down. Dozens of Baldock punches were right on target but never once caused his 'chasseur' to falter or ease up his attack.

In the fifth, Merlo rushed across the ring pushing Baldock to the ropes where he heaved a tremendous uppercut into the Englishman. Baldock was shaken, but his only options were to take more pain and punch it out with Merlo. The two men stood toe-to-toe for 30 seconds or more, firing out their hardest shots; either man could have fallen at this point. The spectators of course loved the little war, but there was no way the fighters could have kept such a vicious exchange going, and Baldock broke away to circle Merlo, stabbing him with left jabs as he went.

Baldock was desperately in need of a respite, but the Frenchman looked relatively fresh. Teddy began to think that his accident the previous day was having an effect. Merlo was doing well for several rounds, and it looked as if the fight was slipping away from the Londoner.

In the 11th, Baldock found a second wind from somewhere, and started getting back at his opponent. He made the final five rounds his own, but his opponent refused to slow up, battling his way in close to let loose a barrage into Teddy's ribs, which the Poplar man would feel for days after.

As Baldock returned to his corner at the final bell, part of him was resigned to taking a draw, but the referee gave him the verdict. It was a popular decision, and his victory was met with a resounding roar of approval, but Merlo also received loud applause as he left the ring. He departed with his dignity intact, having proved himself a worthy warrior in the lion's den.

Baldock's first big West End fight had ended in a victory that gave him a profile of international proportions, but, even given his achievement, the welcome on his return to Poplar would have been hard to predict. People lined the streets and roads awaiting their hero's return. A huge group had gone to the Albert Hall in a convoy of charabancs, and there was something close to pandemonium as they disembarked back on home turf. Those who had been unable to make the trip were clamouring for every detail of the contest, and stories were told of 'the greatest fight in the history of boxing' when East London had defeated France.

The ever-diffident Baldock fell asleep in his family kitchen while the entire area outside remained enthralled by his success. In his own home, the 15 rounds had been relived time and again and as such he was obliged to effectively repeat the psychological effects of the contest. As soon as he was able Teddy went to bed but could still hear people talking in the streets of their local hero who had put Poplar on the continental map.

6

THE UNBEATABLE STRAIGHT LEFT

1926

Baldock's Albert Hall performance demonstrated that he was a real draw, and as such Harry Jacobs booked him for a sequence of monthly fights, promising Joe Morris that a catchweight match with Elky Clark (ominously a riveter by trade) would result and, depending on how he fared against the British Flyweight Champion, a title fight at the NSC was a distinct possibility.

Jacobs himself could have organised a Championship fight, but Lonsdale Belts were an attraction at that time, particularly for boxers (like Clark) who had marked up a Lonsdale victory and wanted to take another step towards winning one outright (even though boxers at that time were starting to value purses higher than trophies). However, in those days, only title fights that were staged at the NSC could offer a Lonsdale Belt.

Clark (who after his boxing career would earn a living playing the dulcimer and accordion) was scheduled to defend his title against George Socks at the NSC on 22 February 1926, and it was agreed that he would meet Baldock at 8st 2lb four weeks later.

But, before that, Teddy's first fight of the year was a return bout with Frankie Ash, around seven months after their first encounter. Ash had asked for 20 three-minute rounds and for the fight to be made at 8st. But Morris wasn't going to be dictated to and dominated the terms, afterwards commenting, 'That's halfway towards winning the fight.' Baldock's manager believed in making matches well, and that meant playing the percentages and taking advantage when and where possible.

So Baldock once again decamped to the Chinese Gardens at Hurstpierpoint for training, accompanied by Johnny Curley, then the British Featherweight Champion. Curley, who was looked after by Archie Watson, trained according to his own personal method, and Archie was hard pushed to persuade him to follow any routine. Boxing historian Gilbert Odd wrote of Curley, 'Round-headed and red-haired, he was on the short side, but was a genius at working his way past defensive props. Once inside he would be extremely busy with both fists, hooking to the body and upper-cutting to the chin. His face held a cheerful look, even under pressure, and as far as sportsmanship went, he was the perfect little gentleman'. Johnny's confrontations with Yorkshire's Johnny Cuthbert and fellow Lambeth fighter Phil Bond lived long in the memories of boxing fans.

One evening, members of the Baldock party invited Curley to do some roadwork the next morning, the idea being to run him into the ground. At 7 am, on a frost-bitten February seaside dawn, Johnny met the group wrapped up in a rolled-top sweater, flannel bags, thick woollen socks and a big pair of boots with a large cap pulled over his ginger hair, and, as the runners sped off at a more than healthy pace, the Featherweight Champion was working hard to stay with the pack. Johnny had extraordinarily splayed feet, a genuine drawback when it came to roadwork, and, looking to save some dignity (and probably some energy), he told the others that he was going to take another route and made off alone in a completely different direction.

On return to their camp, the runners were ready for a big breakfast. Watson asked if they had seen Curley, to the surprise of the others, who had expected him to make it home before the group. When the afternoon came and it was time for gym work, there was still no sign of the Lambeth fighter, understandably causing his trainer to be beside himself with worry.

After the training session, the party had their main meal of the day, which was followed by rest and recreation and a light tea. In the evening, it was decided that they would catch the bus to Brighton, at which point Curley turned up, with a big smile on his face. He told the avid listeners that he had been to the races: 'After I left you blokes, some old Chinas of mine passed me in a car going to a point-to-point meeting, and they asked me to go with them. So I went.'

Pointing to Curley's outfit (which of course was the same one he had been wearing for training that morning), Teddy asked, 'You didn't go like that?'

Unabashed, the South Londoner replied, 'Why not? And I went into the ring, too.'

He was quickly warned to look out for Archie, who by that time was out for his man's blood, but Curley strolled off with the huge grin still lighting up the evening.

Teddy made his way back to London the night before the return contest with Ash and stayed at home. During the afternoon before the fight, he went to the weigh-in with Morris and Lakey. A meal was followed by some time out of the limelight before the drive to the Albert Hall.

An impressive bill had been put together by Harry Jacobs, and the main event of the evening was a Lightweight Championship meeting between the fine Jewish boxer Harry Mason and Ernie Rice. This was their second meeting too, and a somewhat acrimonious one, which would have added to the size of the crowd for the night, which had a definite East London flavour: Harry Corbett (like Mason from Bethnal Green) was fighting Whitechapel's Kid Berg; and Teddy was of course Poplar's representative.

In terms of 'rabbit' Mason was something of a precursor to Muhammad Ali, being seen as one of boxing's showmen in the mid-1920s. A defensive master, it was Mason's boast that no opponent had ever ruffled his carefully parted hair. He played the violin before fights to unsettle opponents and was also apt to address a crowd and recite verses from inside the ropes. Love him or hate him, Mason always entertained.

Harry's home in Fellbrigg Street, was not too far from where Teddy was born, but he began is boxing career in Leeds while working as a trolley boy for the London and North East Railway.

Following a string of victories he made his way back to East London, and within three years became British and European Lightweight Champion. He spent time in the USA before returning to the UK to challenge Scot Johnny Brown for the British Welterweight title. Brown came out on top but Harry won the Belt after the return match. His first defence of the title against Len Harvey ended in a draw, but in 1926 he lost his title to Jack Hoold (from Birmingham). But Mason wasn't done by a long chalk and, in 1934, his 32nd year, managed win back the Welterweight Crown in 1934. He hung up his gloves three years later.

Harry successfully defended his title against Ernie who was ruled out in the fifth round after an accidental low blow.

The experience Baldock had gained in his first bout with Ash gave him the belief that he could get another win, and his victory was a great deal easier in the second fight.

Ash weighed in at 7st 13½lb; Baldock was exactly a pound heavier. Teddy thought his opponent seemed even shorter than last time, and he was seemingly able to strike Frankie as he liked, using his harassing straight left as Ash worked his hardest to get under Baldock's lead hand.

But Baldock's opponent remained a perilous threat as an in-fighter. He had learned a great deal during his time in the US, but since their last meeting Teddy had also been studying his craft and was efficient in tying up his rival, causing his work to be less effective, and then, on the instruction to break, he returned to the long-range attacks to which he was best suited.

Ash had entered the ring with a slightly damaged left eye and in his anxiety to protect the injury was holding his right glove high across his face. This didn't complement his style and Baldock's left lead picked him off at will.

However, Ash looked to progress, bobbing and weaving energetically as he attempted to move inside, and Baldock was left to speculate where his target might be each time he fired a left; it was a waste of time aiming for his opponent's head as Frankie had dodged well before the punch was able to find its target.

But in the second round Baldock clipped Ash with a right uppercut that stopped him in his tracks; the left followed up, which was pursued by a right and left to the head. The last right once more tore open Frankie's left eye and the blood flowed.

A wave of confusion hit Ash, who was suddenly lost in the few square yards contained by rope; another right found his chin to send him reeling. After a short count he was back to his feet, but Baldock freely punished him with both hands, landing solid, scoring blows.

Frankie hit the canvas two more times, but, for Baldock, Ash was 'living up to his name and being as tough as the tree'. He seemed to get a second wind during the middle rounds, and Teddy prudently chose to keep him at the far end of his jabs, converting the bout into a running fight, swiftly circling his opponent and firing constantly, which stopped Frankie moving in close and prevented him from setting himself to deliver a telling blow.

Baldock's camp had agreed to covertly let their fighter know that, as a round was entering its final 10 seconds, there would be a quiet 'click-click' as he came near his corner. At the signal, Teddy changed gear, punching freely. He ran, two-fisted, into Ash's attack. Baldock knew his man would respond with like for like.

There was little risk of a knockout because of the lack of time, but this roaring finish by Baldock impressed both the crowd and the referee. Ash started to live in expectation of this regular, although sudden, assault, but he could not be sure when it might start, which made him a little guarded. As such, Teddy was dictating the tactics of the fight, which placed his rival at an increasing disadvantage. These bursts of power from Baldock began to wear Ash down and towards the end he was tiring considerably.

Teddy strolled the final two or three rounds and claimed a victory by a good points margin.

In Frankie's corner, he told Baldock, 'Blow me, Ted, I'm your best teacher. You get better every time you box.'

After a short holiday, preparations for the meeting between Elky Clark and Baldock got under way, but the Flyweight Champion was to pull out of a title fight against Kid Socks because of illness, requesting a postponement of two months and so ending the prospect of a contest with Baldock. Frankie Ash offered to stand in but Morris felt a third Baldock versus Ash fight would do nothing for Teddy, and Harry Jacobs could see no financial sense in staging such a bout. Instead, he suggested Baldock take on Alf Barber, a Brighton fighter with an outstanding record in the amateur ranks. In his professional career, Barber had claimed victory over Tiny Smith, Johnny Haydn, Kid Kelly, Frankie Ash, Kid Socks and had overcome Young Bill Lewis on two occasions.

But he lost to Socks in his last fight five months earlier at the NSC, which had been an eliminator for a chance to fight Clark for the title.

Alf got involved with Alec Goodman's training camp at Brighton and became Harry Mason's sparring partner. He trained well for his meeting with Baldock on 18 March at the Albert Hall, and he looked fit and dangerous for the scheduled 15 rounds at 8st 3lb. Frank Goddard, defending the Heavyweight Championship against Phil Scott, topped the bill. There were other 15-round contests on the night: Young Johnny Brown against Antoine Merlo, Jack 'Kid' Berg took on Andre Routis and Tom Heeney met Charlie Smith. Every man on the card, apart from Merlo, fought for a Championship during the course of his career; Scott, Heeney, Berg, Routis and Baldock all contested world titles.

It had originally been arranged for Goddard and Scott to fight for 20 rounds, in order to make the whole bill an 80-round package.

The Albert Hall was again packed, so much so that the Baldock camp had to struggle to make a path through a crowd to get into the great building via the 'tradesman's entrance'. Teddy recalled that it was 'a relief to reach the dressing room'.

Many believed that Barber was capable of inflicting a first defeat on Baldock, and he certainly meant business. As the opening bell rang, the Brighton man flew at his opponent, nearly catching him with a lethally destructive right. Barber sustained his energetic attacks, but Teddy used his feet well and his left jab kept him at bay. But as the first round matured the Londoner's long left was landing with a cruel and telling rhythm, while his right glove acted as a hurtful and repetitive encore.

Like most of Baldock's opponents around that period, Barber could not match his reach and Teddy drove home his advantage via his firm and accurate left fist. But Barber was ambitious and, despite the constant direct hits on his nose and heavy rights to his jaw, he kept coming. He absorbed more punishment than Baldock imagined possible. The East Ender felt in top form and seemed to be hitting harder than in any of his previous encounters.

The third round saw Teddy land a peach of a right that connected perfectly with Barber's chin; he toppled and took a count of eight. But once back on his feet there was more punishment awaiting him and he walked back to his corner with his left eye closing. Over the next two rounds, Barber became a simple target for Baldock; a large swelling was growing under his left eye and blood gushed from a nasty cut under the right.

Despite the ordeal, Barber bravely continued his attempts to close the distance between them, but his way was barred by Teddy's attacking defence. Barber had become Baldock's punchbag by the fifth round, and, despite the battered man's protests, the referee decided he had seen enough.

Teddy was relieved to see the ref come in, as he later said, 'No matter how much you want to win a fight, there's nothing clever in cutting another bloke to ribbons. Sure, I might have knocked him out if it had gone on much longer, but it wouldn't have done Barber or me any good.'

Once more, a night of merriment in Poplar followed, as the charabancs got their passengers back to the East End to celebrate another Baldock victory. Although it was close to midnight, the newsboys were doing a fast trade in late copies of the *Star* and *News*, and that night Teddy's result was stamped in by hand in the thousands of 'Stop Press' columns.

At the top of Byron Street, Joe Morris stopped the car to purchase a newspaper, 'Just to see if they've got the result right.'

A FIERCE-HITTING FRENCHMAN

Many 'knowledgeable commentators' believed Joe Morris was over-ambitious when he arranged for his fighter to contest 15 rounds against the French Flyweight Champion François 'Titi' (street urchin) Moracchini. Harry Jacobs put the fight on at the Albert Hall as a 'second-liner' to his Welterweight Championship bout between Len Harvey and Harry Mason exactly six weeks after Teddy's win over Alf Barber. Moracchini had a reputation as a durable and tough fighter as well as a hard two-fisted puncher. In his six-year career, the majority of his opponents had failed to last the distance against him. But Kid Socks had travelled to Paris a few months earlier for a 10-round contest and taken the decision.

Moracchini had never fought in Britain, and Baldock's manager and the promoter were a bit taken aback at the weigh-in. The Frenchman had extremely broad shoulders and a deep chest; he looked bull-like alongside Teddy's lean, wiry figure. He was also fairly tall, so Baldock was denied his usual height/ reach advantage.

But when Teddy ducked through the ropes he was in peak condition at 8st 3lb, although he was to admit he 'couldn't have made half a pound less'. It was starting to become clear that Teddy's time as a flyweight was over, and Joe Morris began to turn his focus on the bantams.

It was just as well that Baldock had trained so hard as Moracchini was to prove to be arguably the strongest and toughest Frenchman to land in Britain. As the bell signalled the start of the fight, he was on Teddy and swinging, machine like, with both hands. The crowd let out a collective shocked gasp at this furious assault, and for the first minute or two the homeboy had to call on all his knowledge and put in his fastest footwork to avoid demolition. It was clear that Moracchini was going for an early knockout. According to Baldock, 'he made the wind whistle with his hooks and swings' and he was frightened that, if Moracchini caught him on the chin, he would go down and not get up. Teddy knew he had to move, and, dodging punches with swift turns of the head and body, Baldock matched his opponent's speed and began to beat him to the punch with his incorrigible straight left.

Soon Teddy was finding it relatively easy to get through to the Frenchman's face, although Moracchini kept his gloves high until he got close enough to force them in Baldock's direction. This kept Teddy on the retreat for a lot of the time, but occasionally Moracchini would have an instant of hesitation and Baldock was rapier quick to spot the chance this offered, coming forward with a destructive, jabbing attack; the reliable tempo of left followed through with right.

In the corner following the initial round, Morris implored Baldock to keep out of the Frenchman's way and avoid any risks. But Teddy felt that Morris 'wasn't by any means the best man to have in a corner because he got too jittery. For every punch I took, poor Joe took a hundred, and I honestly believe he felt worse than I did when I came back to my corner after a hot session.'

Lakey was more encouraging, often telling his fighter that he was doing fine and winning, and throwing in occasional suggestions about tactics. But Teddy really didn't need instructions as he respected Moracchini's punching power. He also understood that this was going to be a long fight; he had struck the point of Titi's chin with a force that would have dropped many fighters but he had seemed totally unperturbed, merely moving forward more fiercely.

Moracchini's persistence in attack began to be the feature of the fight as the rounds went by. It was a fantastic spectacle and it seemed it was only a matter of time before Baldock would be tagged. It became obvious that Teddy only had to miss once with his left, or duck the wrong way, and the fight would be over. Baldock constantly told himself, almost mantra-like, that he had to hit his man flush every time.

However, Teddy was proficient in beating his opponent to the punch; in fact, he confessed that at one point he was concerned it became monotonous. Just as the Frenchman was lunging forward with a swing, Baldock's left would catch him just under the nose. These blows pulled Moracchini up short and knocked his head back, but he recovered his balance and was back into the attack almost immediately.

Having made no ground using right crosses, in the third round, Baldock tried the uppercut, which resulted in some significant blows that were delivered with good weight behind them. Teddy landed several of these under the Frenchman's chin, but, once more, the man waded on seemingly impervious.

Although Baldock was catching punches, he was dodging many more. The majority of the blows that hit him did so when he was moving away, and, as such, much of their power was dissipated by the time they connected. Teddy was also landing half-a-dozen blows for every one he took, so the occasional hard knock was not enough to weaken him considerably.

Baldock had been working on Moracchini in a deliberate way, concentrating on doling out his punches effectively. But midway through the fight he became weary of this approach and decided to go for the knockout in the ninth round. The Frenchman appeared to slow in the second half of the bout, and Teddy took the chance to work on his body and hook hard to the chin. But his attacking attitude overcame his instinct to defend and gave his opponent a chance to score. Moracchini whipped in three rights to Baldock's body, inflicting a wide and deep valley of pain.

Teddy grabbed hold of Moracchini looking to prevent more of the same. He was cautioned by the referee but had gained vital seconds to take a breather and gain his composure before the instruction to box on. Baldock had enough sense to revert to long-range work, keeping danger at bay with the left, no matter how monotonous it got!

There was another scolding awaiting Teddy in his corner. His manager ranted, 'Think yourself clever, don't you? Now you've shown him just how to beat you, so will you use the ring and keep out of his way?'

Morris was proved right in the next round. Moracchini steamed into Baldock with a greater fury than ever before. Teddy answered with a succession of left-hand blows and a well-placed right to the jaw, along with repeated uppercuts. But fighting François kept firing back with bombs of his own and the hardest were set off around Teddy's body, delivering a pounding of rib-bending proportions. However, Moracchini could not trap Baldock in a corner. Teddy was well aware that if he got pinned he would very likely be pummelled flat before he could escape, so, as soon as the threat of being cornered seemed to loom, he turned his rival into the ropes and slid away, or he fought his way to freedom.

A dozen rounds in, Baldock took a smash of a left hook to the short ribs, and he dropped for a short count. The punch stole much of his energy and the whole of the Albert Hall, including Moracchini, could see that Teddy was both shaken and hurt.

The Frenchman, sensing the potential to end the fight with a knockout, came wheeling into Baldock, forcing him to go on the run for the remainder of the round. His retreat continued until the 14th, at which point Morris let him know that if he kept his feet victory would be his. Moracchini must have shared that opinion, as he pressed forward with what seemed like double the brutality. But Baldock took advantage of his opponent's abandonment to attack, grabbing points with his left jab, even though this was not pulling up Moracchini. With half the round to fight, the Frenchman bullied Baldock on to the ropes, and it seemed he had him where he wanted him; at this point Teddy had to forget defence and fight his way out.

It became a last-man-standing street brawl, made all the more frantic by the crowd jumping to their feet and roaring with enthusiasm for the battle. It was hard to say who came off worse, but the pair continued the wild war right up to the gong.

The touching of gloves that opened the final round was immediately followed by Moracchini letting go with a two-handed assault on Baldock's chin, but Teddy was quick to get his head beyond the Frenchman's range and he only felt the tail winds from Moracchini's gloves as they whistled past. For the best part of the three minutes, Baldock stayed out of trouble by sticking out the left and making the Frenchman miss. This was excruciatingly hard work in itself, requiring attentiveness and physical exertion, and Teddy was more than relieved to hear the final bell. Baldock was to say at the end of the fight that he wasn't very worried who the referee might decide was the winner, as he was just happy to finish the fight on his feet.

The announcer climbed into the ring and pointed in Baldock's direction, signalling the fact that he had been given the decision. Teddy was told the bout was a 'brilliant exhibition of boxing', and that he had won by a good margin, but he saw the contest as the hardest of his career thus far, and felt he had come close to defeat several times during the fight.

Teddy Baldock – The Pride of Poplar.
The Story of Britain's Youngest Ever Boxing World Champion

7

BANTAM BALDOCK

When the announcement was made that Baldock would fight at bantamweight in future, challenges came in from all points of the compass. Young Johnny Brown, a Jewish boxer from Spitalfields, based in St Georges, and brother of the British and European Champion, was very keen, and so was Mick Hill, who had just been defeated in a title fight by the elder Brown. (Both brothers fought under the name Johnny Brown, as, in those days, when a younger sibling started fighting they were often tagged with the prefix 'Young' to the elder brother's name and sometimes promoters would start billing them as such. If they were successful, it would be difficult to revert to a proper birth name, as people would not recognise it!). Morris and Baldock were well aware that Brown and Hill and many others would need to be defeated before Teddy could press for a title fight. The Champion at this time was in the US, where, while not doing well, he was rumoured to be making a lot of money.

Baldock wanted to experience America for himself. There was money to be made but he also saw it as the place to extend his ring knowledge. So, when he learned that Ted Broadribb was considering taking Jack Hood and Alf Mancini across the Atlantic, he was keen to join the party.

Neither Teddy's father nor Joe Morris thought that the trip was a good idea. Morris told his fighter, 'You're doing very nicely over here, you young idiot. They'll knock hell out of you in America. Not only that, you're underage and won't be allowed to box more than six rounds.'

But Baldock was determined that the US held the key to his future, and talked to Broadribb about the possibilities. The former 'Young Snowball' told Teddy that he would look after him. Edward Alfred Broadribb was born on 4 December 1888, at 219 East Street, Wandsworth (then part of Surrey). After his boxing career, Broadribb went on to manage the likes of Don McCorkindale, Johnny Williams, Tommy Farr, Ernie Roderick, Freddie Mills, Len Johnson and Ernie Jarvis, so he was a good mentor for Baldock.

But Teddy's father and Joe would have none of it, and this caused something of a split in the Baldock camp. Morris insisted that Teddy was contracted to him, but the fighter reminded Joe that, as he was underage, his contract wasn't binding. But his dad told him that because he was underage *he* had the last word in all matters.

Teddy caught them both unprepared when he asked them what they were afraid was going to happen if went to America. He told them, 'I think I ought to go. I want a holiday, anyway, and it won't do me any harm. I'll have one or two contests, and, if it doesn't work out well, I promise you both I'll come back straight away.'

Baldock's decision to be a member of Ted Broadribb's party for the US upset the rhythm of his previous training and home life. Even his usually supportive mother believed her boy was too young to be going overseas. But the fighter was naturally excited by the prospect, feeling he needed a change and that the opportunity came at the right time.

Morris believed that the unfamiliar environment and opponents with foreign styles, temperament, approach and attitude would not be helpful to his fighter but Teddy argued that his ambitions to one day fight for a world title meant that he would be well advised to acclimatise himself to the American fighting style.

Eventually, it was agreed to let the lad cross the pond, and, although Baldock had not stopped arguing with Morris and his father about the trip, he had still been purchasing all the necessary items for his journey. The mood at the gym and at home was tense, but far from changing his mind this made Teddy look forward even more to boarding the ship.

But, before leaving, he had two further fights scheduled to take place at Premierland. The first before sailing was with Tiny Smith who had been 15 rounds with Baldock the year before. The venue was filled to capacity for Teddy's return to the East End following a seven-month absence and the two fighters gave the packed audience value for money.

Ploughing into Baldock in his customary resolute manner, Smith looked determined; however, Teddy felt he could manage this. The tough Sheffield warrior made an impression in the first round, wading in with two-handed attrition, but that afternoon Baldock was at his best; his left seemed to hypnotise Smith. The jab was so swift that the Yorkshireman appeared disoriented and was hit at will. When he did try to strike, favouring a furious hook, Teddy's defensive body-swerve caused him to repeatedly miss. Smith continued to try to pursue his prey but when Baldock called on his right hand it was clear that the fight would not continue for much longer. It cracked into Smith's jowl so quickly that he was forced to try to absorb some of these blows, while attempting to elude the rockets that would relentlessly follow to his head.

Smith was boxed to a standstill by round five, providing little more than target practice for Baldock from then on, and the referee Sam Russell stopped the contest to lead Smith back to his corner.

After the fight, Phil Lolosky climbed into the ring to challenge Baldock at 8st. Teddy had found it hard to make 8st 4lb for Smith, as Phil knew. It was by now also common knowledge that Baldock was on his way to the US and so challenges of this type had to be expected.

Harry Mason, who was matched to fight Jack Hood in a return contest for the Welterweight Championship and Lonsdale Belt, was at Premierland that afternoon. He conducted an auction in aid of the striking miners' wives and children and was a one-man variety act. He was offered a pound note to sing a song, and he gave a rendition of the West Ham United anthem 'I'm Forever Blowing Bubbles', followed up with a performance of the Charleston to his own accompaniment on the violin.

Around a week before he was due to sail across the Atlantic, Baldock made his final appearance at Premierland against another Yorkshireman, Kid Nicholson, a good-class bantamweight, who had quite a reputation in the Northern rings.

Morris hadn't wanted this fight and pressured Baldock to call it off, but Teddy thought the money would be helpful for his forthcoming trip, going towards paying for his passage. The promoters had directly approached Baldock about the fight, and Teddy felt it was likely that they knew Morris would not have taken it at any price. But having given his word Baldock was loath to cancel. He struggled to make 8st 4lb, and there was all-round surprise at the weigh-in when, as he boarded the scales, they went down with a clatter. He had trained hard, but didn't feel at all in fighting condition; however, Teddy was conscious that he had to do his work that night.

The crowd that filled Premierland were of course ignorant of their favourite's problems. As Baldock walked along the gangway to the ring, he heard a bookmaker wager £20 to a cigar on his winning the fight. Not feeling at all right, he had the urge to warn him to shorten the odds.

Nicholson was being given no chance, and, sitting in his corner, as his gloves were being adjusted, Teddy could hear the offers of six to one against the Leeds man.

Later, Baldock was to concede that his opponent that night was a good fighter but believed that he should have 'licked him without any bother'. However, from the first round, Teddy was missing badly with the left, and his right was even more wayward. He felt sluggish and thought that he would have been better off anywhere but in a fight.

The fans at Premierland watched in amazement, as the Yorkshireman beat Baldock to the punch with a straight left in the initial rounds, and when he dived in and trapped Teddy on the ropes with a two-fisted barrage the local man was powerless.

Baldock's corner was animated like never before, and he was scolded and berated between the rounds. But, despite all the advice, he was unable to get himself going and it was lucky that Nicholson didn't seem to be equipped with a one-punch finish.

The Kid was in front by round five, but Teddy's supporters continued to hope and urged their man on with shouts of 'Do something, Baldock,' and 'Wake up, Teddy'. This seemed to have some effect, as his combative spirit asserted itself, and Baldock began to drive the surprised Nicholson across the ring with an all-guns-blazing attack. It seemed Teddy had begun to turn the tide!

Nicholson was falling prey to long lefts as well as both left and right uppercuts to the body and it became clear that he was uncomfortable with the digs downstairs. Teddy now concentrated on the body, hoping to bring the Kid's guard down when he could then switch to the head. He walked the seventh and eighth rounds and was now back in the fight. Nicholson made a great effort in the ninth, fighting back fiercely with lefts and rights to the head, but Baldock's blows carried more weight and midway through the round he found a punch to send the Yorkshireman tumbling. Teddy could not believe it when Sam Russell instantly ruled him out, declaring the punch to have been low, and Nicholson was declared the winner.

Uproar followed. Baldock's first loss had come by way of a foul. Following the fight he told the referee that he would rather have lost it any other way, to which Russell replied, 'You ought to feel pleased I didn't disqualify you a few rounds earlier. You went very low then, and, if Nicholson had gone down or claimed a foul, I'd have let him have it.'

Teddy chose not to respond to this.

There was some talk of Russell having taken advantage of the generous odds on Nicholson, but, according to Baldock, the well-known referee had officiated at many of the contests he had been involved in and Teddy had never had occasion to be critical before. So he decided to 'just take it with a smile knowing that Sam did his duty'.

Nevertheless, the defeat was a painful experience for Teddy, especially in front of his home supporters at Premierland. But, with the prospect of boarding the *Berengaria* for his first trip to the United States, Baldock at least had something to take his mind off his loss and the end to his unbeaten record. When the time came for him to leave, he got a great send-off from the East End and it was thought that the land of opportunity, home of the brave, would quickly take a liking to the modest young man from Poplar.

Teddy Baldock – The Pride of Poplar.
The Story of Britain's Youngest Ever Boxing World Champion

8

TO AMERICA

The party that looked to America were a convivial bunch. Alf Mancini in particular was to become a good friend to Teddy. They bunked together and trained as a pair in the ship's gym. Both men provided several exhibitions for their fellow passengers. For the young man from Poplar, the voyage was a wonderful experience in itself, but the Londoner would never forget the sensation of seeing New York for the very first time. As the liner approached, Teddy watched in wonder from the upper deck, to him, the City's magnificent skyscrapers seemed to rise from the sea like magnificent fingers of marble pointing to heaven. The appearance felt threatening, forbidding, cold and mechanical, with none of the grimy, homely welcome London gives you as you sail up the Thames, between the long miles of docks and factories.

Mancini was delayed on Ellis Island on a technicality, so Baldock stayed with him while Ted Broadribb and Jack Hood went on to organise the party's affairs. Eventually, it was arranged for Mancini and Baldock to stay with a German family at Woodhaven, Long Island. They were made to feel at home and found the lodgings comfortable. But the first time their landlady saw Teddy she threw up her hands in shock, telling him that he needed 'feeding up', and the wiry East Londoner feared she would make him a heavyweight if she had her way. He was a bantam at this point but he couldn't allow himself free rein. He soon convinced her of his situation and, in his words, 'she looked after me like a mother'.

Mancini and Baldock quickly found their way around and made friends in the neighbourhood. They would travel into New York on the overhead railway for a nickel. Looking back, Teddy declared that it was 'the cheapest ride in the world and we couldn't get over it'.

The party trained at the St Nicholas gym, which later became a fight arena and a nursery to Madison Square Garden. Baldock found it to be 'businesslike' compared to what he had known before, with its three rings simultaneously in use. When the three 'Limeys' put in their first appearance, the Americans crowded round to assess their ability.

Hood did his stuff first, followed by Mancini, with Baldock last on show. Few remarks had been made when Baldock stepped up. He was keen to demonstrate his ability but at the end of a round there was still little comment. Jack came to his corner and told him, 'Don't show them all you've got and don't let that fellow [he nodded towards the sparring partner assigned to Teddy] mess you around. Just let 'em see you're no mug, but no more.'

Hood, who was five years older than Baldock, would be very supportive throughout the whole trip, always ready with encouragement and advice.

Ted let the lads have some time to find their land legs, but eventually came into the gym to let Baldock know he was to meet Mickey Gill (also known as Irish Terror, Homer Smith and Irish Mickey Gill), an Irish-American (born in Dublin on 1 January 1905), over half-a-dozen rounds at Rockaway Beach in the Steeplechase Arena.

For his first contest in America (indeed, his first outside Britain), Baldock could boast just three supporters (Ted Broadribb, Alf Mancini and Jack Hood) as he climbed into the Steeplechase Athletic Arena ring. But he was glad to have at least these friendly faces, because although the environment at Premierland was usually dense and filled with sound, the New York fight fans were completely different. They gave off an aura of suspicion coupled with an expectation that they would get a fair return for their admission fee, plus interest; they wanted to see a performance that would truly impress them and sustain them until the next fight night. And, while, of course, this is to some extent true of every boxing arena, in New York, in the 1920s, there was a chill of cold aggression in the fight audience.

Then, even more so than now, New Yorkers were sceptical about foreign fighters coming to their rings, and Englishmen in particular, who were often seen as pallid, effete weaklings all too ready to go to the canvas or as physical representations of ancient colonialism (certainly by locals with Irish and to a lesser extent Scottish ancestry) or sometimes both.

This atmosphere made Teddy feel nervousness like he had never known before, but when he got to his corner, supported by his compatriots, he soon regained his poise.

Mickey Gill was a few years older than Teddy. Dublin born Gill had been based in Vancouver (British Columbia, Canada) before coming to New York. He appeared very organised and concentrated, but Baldock wondered about his opponent's know-how and experience.

Mickey came whirling out of his corner firing two-fisted, but Teddy detected that he had almost no defence to the straight left, and soon Baldock was jabbing him so often that the crowd began to deridingly whistle their own man.

Gill might have thought that his opponent would slow after the first round, but Teddy kept up his bombardment. The Irish-Canuck/Yank was punched dizzy for two minutes before making a forceful rush, looking to get inside, and on making it in close he hit out with all he had, but Teddy fought back with matching gusto. The pair provoked enthusiastic yells from the crowd as they traded leather. As the bell went, Baldock felt he was taking no chances as he assessed that his opponent had nothing big in his armoury.

As the fight progressed, it was clear that Teddy was in control, hitting Gill with left-right combinations almost at will, but not quite finding the knockout blow. The six-round limit (Baldock's age restricted him to six-round bouts within New York City State) made this an easy fight for the Londoner as he was already well conditioned to 15-round bouts in London arenas. He was the obvious winner and received a great ovation as he left the ring.

Later Teddy was told he was among a very few that had been so well received at the seashore club and that he had made a lasting impression. Ted Broadribb was pleased, and alongside many others saw the fight as a good start to the tour.

Gill went on to enlist in the American Army at the start of the Second World War and volunteered as a paratrooper. Private First Class Mickey Gill was killed in action in France on 3 November 1944 aged 39.

The day following Baldock's first showing in a New York fight arena, local newspaper scribes raved about the new 'English Invader';

'Wizardly boxing skill combined with blinding speed and aggressiveness, marked Baldock's display. Baldock lived up to all advance praises extended in his behalf, and showed form somewhat reminiscent of the style of Jimmy Wilde, the Mighty Atom, with a dash of Bud Taylor thrown in for his aggressive nature. Judging him by his showing last night it will take nothing less than a champion to beat Baldock. His future is established in American fistic circles'.

Teddy sent a few cuttings home and celebrated with Mancini at a local drugstore, a block away from their lodgings, which was to be a nightly venue for the two pals. Another German woman ran the store and made a great fuss of the two Brits, despite the fact that it took her a while to understand East End slang and the Cockney sense of humour.

Broadribb pulled off something of a coup getting Jack Hood a fight at Madison Square Garden against Jimmy 'The Fighting Welshman' Jones, from Youngstown, a man with much experience. The Swedish heavyweight, Harry Persson, who had caused a sensation by knocking out the former Scotland Yard detective Phil Scott, was top of the bill, and managed to gain a points decision over Carl Carter, a gangling black New Yorker.

Mancini and Baldock went along to the Garden to support Hood. Teddy had heard plenty about the famous New York venue, and it certainly met his expectations, both inside and out. Baldock asked Broadribb about the chances of his getting a bout at the great arena, and Ted told him that if the Brummie welterweight put on a good performance, it would ease the way. But Jack's fight did not impress the locals. In Britain, he would have been given the decision. At the same time, he hadn't lost, but his stand-up style did not endear him to the New York fans who looked for something more dynamic in their boxing. Added to this, Americans don't like 'ties' and Hood got a draw. But Broadribb was content that Jack had shown his superb skills as a boxer and he still had Mancini in hand.

The three Englishmen were keen to fight, not being happy to remain idle, because although the purses were relatively fat, the cost of living in New York was high. Every day they trained, mostly up to noon. During the afternoon or early evening, the three boxers would take in a movie at one of the many cinemas in New York. Mancini and Baldock shared a love of the cinema and were taken with the fact that 'the pictures' were well in advance of anything they had experienced in London.

Wild West (western/cowboy) films were Mancini's greatest love, and names like Tom Mix, Hoot Gibson or W.S. Hart would never fail to lure him in. This was a time before 'talkies', when the story was flashed across the screen and all the dialogue was delivered in writing on a separate frame. The two film buffs would get excited as they read the wording out loud. Sometimes, when the guns were whipped out onscreen, Mancini would become particularly thrilled, especially if the cinema deployed 'special effects' so it seemed like the cracking of the pistols and Winchesters were going off around them.

While enthralled by one such movie, Baldock noticed two hard-looking blokes sitting in front of him and Mancini. They seemed restless, and Teddy nudged his pal, telling him to 'shut up'. But Alf took no notice.

Eventually, one of the tough guys turned round and growled, 'Will you two goddam Limeys quit yapping, or else…' His hand went inside his coat and he began to pull something out.

Neither of the English lads had any desire to see a gun off-screen, so they swiftly changed seats. On the way out, an attendant informed the two Londoners that the threatening-looking pair were known gangsters. Teddy felt more excited than intimidated; he'd met a couple of 'real' New York bad guys!

Another time, Mancini and Baldock were walking along the New York streets when a car came speeding past. It was quickly followed by another, and they were exchanging fire. The Londoners threw themselves into a shop doorway, and watched what seemed to be criminals in the front car trying to shake off the chasing police. For a while, that put both of them off films featuring gunplay.

Two weeks after Hood drew with Jones, Baldock outpointed the Filipino fighter Tommy Abobo over six rounds at Mitchel Field; a military airbase that staged many boxing shows in the 1920s. It was from there that Colonel Charles Lindbergh had made his historic solo flight to Paris. (Mitchel is often misspelled as 'Mitchell' but it was named after the former New York City Mayor

John Purroy Mitchel and not, as many have thought the flying ace Billy Mitchell.)

At the venue, the English party ran into Ernie Jarvis and Phil Richards, brother of Benny Caplan, who was doing well as a lightweight. The Caplans came from St George's, the same East London area as Jack 'Kid' Berg, and, also like Berg, they were of Jewish heritage. As an amateur, Benny Caplan was the 1931 ABA Featherweight Champion, and, in February 1939, *Ring* magazine ranked him as the number nine featherweight in the world. They were living in the district at that time, and arrangements were made to meet up.

A week later, Broadribb got Teddy a fight at Madison Square Garden against Arthur de Champlaine. Meeting the Canadian Bantamweight Champion at the Garden gave Baldock the feeling that he was getting somewhere, and he was determined that he would impress everyone concerned.

Tod Morgan, a fine fighter, topped the bill, defending his Junior Lightweight title against New York's own Joe Glick, and Baldock was very pleased when he was told he would be on first, which meant that he would be able to see Morgan fight.

Tod was born Albert Morgan Pilkington on Christmas Day 1902 in Dungeness, Washington, his stepfather, Fred Morgan, got him into boxing as a means of putting some muscle on the scrawny kid. He began training him in the backroom of the Hoffman House in Vallejo, a soft-drink parlour and lunch room (during the Prohibition years in America), and, much like Ted Baldock's attitude towards his boxing baby, Fred had no ambition for his son to become a paid fighter, much less a World Champion, but Tod liked the game and started boxing professionally.

During World War II, Morgan served in the Australian Army, fighting against Rommel in North Africa. He later returned to the US, doing some refereeing, and he worked as a bellboy in a number of hotels before he passed away in 1953.

Mancini and Hood came along to support Baldock in his bout with de Champlaine. In the corner before the first round, Broadribb told him, 'This geezer's got a bit of a dig. Go out, size him up, and then drop a right on his chin before he starts to try one himself.'

As soon as the bell sounded, Baldock was up and stabbing half-a-dozen lefts at the Canadian's head, before slinging a right that landed on his jaw and de Champlaine fell like a sack of bricks. The referee pushed Teddy back before beginning his count, so giving the Canadian added time to rise. Jack Dorman, the timekeeper, reeled off the seconds and when he reached 'nine', Arthur was beginning to recover his senses. At 'ten' de Champlaine was still down, but got up just as the count was completed. However, the referee, Johnny Marto ordered the fighters to box on, claiming not to have heard the timekeeper.

Still dazed, de Champlaine was caught with another right that landed almost exactly on the same spot as the blow that had floored him and he hit the boards for a second time. At 'nine' he was up, but, anticipating another right, he left the right side of his head unprotected. With a predictability that was almost as painful as the blow itself, Baldock's left hook finished it. The contest was over in 63 seconds.

It was Baldock's best win to date and the next day the newspapers gave as much room to his performance as to Morgan's successful defence of his championship (outpointing Glick after a 15-round war). Teddy's left was compared to a piston, and it was claimed nothing like it had been seen before.

A week later, both Mancini and Baldock appeared at Mitchel Field. Mancini faced Milton Jampole in a 10-round bout, while Baldock met Johnny Erikson. As Mitchel Field was outside the jurisdiction of New York City, Teddy's eight-round contest was legal.

Ernie Jarvis, Phil Richards and Pop Humphries were at ringside that night and to Baldock it seemed that America was full of British boxers at that time. With their compatriots' encouragement, both Mancini and Baldock achieved good victories.

Mancini probably worked harder than he needed to. The contest wasn't a minute old when he landed his famed left hook on Jampole's chin, sending him through the ropes and out of the ring. But the referee did not start the count, allowing the American to be helped back through the ropes; he should have been counted out, as about three minutes had elapsed before the fight was resumed.

Baldock faced a consistent winner in the Italian Angel Azzolina, who was known as Johnny Erickson (it seems Italian fighters were not popular at that time in New York). But Teddy fought hard from beginning to end, and had he not been so fast he might have had a much harder fight. But as it was the Londoner overwhelmed Erickson with his ever-reliable left, but also tagging him repeatedly with rights. At the finish, his opponent's nose was swollen, his mouth cut and both eyes blacked.

Whenever Erickson attempted to throw a punch, Baldock had sidestepped it before it was halfway to him. The Italian missed so often it was surprising he didn't get discouraged, but he kept going to the bitter end. Teddy got the verdict by a wide margin; both he and Mancini were given huge applause by the big crowd.

With their pockets full of dollars, and on Jarvis's suggestion, the tourists agreed to buy a car. They paid $95 (at just under five dollars to the pound) for a vehicle with slightly dodgy brakes; in fact, according to Baldock, 'It was safer to run it alongside the kerb to bring it to a halt.'

With no fights scheduled for a few days, they decided to drive to Philadelphia to see Jack Dempsey training for the forthcoming defence of his heavyweight title against Gene Tunney. Mancini drove, and Jarvis's brother Joe came along.

Gus Wilson, a French-American who had initially come to the United States in 1921 with the great Georges Carpentier, acting as his French–English translator for his bout with Dempsey, was in charge of the old Manassa Mauler's camp, and he made the Englishmen very welcome. With him was Johnny Sullivan, the Covent Garden middleweight, who was pleased to see his countrymen. The tourists stayed with the camp for four days and were among more than 120,000 who witnessed the World Championship fight in the pouring rain at the Sesquicentennial Stadium in which Dempsey lost his title.

Although he was beaten and appeared ring rusty, Teddy thought Jack Dempsey was the greatest fighter he had ever seen; he was to hold that view for the rest of his life. According to Baldock, if 'he had been given a warming-up fight and the ring hadn't been so slippery, I'm sure he would have retained his title'.

Teddy and his travelling companions kept their car going until it ceased to be remotely safe to drive and then parked it by the side of the road one night, got out and crept away. It was gone the next morning and was never seen again.

Broadribb arranged a New York date for Hood, against 'Sailor' Darton, the former Welterweight Champion of the US Navy; Mancini would perform two days later at Madison Square Garden in a contest with the rather ominously named Paul de Hate; Baldock was booked to fight Mexican San Sanchez four days later.

The arrangements marked the start of some hard training for the Englishmen at the St Nick's gym. Baldock became known as 'Red', in recognition of his auburn hair and freckled face, and the nickname was to follow him round America. During this time he met 'Bermondsey' Billy Wells, who had been in America for several years and was a boxer with huge experience. In Britain he had won the 'John Bull' Welterweight Belt, but, having not seen an opportunity to get a title fight, had travelled to Canada in 1922, where he won the Canadian Championship, before moving on to the US, fighting throughout the country. When Teddy met him in New York, he was close to the end of his long career, and had fought some of the best welterweights in the world, including Jack Britton, former world title holder Pete Latzo (also known as Young Clancy), World Champion challenger Pinky Mitchell, as well as Dave Shade, Jock Malone, and other notable Americans.

Wells treated the lad from Poplar kindly and taught him a lot. His first words as he shook hands with Baldock were: 'Take no chances, here, son. Never drop your hands – come out with 'em up and, when the bell goes, keep 'em up.'

They sparred together on several occasions, and Teddy found Billy to be an intelligent fighter with a gift for evasive action. Baldock had seen himself as well versed in the art of ducking and dodging, but Wells was able to make him miss by drawing in his breath. Teddy soon understood how he had been able to battle for so long with the best in the game. The first time they sparred, Baldock threw out a fast left causing Billy's nose to bleed. He apologised but, dabbing his nose with a towel, Wells told him, 'My nose hasn't bled for years and it has to be a little red-headed basket like you to do it. Well, keep that left hand going fast, and you'll do.'

Wells dressed immaculately and told Baldock that he had around 50 suits. He would wear a different suit every day. Even today that's quite a wardrobe, but in a time when all suits were made to measure, and when most men had just one that they kept for decades, this was phenomenal. Billy was also a fine snooker player, who took Mancini to the cleaners, when he was unwise enough to play him. The South Londoner, up until then was not averse to supplementing his boxing purses on the side, via his cue-craft.

Hood beat Sailor Darton on points, but he was again unable to impress New York. He appeared well out of form, but it was hoped he would put on better shows as he acclimatised to the American environment.

However, New York seemed to suit Mancini and Baldock. Alf had a tremendous contest with Paul de Hate at the Garden, and Teddy would never forget the terrific enthusiasm the fans showed all the way through that fight. Mancini leaped in to rip in a tearing left hook in the first round, but he got crossed by a right to the jaw that had him on the deck. However, he seemed to rebound almost straight away, rising to fight furiously and throw the American's rhythm.

Putting up a non-stop salvo, Mancini had exhausted de Hate by the final bell to win on points. The crowd were ecstatic, throwing their programmes into the ring to show appreciation. When Baldock chalked up his fourth victory, beating Sanchez on points over six rounds, the tourists had collectively won eight out of nine starts with one even. It was a better record than they might even have dreamed of when they left London.

Six days later, Hood and Baldock had engagements on the same evening. Hood beat Los Angeles-born Paul Doyle over 10 rounds in Newark, as Teddy met Jackie Cohen at the Broadway Arena, a recently opened New York fight venue.

Cohen was a Brooklyn bantamweight (although he was the New England Featherweight Champion at the time) and his fans went mad when he bowled over a right that caught Baldock unprepared, sending him to the resin-strewn floor. Teddy bounded to his feet, avoiding a count, and set on Jackie at a tremendous pace that caught the American by surprise, leaving him totally shocked. But Cohen didn't go down, and at the conclusion of the six rounds, although

Baldock was convinced he'd done enough to win, the bout was declared a tie. The knockdown had been crucial, because Teddy had outscored his rival from getting up off the floor to the end of the fight, even though he had picked up a nasty cut above his left eye in a collision of heads in the first round. After the fight, Baldock was told that his hair had stood on end as he launched into Cohen.

Despite this slight setback, there was a big demand to match the Poplar lad. In 18 days, he had four contests in various clubs and arenas around New York, all of which he won.

This run started with a bout against Billy Marlow at the Mitchel Field Arena and, as Baldock had built up quite a reputation, the large venue was packed out. The fight had been scheduled as an eight-round contest, but it ended in the first. According to Teddy, 'Billy was easy, and was being punched around the ring, when he decided to act the goat and used the top of his head as an extra weapon. Having been warned for this, he started to use his knee at close range, whereupon the referee stopped the affair and disqualified Marlow, leaving me the winner.'

Eight days later, Baldock met Tommy Lorenzo at the Pioneer Club, at 155 East 24th Street, Manhattan. It was originally known as the National Athletic Club and usually staged fights on Tuesday evenings. It could hold around 3,500 spectators and there was a capacity crowd for the fight between the New Yorker and the Londoner. But local fans were to be disappointed when Teddy outpointed their man over six rounds.

The tough Italian, from the East Side was by now building up quite a record. Reports had already been circulating that during his preparation at Stillman's Gym he was giving Carl Duane, his junior lightweight sparring partner all he could handle.

Local fans were not disappointed; 'the little Englishman, gave an amazing exhibition of cleverness that bewildered his opponent quite as much as it fascinated the crowd.'

Twice Baldock staggered Tommy in the first round, once by feinting him and shooting over a long right and again by a combination left hook and short uppercut in close.

In the second Lorenzo was twice dropped to the canvas after being worked from one side of the ring to the other, but the Italian rallied and nailed Teddy with a huge shot that visibly shook him. He wasn't going to allow himself to be caught like that again, so was all over Lorenzo in the third before knocking him to the boards for a count of eight in the fourth.

Teddy put on an impressive performance and although he was not able to stop his opponent, he had dominated the fight and won comfortably on points.

Alf Mancini was also on the card and beat Paul Gulotta of Brooklyn over the six round distance. Another fighter, hoping to add a further win to his unbeaten record that night was none other than James J. Braddock, who eased through a six round points victory over Lou Barba. He would go on to win the world heavyweight title after beating the champion Max Baer as a 10 to 1 underdog in 1935. It would go down in boxing history as one of the sport's greatest upsets. Seventy years later in 2005, Braddock would be the subject of director, Ron Howard's Hollywood blockbuster, *The Cinderella Man*.

The Manhattan Casino Sporting Club had just re-opened its doors and just five days after the Lorenzo contest a large crowd was in attendance to witness Baldock adding another points victory to his tally, this time against Billy Reynolds of Brooklyn. A further five days later, the last of this series, a six-round fight against Ralph Nischo again ended in a points win for Teddy. The young lad from Poplar was making quite a name for himself in New York.

Baldock's fellow travellers were also staying busy, although they were not quite as active as Teddy. Jack Hood fought a tough 12-rounder with a black fighter named Jack 'Pride of Harlem' McVey (although his real name was Julius Williams and he was born in Athens, Georgia), who put Hood down for a count of nine in one of the early rounds. The Brit got up to out-box McVey, but it was judged to be a 'no decision' contest, and the majority of reporters voted for McVey.

Mancini beat Sid Berts at the Pioneer Club and fought a 10-round draw with Henry Goldberg, while Baldock defeated Belgian Featherweight Champion Pierre de Caluwe over his usual six rounds at the New Broadway Arena, Brooklyn, New York.

Baldock with trainer Jim Varley (c. 1919)

Below: Young Teddy (c.1924)

Teddy Baldock (seated left) Ted (Teddy's father – standing behind Teddy) and Jack 'Kid' Berg (seated right) 1925/1926

Below: Teddy (right) in training with Jack 'Kid' Berg - Jan/Feb 1926 at Hurstpierpoint, Sussex, in preparation for his contest with Frankie Ash. Berg was facing Harry Corbett on the same Albert Hall bill but lost on points.

Baldock, Alf Mancini and Jack Hood (from left to right) USA 1926

Training aboard ship (Baldock far right) August 1926 along with Alf Mancini (far left) and Jack Hood (to Baldock's right).

Chopping and Training

Teddy Baldock and Archie Bell slug it out on 5 MAY, 1927 for the vacant World Bantamweight Title at the Albert Hall, London

Teddy and his mum (Louisa Rose), May 26, 1927

Below: From ring to table, canvas to baize – Teddy takes on The Middleweight Champion Len Harvey 22 Nov 1929

1927 - Teddy receives an 'illuminated address' from the Mayor of Poplar

Baldock on the ropes but still punching 16 May 1929

*Baldock presented with his
Lonsdale Belt (by Lord Lonsdale)
May 16, 1929, Olympia, London*

*The Pride of Poplar (with Lonsdale
Belt) 1929*

Above: Teddy being seen off on his way to America – 1929

August 1926 - All at sea – Mid-Atlantic Teddy challenges Lord Lipton but it's not his cup of tea

Jack Sharkey (left) with Teddy Baldock - Teddy's training alongside the future heavyweight champion of the world! (Gerald Ambrose 'Tuffy' Griffiths on left – 'The Pender Pounder'/Terror from the West'- Tuffy had the unenviable distinction of being knocked out by James Braddock in 1928)

Boxers v Jockeys at West Ham Stadium 1931. Boxers won 4-3 with Teddy scoring 2 of the goals and Alf Goddard scoring the other 2. From left to right boxers team Dick Corbett, Jack Hyams, Jack Hood, Alf Goddard Teddy Baldock and Team Captain Jack Bloomfield (holding the ball) chatting with Lord Lonsdale

Baldock walks back to his corner after flooring Mick Hill as referee Sam Russell counts. This was the 14th round knock out at The Ring, the legendary Blackfriars venue, London

1929 Teddy training at Blackpool Cricket ground for his contest with Gideon Potteau. Accompanying him is Jack Lakey his trainer (right) and Cecil Parkin (left) the England and Lancashire bowler.

22nd January 1930, Albert Hall, London – Baldock gets the decision following a 6th round foul by Frenchman Emile Pladner

Early part of the Baldock v Plandner fight - 22nd January 1930, Albert Hall, London

*Above: Early morning work
out on Brighton Beach with Sid
Raiteri 14th January 1930*

*Al Brown in training at the
National Sporting Club for his
meeting with Teddy Baldock –
May 1930*

Above: 1931 – 20th May,
Olympia, London – referee
Owen Morgan stops the fight
in the 12th round, giving
Al Brown the decision over
Teddy Baldock

Teddy Baldock and Dick
Corbett weigh in at
The Ring, Blackfriars –
September, 1931

*Teddy Baldock (right)
fighting Billy Reynolds
at Lea Bridge, May
1933 (intended as
the first of a six fight
comeback for Teddy)*

*October 6 1959: Teddy appears as a guest on the BBC programme "It happened to me"
(left to right) Len Harvey (former World Light-Heavyweight Champion) Dom Volante
(ex-British Featherweight title challenger), Jock McAvoy (former British and Empire
Middleweight Champion).*

'I'm proud of Poplar. It made me.'

Teddy – Fallen Star (1956)

Teddy's daughter Pam, grandson Martin and great-grandsons Danilo and Lito. Martin has a twin brother, Robin, who lives in Canada

It was getting close to Christmas and there were plenty of opportunities to be had for the three tourists. The cash incentives were not massive, although they were getting good paydays for relatively short-distance contests. But Teddy was starting to feel a tad homesick, and the thought of being so far away from home at Christmas time did not appeal to him. So he told Broadribb that he wanted to return to London. Ted believed that leaving at that point was a mistake, and he was staying on, along with Hood and Mancini, but he said Baldock was free to do as he saw fit and he told Teddy that he could rejoin them in the New Year if he wished.

Before he left, Baldock had one more contest at Madison Square Garden, matched with Joe Clifford. Mancini was also on the bill, meeting 'Farmer' Joe Cooper, a tough welter out of West York, Illinois (although Terre Haute, Indiana, was where he called home). In a recent fight Cooper had gone the distance with the famous Philadelphia southpaw Lew Tendler, who had fought for the World Lightweight title against Benny Leonard in 1922.

Mancini's 10-rounder was gruelling, and Cooper steamed in constantly, although most of his shots were off-target. Mancini's snappy left picked him off with some ease, and Joe's nose was bloodied in the early rounds. Mancini had to be sharp to keep out of harm's way and managed to stay clear of danger. Teddy believed the draw, a result that was soundly booed, was an injustice to Mancini.

As he had disposed of his opponent in little over a minute in his last visit to the Garden, Baldock thought that he would try to make this fight another quick one. He outclassed Clifford and, although Joe was game enough to stay upright for the first round, he was hit with every punch in Baldock's growing repertoire. Teddy's speed overawed his opponent, who was well beaten in the second round when the referee stopped the contest five seconds before the bell.

Teddy left the US just under four months after he arrived. During that period he had fought a dozen times, winning 11 and drawing one. Perhaps more importantly he had learned a huge amount about American methods, and saw himself returning to London as a better more rounded fighter for his experience. He had learned a huge amount about American methods, and saw himself returning to London as a better 'fighting machine'.

This is reflected in a letter he wrote home just prior to his departure;

'The ring experience I am enjoying is wonderful and will stand me in good stead when I return to dear old England a few days before Christmas. I found nothing but welcome and appreciation awaiting me here, and I find nothing wrong with American boxing audiences. They like a good fight and when they get it they are unstinted in their approval. All the boys I have been up against are very tough and in most cases I have had to concede weight. I am receiving all sorts of offers, but am accepting none until I return to think it over. Give all my best wishes to all my boxing friends, and tell them I would not have missed this experience for worlds'.

Boxing promoter Tex Rickard, a former cowboy who had herded cattle from Texas to Montana and Kansas City, one-time Town Marshall of Henrietta, Texas, ex-Klondike Gold Rush prospector and gambling-house proprietor, was the man primarily responsible for building Madison Square Garden in 1925, and in his highly regarded ratings at the beginning of 1927 he included Baldock in his top-12 best bantamweights. Bearing in mind that Teddy wasn't a British or European champion, and was just 19½, that ranking was something better than special.

Baldock was met at Southampton by Joe Morris and they were pleased to see each other. On the train back to London, Joe told Teddy about what had been going on in his absence, and that, if all went according to his plans, Baldock would make a good deal of money and maybe fight for a Championship, Teddy's ultimate ambition.

A group of celebrities from the world of boxing (including Moss Deyong, Bernard Mortimer, Bernard Dorris and Harry Lee, father of Sydney Lee, the champion billiards player, and Johnny Bucknell) had created the International Sports Syndicate (ISS). The ISS had taken over the Royal Albert Hall from Harry Jacobs, who had moved his operation to Olympia. Baldock was offered £1,000 by the ISS for three fights; one contest, provided he met their expectations and became a contender, would be for the Bantamweight Championship of the World.

Young Johnny Brown, brother to the British and European bantamweight champion, was to be Teddy's first opponent. If he defeated Brown, then next would be the titleholder, Johnny Brown himself. Following a successful result against the elder Brown sibling then Fidel La Barba would be brought over to London from Los Angeles to fight Teddy for the world crown.

LaBarba, who had in recent times defeated Elky Clark for the world flyweight title, had chosen to continue his career at 8st 6lb, and because of his reputation believed that he had the right to be considered as a contender for the NYSAC bantamweight title that had been vacated by Charley (Phil) Rosenberg.

On 25 March 1925 Rosenberg (born Charles Green) shocked fellow American, Eddie Martin by beating him over 15 rounds on a unanimous points decision, at Madison Square Garden, for the World Bantamweight Title, sanctioned by the NYSAC. The odds were against Charley after it had been reported that he was struggling to make the weight, having to lose 39lbs in only a few weeks leading up to the contest. Strangely, *Ring Magazine* continued to refer to Rosenberg as a 'mythical' champion and it wasn't until June that the National Boxing Association of America (NBA) announced that they recognised him as the titleholder and expected him to defend the championship against the best men available.

Only three months later on 23 July, Eddie Shea challenged Rosenberg for his title at The Bronx Velodrome, New York City. The fight was a savage affair and after a blistering exchange in the fourth round, Shea was dropped to the canvas by two heavy rights to the jaw. As the referee reached a count of five, his corner threw in the towel (it appeared they wanted to save him from further punishment). However a suspicious fluctuation in the betting odds just before the fight, prompted the Commissioner to carry out an investigation. Further rumours and allegations that Eddie Shea's life had been threatened unless he 'threw' the fight, resulted in the NYSAC suspending Rosenberg indefinitely and Shea for life.

Controversy was never far away when Rosenberg was around and on 26 October 1926, following the failure to post a forfeit for a forthcoming title defence against Bud Taylor in Chicago, the NBA stripped him of their version of the championship and Taylor was nominated as the new champion.

Somewhat surprisingly, Rosenberg had his suspension lifted by the NYSAC for a title defence against Utica's Bushy Graham (who also fought under the names 'Bobby Garcia' and 'Mickey Garcia') in New York City on 4 February 1927, but then forfeited his title on the scales after weighing in over the bantamweight limit. The fight went ahead as planned and had Graham won he would have been proclaimed champion by the NYSAC. However, not only did Graham not win, with Rosenberg receiving the 15-round points decision, but both men were suspended in New York for a year following the discovery of a secret agreement regarding purse money.

The situation led to a state of confusion, with three governing bodies, the British ISS and the American's NYSAC and NBA all making claims for their nominated champions and staging fights, for what they felt were legitimate versions of the World Bantamweight Title.

The Albert Hall promoters believed that, if Baldock defeated LaBarba, any other claimant would have to come to Teddy in order to settle who was the worthy Champion.

However, the NBA, then a powerful body, named Charles 'Bud' Taylor as the new Champion, but the ISS believed that, if Baldock defeated LaBarba, any other claimant would have to come to Teddy in order to settle who was the worthy Champion.

But it all hinged on Baldock's fight with Young Johnny Brown; if Teddy lost this bout, Brown, and not Teddy, would become the British challenger for the world title.

9

STRONG AS A BLEEDIN' LION

1927

Johnny Brown was pleased to see Baldock back home, as he had been keen to pit himself against the local hero. Young Johnny had become synonymous with Premierland before Teddy had made his presence felt there and he may have considered Baldock had somewhat usurped his position, but no doubt his priority would have been to cut into Teddy's reputation and at the same time enhance his own status, and he openly declared himself the better man. He trained for the fight at Shoeburyness under Jack Goodwin, a renowned and respected trainer, who would have had a definite plan to stop Teddy's career in full flight.

Baldock took up where he left off with Jack Lakey, preparing at Hurstpierpoint. As Teddy had fought at featherweight in the US, it was naturally thought that he would have his work cut out to make the bantamweight limit. This was central to Goodwin's thinking; he believed his insistence that the match be made at 8st 6lb was a masterstroke and a trap the Baldock camp had fallen into all too readily.

Teddy's initial training session included a seminar with Lakey, who told his fighter that he would have to get below that weight and still 'be as strong as a bleedin' lion' and the trainer immediately set about planning a tailored but strict schedule for Baldock. Jack watched Teddy almost constantly, taking note of every fraction of an ounce as the weight came off.

At the weigh-in for the fight at a hotel in Leicester Square, Goodwin looked taken aback when he saw Baldock make 8st 4½lb (dead on what Lakey wanted) with no difficulty on the jockey scales. Brown's trainer insisted that the scales were faulty, so everyone had to tramp to a nearby gymnasium to repeat the process. Once more Teddy tipped the scales at the same weight. Although he had to be satisfied, it was plain that Goodwin was disappointed.

Lakey, Morris and Baldock, having got some idea what shape Young Johnny was in, talked tactics after the weigh-in. Whereas previously strategy for Teddy's fights had been pretty ad hoc, it was thought that, as Baldock was close to his biggest ever fight, the time had come to get tactical. It was decided that Teddy should keep Brown on the end of the straight left until he began to tire, but look to take the fight on points and on no account get involved in any prolonged exchanges or be tempted to take part in serious in-fighting. It was expected that Brown would try to get inside and draw Baldock into a scrap.

The fight was a 15-rounder, with two other fights of similar distance included in the programme. The bigger of those two bouts saw Roland Todd meet Frank Moody, from Pontypridd, Wales. This fight was billed as being for the British and European middleweight titles (although Tommy Milligan was recognised by the NSC as Champion, Todd had never been defeated, and maintained he was the rightful middleweight titleholder).

Todd was born on 14 January 1900 in Marylebone, London, the great-great-grandson of John (Jack) Musters, the Squire of Annesley and Colwick Halls, Nottingham, a well-known fighter in Nottinghamshire in the early 18 century. In 1923, Todd had met Tommy Loughran (who later became a well-known bridge player) at Madison Square Garden and went on to meet Pittsburgh's Harry Greb (the World Middleweight Champion). But the fight contract stipulated that the referee was not allowed to give a decision for the fight and that Todd would come into the contest 2lb over the middleweight limit, making it impossible for him to claim the title in any circumstances. However the weight was just a formality as the Englishman lost on points over 12 rounds.

Frank Moody began his career in 1914, and later won the Middleweight and the Light-Heavyweight Championships of Great Britain. During his career he fought Ted 'Kid' Lewis, Harry Greb, Tiger Flowers and Maxie Rosenbloom. While campaigning in the US, Frank's most impressive win was over Kid Norfolk who he knocked out in the fourth round in a contest held at New York's Yankee Stadium.

Frank Moody beat Roland Todd over the scheduled 15 rounds in what could only be described as; 'a rather dull affair'.

In another bout that evening, Scot Johnny Hill (who would become British Flyweight Champion) stopped Londoner Phil Lolosky.

The incoming Albert Hall promoters broke with boxing tradition by reducing their Championship title bouts from the normal 20 to 15 rounds. The programme was made up with contests of 12, 8 and 6 rounds, and on this evening they presented 71 rounds of boxing at prices ranging from 5s 9d (about 29p) for the top balcony to two guineas (£1 1s, £1.05) for a ringside seat.

Alf Mancini, Teddy's companion during his trip to New York, faced the tough Frenchman, Emile Romerio in the 12 round contest. Alf was not at his best as he had been suffering from flu, so Romerio was certainly the strongest of the two. There was not much in it by the halfway stage but Mancini now had the measure of his man and his more accurate punching in the latter rounds won him the referee's decision after a stubborn and thrilling battle.

The supporters from Poplar in the sell-out crowd gave their man a fantastic welcome. As Teddy emerged from the dressing room and made his way through the ringside seats to climb through the ropes, they lifted the roof off the grand old venue that even then was over 50 years old. They had been working up to this reception since Baldock's first fight after his American odyssey had been announced; many had arrived via charabanc parties organised by local pubs and the majority had made more than a few toasts to Teddy en route. As such it was a great night out for Baldock's loyal fans.

Brown was waiting in his corner as the now well-travelled Baldock entered the ring. Having climbed through the ropes, Teddy walked over to his opponent and shook his hand. Young Johnny smiled with self-assurance, and it was obvious to Baldock that his rival fancied his chances. After the fight Teddy was told that Brown's confidence was based on his observations of Baldock before he had made his trip to the US, and he had something of a shock at the extent to which Teddy had developed in New York; for many Baldock had left British shores as a boy and arrived home a man – he certainly had matured as a fighter.

Looking back, Baldock confessed, 'I didn't really appreciate the fact that I was any better than when I went away.' He had found the Americans swift, dynamic and strong, but he had been able to manage them well. What he failed to comprehend was how much his stateside experience had honed his awareness and skill; his boxing had a professional polish that it had lacked previously and with his rough edges smoothed it was likely his overall ability was now well above most of the bantamweights in the UK.

At the opening bell, Baldock headed straight across the ring and started shooting lefts to Brown's head as often and as quickly as he could, these were followed by swift rights. It was all Brown could do to defend himself; anything in the way of retaliation was minimal and as such ineffective. He caught a few on his gloves and ducked some others, but most of Baldock's blows hit their target, each one jolting him to the core.

The one-way pummelling continued for about 90 seconds before Brown tired of his role as punch-bag. He dropped his defence and waded in, attempting to get close enough to Teddy to make a telling attack to the body, but, as he came in, Baldock punished him with both gloves. Brown was visibly shaken and was obliged to grab hold of the opponent he was beginning to think he just might have underestimated.

Young Johnny made another run through Teddy's onslaught, but, rather than allow Brown to seize hold of him once more, Baldock shortened his blows, hooking and burying uppercuts into his man. Brown fell back harmed, but he was chased and could not escape the relentless straight left.

As the first round concluded, thunderous applause sent Baldock back to his corner. That initial salvo, although quite one-sided, had been action packed.

In the second, Brown drove himself forward, looking to put an attack together on Teddy's mid-section, but his efforts were met with a profusion of hard lefts and rights, the effects doubled as he walked on to them. He must have been in top physical condition to have survived the level of attrition he was experiencing, never once recoiling. Even as he was beaten into retreat, the smile did not leave his face, giving the impression that Baldock's punches were falling off him like raindrops. Teddy recalled Jim Varley's view on smiling boxers and he realised Brown's outward expression was little more than transparent bravado, which was confirmed during a brief clinch in his corner when Baldock glimpsed over his opponent's shoulder to see Brown's seconds looking anxious.

Connecting with an uppercut to Baldock's body seemed to give Brown's supporters some hope, and when he planted another fast right uppercut squarely on Teddy's chin it looked like Young Johnny was rallying. But he had been repaid dozens of times over, mostly to the head; by the time the bell ended the second round.

As Baldock returned to his corner, Morris showered him with praise, telling the fighter to keep up his work rate. 'Do what you're doing, and he won't last the distance.'

Teddy replied, 'I don't see why he should last out the next round.'

But Morris was his usual cautious self and, thinking Teddy might start to take unnecessary risks, pleaded, 'Now be careful, Alf. He's a stiff puncher, and he's still strong, so just box him.'

This was a reminder of the pre-fight plans for a relatively cautious campaign but Baldock turned to Lakey, saying, 'Pull up my right glove.' This was their shared sign that Baldock was going to attempt a knockout.

Jack did what he was asked; although he was concerned that this was a departure from the strategy they had so carefully laid out, he knew Teddy well and that his fundamental gift lay in his instinct and the ability that arose out of that.

At the clang of the bell, Baldock clasped his right tightly and ran at Brown. Young Johnny was peppered with a spray of straight lefts, many quickly followed up with solid rights. He retreated under the fire, but Baldock followed, pelting his foe with both fists. Brown swerved, ducked and ran, but Teddy felt he couldn't miss even if he tried. Striking with precision and at an astounding pace, Teddy showed how he had benefited from his encounters with the two-fisted New York scrappers.

However, like a wounded animal, Brown impulsively began to lash out, desperate to beat off his relentless attacker. This was his final mistake. Toe-to-toe, exchanging blows, this was Young Johnny's last stand. Baldock's fists were peppering Brown, whose replies were merely falling short around Teddy's arms. Baldock saw Johnny's chin exposed, an open and vulnerable target, seemingly impossible to miss. The right was fired by intuition; it was his hardest strike of the contest, and it was planted flush. On impact Brown's head turned. Another right, then, instantly, a third blasted home. Baldock had landed a dozen when Brown finally dropped. As he tumbled Teddy stood watching him fall away, speculating on the likelihood of Brown getting up before 10. He stirred on the floor, then he was up at eight. Although he was swaying, he bravely waved Baldock in; surrender was not an option.

Teddy came forward to end it. A left measured the job and a right crashed on Brown's head. He should never have got up, but he dragged himself to his feet. He lifted his fists and gazed glassy-eyed at Teddy before falling forward on his face.

As the count ended, Brown's corner men dashed to his aid. To a deafening roar of approval the Master of Ceremonies made Teddy's win official.

Baldock went to Brown's corner to shake his hand. But he was still out, and Teddy heard later that, although Johnny ultimately came round, he was unable to get out of the ring for a while and when he did finally get back to his dressing room he immediately collapsed again.

Back in his packed dressing room, everyone in the Baldock camp was exuberant. Friends, associates and complete strangers vied to congratulate their hero. Baldock was to recall that 'everybody was talking at once' and, bothered by the cacophony, he asked Morris to get rid of everyone and lock the door. The manager did as requested and only a select few were left to contemplate events. But shortly after someone came to the door to let Teddy know he was wanted at ringside to shake hands with the Prince of Wales. Baldock felt this was something he was unable to do. His father and Morris badgered him to make the effort to meet the Prince, but he totally refused, completely overawed by the prospect of meeting the future Duke of Windsor, so much so that he was shaking. However, Moss Deyong and Sam Russell turned up and more or less dragged Baldock back into the arena, and placed him in front of the man who would one day, for a short time, be King and Emperor. Once he shook hands he felt fine. He was to remember, 'We had quite a conversation, although I only made the answers. The Prince said I had put up a magnificent performance, and he hoped I would go on and win a World Championship. I said I would do my best if the chance came my way, then he asked me how many fights I'd had, how old I was, and what

I thought of America. He was very kind; even so, I was glad to get in my dressing room.'

The following day details of the fight filled the sports columns of the national newspapers, while exclusive pictures, with the headline; 'Albert Hall Boxing Thrills' made a double page spread in the *Daily Sketch*.

The manner in which Teddy had dispatched Young Johnny Brown was the talk of the boxing press. The weekly edition of *Boxing* (forerunner to today's *Boxing News*) trade paper for the sport, featured Baldock on their front page as 'The New Terror', it was clear that the editor, amongst many others, saw this young man from Poplar as a prospect;

'We cannot congratulate ourselves on the possession of a world's champion yet awhile, yet we can feel reasonably confident of owning the world's bantam crown, should the International Sports Syndicate succeed in persuading Bushey Graham, or whoever is now regarded as America's best bantam, to pay us a visit. On the form he displayed at the Albert Hall on Wednesday last we can confidently look to Teddy Baldock as a real world's champion, who has been jewelled in every hole'.

It was also noted that a number of American boxing critics who had been present at ringside, openly declared that Baldock was the very best they had seen anywhere in a number of years.

Not only did the win increase his status in boxing circles but also as a sporting celebrity. Twelve days after the meeting with Young Johnny Brown, a publicity stunt was organised in which Teddy would play Sydney Lee, the boy amateur billiards champion, in a 'battle of the baize' match, at the Camden Terminus Club in London. Although this was basically a publicity stunt, games like billiards were seen as therapeutic while benefiting hand/eye coordination.

Baldock's second fight for the ISS was due to take place on 30 March against Champion Johnny Brown (the elder, born Philip Hickman), which gave him six weeks to prepare.

However, Fidel LaBarba was beaten by Italian-born Bostonian Johnny Vacca, which was a bit of a shock; not a few thought it to be something of a fluke. Vacca's performance was all the more remarkable as he knew he would get no financial reward from the fight. Heavy snow had limited attendance to such an extent that the bout might have been called off, but, as Johnny said he would fight for nothing, the show went ahead. Vacca showed the first result was no accident by beating LaBarba in the return fight, meaning the flyweight champion would not be given a chance to take a shot at the world bantamweight title.

Since the NYSAC had recently suspended Bushy Graham and Charley Rosenberg due to their 'financial arrangement'. The ISS took this opportunity to announce that Baldock's fight with the elder Johnny Brown should be for a World Championship. However, the Americans matched Bud Taylor with Tony Canzoneri, this pair was recognised in America as the most worthy contenders for the vacant title (Canzoneri was to better a dozen different World Champions and got a draw with another for the title). The Canzoneri and Taylor fight ended in a draw at the Coliseum, Chicago, and a rematch was arranged. It is worthy of note that both the first fight and rematch in the USA were contested over 10 rounds, a championship contest in Britain at the time, was fought over 15 and a Lonsdale Challenge Belt match at the NSC, could still be made at the 20 round distance.

After hanging up his gloves Canzoneri ran a 144-acre ranch and orchard in upstate New York, a clothing store, had a song-and-dance nightclub act, and a part interest in Tony Canzoneri's Paddock Bar and Grill on Broadway near 50th in New York City. However, he was to lose it all. On 10 December 1959, in Hotel Bryant in New York, a few blocks from the bar that still bore his name, he was found dead by a maid in a $21-a-week room. He had lived in the hotel for a year and had no other assets. His death was recorded as the result of a heart attack.

Baldock was relaxed at the prospect of fighting the 'other' Brown, although he considered him to be a fine boxer and a worthy champion. This Brown had been to the US, but he hadn't prospered against the American featherweights. He had recently returned from South Africa, where he had been beaten by Willie Smith, the 1924 Olympic Games bantamweight Gold medallist. At the time, Teddy believed that Brown was just past his peak, and that he should overcome him to claim the British, European and World titles. It is hard to fault Baldock's assessment. Relatively few champions at the lighter weights went long before being deposed and Brown's fight with Smith at City Hall, Johannesburg, was his sixth consecutive defeat (five of which had taken place in the US and Canada) since he had reclaimed the bantamweight crown by beating Mick Hill close to four months earlier, and in his last seven bouts (in the year from November 1927) he would lose five. But Brown broke down in training and had to withdraw from the scheduled bout with Baldock.

Vacca was matched with Baldock as a substituted contest for the scheduled fight with Brown, but Vacca was defeated by Brooklyn's Archie Bell just before he was due to leave the US. The ISS cabled Bell with a $5,000 (£1,000 at the time) offer to meet Baldock at the Albert Hall on 5 May, which Bell accepted.

Bell (born Archie Salon on 12 November 1904) was not originally carved out to be a fighter. His father had insisted that he take up a college career after graduating from his elementary school education. However, Bell was tempted into the amateur ranks in 1921 after meeting a young fighter named Lew Goldberg who would often flash prizes that he had won in the ring, such as gold watches and pins, in front of Archie. Over a two-year period, Bell contested more than 100 fights, losing only four and winning around 60 by knockout. He held the Metropolitan and Brooklyn-Long Island flyweight titles.

In 1923, Archie turned pro and, on 25 June 1926, he met Tony Canzoneri (on the undercard of the Ruby Goldstein match with Ace Hudkins) but was knocked out in five rounds. Bell was to face some of the best at his weight during his career and defeated many but he was never to win a Championship fight. A tough Brooklyn fighter, Archie fought twice for versions of the World Championship but lost both bouts.

Before Bell left for London, Tex Rickard told him that if he defeated Baldock he would get him a fight with the winner of the impending return contest between Canzoneri and Taylor. Rickard was unable to make Baldock the same offer because he was still not 20 years old; it would be another year before Teddy could be allowed to fight for 15 rounds in the United States.

Meanwhile, Baldock had to be found a match for 30 March. There was an attempt to bring Henry Scillies, who was recognised by the IBO as a Bantamweight Champion of Europe, over from Belgium, but he chose to go to South Africa instead.

It was thought by some that Kid Nicholson, the one English boxer to hold a decision over Teddy, should be given the opportunity, but he had since been 'signed up' by Joe Morris and was now part of the same stable.

Then by luck German bantamweight Felix Friedmann returned from the States and was ready to meet Baldock. Friedmann had a good record and his workouts at Fred Dyer's gym in the Strand were striking, persuading some commentators to give him a decent chance against Baldock.

However 'das Zerstörer', as he was known in Germany, did not begin to stretch Teddy. His best asset was a speedy line in backpedalling and when Baldock pursued him with his majestic left the fight looked more like a game of tag than a fistic contest. Friedmann quickly retreated to the ropes in the second round, and Baldock caught him as he bounced off them; a straight right that hit home with a pleasing crunch seemed to demolish the German.

Felix was on his haunches but seemingly unable to move. He was counted out in this unflattering position. Not many of those present had seen the final blow, and Friedmann caused a deal of puzzlement as he seemingly just hunkered up. But he had to be carried to his corner, still partially stooped (having hardly moved).

That win provided publicity for the ISS's effort to match Baldock with Archie Bell for the vacant world bantamweight title. The newspapers were brimming with anticipation for the approaching contest, as Teddy went away to Hurstpierpoint to prepare for what he saw as the fight of his life.

10

THE WORLD CHAMPIONSHIP COMES TO POPLAR

As soon as the arrangements for the World Bantamweight Championship with Archie Bell were finalised, Teddy had once again made his way to Hurstpierpoint to train, accompanied by Johnny Curley (who up to January 1927 had been the British Featherweight Champion, before losing to Johnny Cuthbert at the NSC, Covent Garden), together with his regular sparring partners. But, before leaving, he met up with Bell and his manager, one-time fighter Eddie Borden. Borden was looking after Bell while he was in Britain, but during his career Bell was managed first by Ike Morgan and then Sol Gold, who also handled Jack Kid Berg. Borden would become a long-time contributor to *The Ring* magazine, where his 'A Corner in the Fistic Market' column, along with his monthly ratings, made popular reading. After they had got to know one another, Baldock walked away from the meeting holding both Bell and his manager in high regard.

To drum up some publicity, they made an appearance at Premierland one Sunday afternoon and received a great welcome from the venue's punters.

Bell was three years older than Baldock and he had 60 pro fights under his belt, which was less than Baldock, but some of the men Archie had fought had been highly rated. Bell was seen to be a two-fisted puncher, with a dangerous left hook, and with this in mind Teddy and his manager built their strategy, which would rely on Baldock's natural swiftness. As such he concentrated on punching rapidly with both hands while using the ring at high speed.

Bell prepared for the fight at the Black Bull in Whetstone, a popular training venue for fighters at that time (the pub still operates as an Ember Inn in N20).

A few days before the fight, Baldock was the guest of a group of admirers at a high-class restaurant in Holborn, who seemed to be celebrating his elevation to World Champion status even before a punch had been thrown.

On the day of the fight, Bell and Baldock met for the weigh-in at Fred Dyer's gymnasium in the Strand. Teddy was just three ounces inside the weight at 8st 5lb 11oz, and Archie was 9½oz lighter. It hadn't been hard for Baldock to make the bantamweight limit, but he did follow a very strict nutritional regime under his trainer's watchful eye and the moment he was off the scales his father passed him a thermos flask filled with his mother's beef tea, which he consumed eagerly.

The two fighters posed for pictures, shaking hands and wishing one another the best of luck. Bell went back to his hotel (the Strand Palace) while Teddy made for his family home and his mum's cooking. Teddy's dad encouraged him to eat a huge steak (which would have taken anything up to eight hours to fully digest) but the fighter, following Lakey's instructions, stuck with chicken together with plain vegetables. He had nothing more until around five o'clock, when he had a cup of tea.

During the early days, when Teddy had trained over the banana loft close to the Baldock home, his father would visit his friend Harry Thorn, a butcher, and would return with the best steak in Harry's Dingle Lane shop. He would hand it to his wife telling her how it should be prepared and as Teddy said, 'I was to eat the ruddy lot.' But, as soon as Baldock Sr wasn't around, Mrs Baldock would produce a pound of sausages and fry them up for her boy, knowing Teddy couldn't eat that steak but loved his sausages. The young fighter would have the bangers while his mum tucked into the steak. Afterwards, they would exchange plates to assure Ted that his instructions had been followed. When he eventually discovered the great mother/son banger conspiracy, he told Joe Morris. Subsequently, Jack Lakey was warned to watch carefully what Teddy ate and was threatened with the sack if the fighter was caught eating sausages while in training.

More than 50 charabancs took the eager inhabitants of Poplar to the Championship fight, and the Albert Hall was full to capacity. Years later, reflecting on his feelings before the contest, Teddy said, 'I must have been the least excited person in the East End.' He left home at 5.30 pm and caught a bus to the Holborn Empire (formerly the famous Weston's Music Hall and The Royal; the Empire was the last surviving hall playing variety in the West End when it was destroyed during the blitz in 1941). Baldock knew the manager of the Empire well, and he let Teddy, who loved music halls in those days, sit in a box for the first house, and the time passed quickly. When the show finished, Teddy strolled to a car that was waiting to take him to the Albert Hall.

The bill got under way at 8 pm, but even early on there was a huge swarm of people outside trying to get in, and Teddy and his friends had to force their way through the crowd to get inside the venue.

Baldock had not been in his dressing room long when Eddie Borden visited to wish him good luck. Baldock thought it was a nice gesture, and Morris, picking up on the hint, returned the compliment to Archie Bell.

As was standard, Teddy's dad, Joe Morris and Jack Lakey were in Baldock's corner. Alf Mancini was more than once to claim that he was there too, but, according to Baldock, 'I never saw him; in fact, the others were only in a misty sort of background. I knew they were there, but my whole concentration was on Archie Bell and the job of beating him.'

The fight itself was to be the hardest Teddy had known, and to a certain extent both men would be destroyed by what was a titanic clash. In Baldock's own words, 'I honestly believe we were neither of us as good afterwards.'

For many it was the most punishing encounter the bantamweight division had ever seen; a grim war, relentlessly fought, but without loss of control on the part of either boxer. As Baldock described it, there was 'no fury and no sentiment'; it was a steely, cold conflict, frozen in a dark haze of finely tuned and managed brutality.

From the instant that Sam Russell called the two men together right up to the final bell, the fight was a confrontation of minds practised in ring intelligence. In the initial seconds, Baldock became aware that he would need to box in a way and to an extent that he had never been compelled to before. He realised that Bell was streets ahead of anyone he had previously met.

Added to this Teddy was to fight 15 rounds, a journey he had not faced for over a year. Although he had been billed in fights of that length, none had gone the distance. His background against Americans consisted of relatively brief encounters; in New York he had not been on his feet for longer than eight rounds.

The American, at 5ft 4in, was a couple of inches shorter than Baldock and as usual Teddy had the superior reach. During the early rounds of the contest, he was able to pile up the points, taking full advantage of Bell's attempts to get into close quarters, which appeared to be his game plan. In his 81 fights, Archie would achieve just five knockouts, but he was an expert at in-fighting with a well-cultivated left and right hook, which he would attempt to land at any given opportunity. Such specialists need to get tight on their adversaries to make their work count.

Baldock fended off Bell with the trusty left for as long as he was able, but, when the Brooklyn man got beyond that lead, Teddy had to rely on his boxing brain to prevent him landing to the body. The American's left hooks were hurtful and, having felt their power, Baldock was loath to endure too much of that kind of pain. To prevent Bell from scoring, the Londoner needed to sidestep, draw back or grab his opponent and turn him so as to nullify his attacks.

Bell was repeatedly manoeuvred to this effect by Baldock tugging his left elbow forward, so spinning Archie round and stealing his balance; he was unable to regroup before Teddy had danced out of range, only to come back at him with rapid lefts to the head, reinforced with rights targeted to his jawline. But Archie was not easy to hit; he soon became adept at ducking into Baldock's right hand, causing those blows to hit high or just swing harmlessly round his neck. With damage limited, Bell would drive into Teddy, aiming for his midriff, forcing him to move faster than his own thoughts, instinctively blocking and parrying.

The pace of the encounter was phenomenal round after round. Bell showed he had those real championship qualities of a world beater, and Baldock became ever more assured that this was the best boxer he had faced, maybe the best all-round fighter he would ever meet. He kept the Cockney working all out, not daring to go into a lower gear, and, had it not been for his lengthy left and swift feet, Teddy would not have been able to grab the slight advantage he accrued in the early part of the fight.

But at the start of each round, Bell came on, bobbing and weaving a potentially injurious path for his rival. Baldock's answer was to skip lively around the ring while shooting out multiple stinging lefts into Bell's face. But he just kept coming.

Harm, damage, destroy were the only sentiments available to Teddy, as each time Bell got through with a solid left or right to the trunk it was doing damage. Baldock would explode a left in Bell's face and follow up with a right; he'd crash in a right hook to his chin but, although he pulled Bell up short on occasion, Archie seemed to register no hint of pain or loss of strength. This was shaking Teddy's morale; what did he need to do to make this man back up?

There was not a single second of a single round when the crowd were not roaring with enthusiasm, confirming that this was one of those fights you see so rarely in a lifetime. The fans witnessed Baldock's finest left-hand work, not so much out of effort but necessity, to stop himself being bulldozed by Bell's onslaught. The American was resolute in his effort to slow Baldock down and move in with his most devastating punches at the closest possible standpoint. But Teddy didn't dare drop his pace; there were literally no options but to run and punch.

As the bout progressed, it became like a fight for survival, the fighters wits and boxing skill being pitted against each other. Baldock began to concede that his opponent's knowledge was at least equal to his own and he became concerned that he might be facing a slightly superior boxing intellect.

When Teddy got through, his legion of followers roared their approval, but if Bell caught Baldock the appreciable number of Americans in the audience made the Albert Hall reminiscent of Madison Square Garden with their whoops and cheers. But at points the crowd were united in their approval of both boxers, such was the quality and keenness of the combat.

Baldock was to recall, 'Each round seemed alike to me and, after I found he could take my best punches without turning a hair, my only thought was to keep on my feet to the finish and hit him twice for every one I had to take. On that reckoning I could see myself as the ultimate winner.'

Teddy's best moments occurred when he drew Bell's lead and countered him quickly with a right, but sometimes Baldock would surprise his rival by allowing him to move in close and then beat him to the punch with a rapid two-fisted barrage to the body. Bell liked to thump hard into the organs, but if Teddy was able to get the inside position he found that he was quicker than his opponent.

At points Bell would attempt an uppercut, but Baldock was generally able to predict the arrival of these bombs and worked efficiently to dodge or suffocate them in their eruption. Archie's left hooks to the body were difficult to escape, so Teddy made sure he moved away from him quickly and, when that failed, he sought to tie him up inside.

In the eighth round, Baldock believed he had got his man. He had scored well with several straight lefts and saw his opportunity to hook Bell with the same hand. Teddy caught his antagonist firmly on the side of the head. The American stumbled to such an extent that Baldock estimated he had to fall. With his equilibrium shattered, Bell went to ground, but there was no time to start a count before he was once more on his feet. However, as soon as Archie was upright Baldock began laying into him with left and right gloves blazing, but Bell was not giving in and seemed to come out stronger for the ninth, somehow having found a second wind.

As Archie had drawn on uncharted reserves, Teddy had to find something more in himself. Each time Baldock returned to his corner, Joe would encourage him: 'That's it, keep away from him – use your left – don't let him get close – you're winning every round.'

However, although Teddy had trained well for the scheduled 15 rounds, he had not experienced this sort of pace before. He knew he was probably doing OK because at points he had struck Bell flush on the nose with his left, as well as hitting him with a range of other blows from both hands. But Baldock could feel his ribs being tenderised with every thump Bell landed. The American, in Teddy's mind, had taken on the persona of a man who didn't seem to rest, tire or idle, and Baldock thought that, even though he might be scoring better than Archie, maybe as much as three to one in terms of blows landed, this also meant that he himself had absorbed dozens of hurtful shots.

At the end of the 13th round, Baldock was relieved to hear his manager tell him that he was so far in front he couldn't lose as long as he avoided getting knocked out. Morris advised his fighter to coast the final two rounds, concentrating on avoiding damage. But, within 20 seconds of Baldock adopting these tactics, Bell flew at Teddy in a blitz that shocked the Londoner. A left and right thudded into Baldock's body and then a right clipped his chin. Before he had time to move, a left hook came over on the other side, and Baldock was on the ropes.

Teddy regained a little composure and began to try to fight Bell off, but leather was coming in fast from everywhere, at every conceivable angle. Baldock was blocking and parrying but he was taking a great deal of punishment. However, by pure intuition, Teddy escaped and as he did so he stuck out the left, but Bell was back in, and once more Baldock was forced to defend. The fight had turned! The shock was felt throughout the great Albert Hall and Morris was pulling out what little hair he had as the bell brought Teddy tumbling back to his stall.

Joe begged his fighter: 'Keep moving. Keep away from him – use the ring, and don't swap punches', but he was only telling the boxer what he already knew he should do.

The American realised he had to knock Baldock out if he was going to win and he certainly had a go at it. As Teddy touched gloves with Bell, Archie's eyes told him there would be no quarter on his opponent's part; somewhere in his mind, Teddy realised that the World Championship hung in the balance and how he performed in the next three minutes would determine his destiny. As such, he decided he too would throw caution to the wind; he would win or lose the contest as a fighting man.

The two men met with an immediate and mutual flurry of punching. This ferocious exchange was indiscriminate, with nothing calculated in the shots. But Bell was stronger than Teddy had anticipated, and he felt himself fading and desperately grabbed hold of Bell to avert certain disaster. However, Archie would not be denied and came after Baldock with both hands.

Teddy threw what remained of his strength at Bell in a broadside of controlled fury, and was even successful in pushing the American back. Against a wall of noise from the appreciative audience, both fighters made one last effort in the dying seconds of the contest, knowing the World Championship crown awaited.

Baldock began to wonder if his strategy had been wrong, thinking maybe he should have boxed Bell off, but as he was to say retrospectively, 'There's a fighting spirit in each of us that can't be suppressed in an atmosphere of this kind. I knew I was taking a trouncing; I realised that Bell was intent on putting me away, but, although I was getting as weak as a drowning kitten, I just couldn't resist making a grand slam finish of it; in fact, I was belting away with both hands, and actually driving Archie before me at the last gong.'

As the fight ended, both boxers dropped their hands and stared at each other, respect and incredulity in both men's eyes. Had they really gone through this battle? Surely not! Who could? Both were worn out, but the gloves touched, and then Morris was in the ring to put an arm round his fighter's shoulders, as Bell's corner men helped him back to his stool.

Between gasps, Teddy asked, 'Who's won?'

Yelling over the great clamour that filled the arena, Morris told him immediately, 'Blimey, listen to 'em! You have!'

With 'For He's a Jolly Good Fellow' belting out of the hall's mighty organ, Baldock was lifted shoulder high and, blushing with embarrassment, he was carried round the ring.

As soon as he could, he got his feet back on the ground and went to see Bell and Eddie Borden, who had no complaints. Then Teddy left the ring as fast as he could and made for home and bed, leaving the celebrations to the people of Poplar.

This was the biggest victory of Teddy's life, but his share of the proceedings amounted to just £350. It was part of a three-fight deal for which he would be paid £1,000. When he had paid his sparring partners, manager's percentage and other expenses, he had £180 left, for winning a world title.

POSTSCRIPT TO BELL

In the last quarter of 1927, a trio of fighters laid claim to the world title. In September of that year Archie beat Ignacio Fernandez and in June the following year he defeated Young Nationalista (both were contenders for the crown), but in June 1929 Archie was defeated by Bushy Graham, the former New York Commission World Title holder.

Bell didn't lose a match during 1930 and appeared ready for another shot at the world title. However, by 1931, the division, which had become unified, was once more on the cusp of separation. In May of that year, Archie went to Montreal for a fight against Norwegian Pete Sanstol, but the contest acquired more significance when the Champion, Al Brown, declined to meet the winner (it was thought in some quarters that he was having difficulty making the weight).

The NBA threatened to strip Brown of his title and let it be known that it was ready to recognise the victor of the Sanstol/Bell fight as their number-one contender, using a 'mail-in' pool to award the title. At the same time, the Canada Boxing Federation and Montreal Athletic Association declared that the match was for the world crown, hoping that the US governing bodies would rubber-stamp their claim. Amid the chaos, the fight became a massive event.

On 20 May, the two fighters met not knowing if the title was at stake. The bout was a gruelling battle over 10 rounds and Sanstol won the unanimous decision (taking seven rounds to Archie's two, with one drawn).

Sanstol was recognised in Montreal as the World Title holder, but most boxing historians see Brown as the undisputed Champion at that time (notwithstanding the NBA's removal of his crown).

In August 1931, Brown beat Sanstol. Bell was never to get a shot at Brown, but he continued to be a contender as one of the best bantamweights of his era until his retirement in 1932 with 63 wins (five by KO), 18 losses, 8 draws and a 'no decision'. He passed away on 15 April 1988.

11

BALDOCK IN DEMAND

The morning after his victory over Archie Bell, Teddy bore little evidence of the epic battle, just a small bruise under the right eye and slight swelling on the upper lip. He started to comprehend that he was the new Bantamweight Champion of the World.

Reporters were already gathering outside the Baldock household, all wanting an exclusive from Britain's new World Champion. Louisa Rose Baldock had already told a representative from the *East London Advertiser* that Teddy had been led to believe that she was going to the pictures on the night of the fight. What he didn't know was that his mother had actually witnessed the event from one of the Albert Hall's upper balconies. All but the last round, when on hearing the final gong, the strain became too much and she left her seat to wait outside in the passageway, beside herself with worry that Bell might stop her son in those crucial last three minutes.

The ISS were pleased with the Londoner's victory, in fact, so much so that they added £100 to his winner's purse. The season at the Albert Hall finished with his fight, but they assured him that they would be calling on his services the following winter.

But Baldock was in great demand. A couple of days later, he attended West Ham United's final game of the season versus Liverpool at Upton Park, where, both before and after the game, despite a thrilling 3–3 draw (that pushed the Hammers up to sixth place in the old First Division, finishing their campaign as top London club), he was swamped with attention and autograph hunters.

Just a few weeks later, Teddy was reported to be earning '£10 a minute' for his exhibition bouts at the Astoria (the new purpose-built cinema in Charing Cross Road had only recently been converted from its former role as the

Crosse and Blackwell pickle factory; it became a famous music venue before its demolition in 2009). Local adulation culminated later that summer when Poplar gave him a 'municipal welcome' and an 'illuminated address' (a grand framed certificate presented by the Mayor of Poplar) together with the freedom of the borough. Baldock opened charity bazaars, kicked off at football matches, made appearances at local cinemas, and was generally kept in the public eye. He also attended music hall engagements, giving exhibitions of his skills.

Teddy had become something of a national sporting celebrity. He frequented some of the best London eateries and clubs, as well as being a regular at the great horseracing events of the time, rubbing shoulders with high-ranking military men, lords, knights and gentlemen. He was every inch the archetypal roaring 20s playboy, often seen in a bowler hat or dinner suit.

Around this time, Teddy, through his father had brought a court case against the boxing-promoting Jacobs brothers (Isaac and Harry), which would be reported in the *Star* on 28 August 1927, under the headline 'Boxer's Earnings. Judge Asks About Baldock's "Immense Wealth." £550 For a Fight. Cancelled Contract With Bantam Champion'.

On his return from America in December, Teddy found that the Jacobs brothers were claiming to have a right to his services under an agreement that he knew nothing about and at once repudiated. Notwithstanding this, the promoters went ahead and billed him to appear at the Albert Hall in a contest on 27 January, against Louis Jerome of France.

The contract referring to the retention of Teddy Baldock's services for the season 1927 to 1928 was purported to have been signed by Joe Morris in his fighter's absence.

During the Court proceedings, Mr Archer, acting in defence of Harry Jacobs argued 'that they gave this boy an extremely beneficial contract when he was unknown and could not command any money at all to speak of. He came from an obscure home in the East End, where there was hardly enough to eat, and he was given this chance. He insisted on having a clause inserted giving him leave to go to America, and, having done pretty well there, the first thing he did on his return was to repudiate this contract.'

When Baldock entered the box, he was asked his age and replied that he was 20 that day, he then gave details of his trip to America under the supervision of Ted Broadribb. When questioned about the alleged contract he stated;

'I never authorised Joe Morris to enter into this contract with the defendants, and I had no communication directly with them'.

Referring to the occasion on which he was billed by the defendants to fight Louis Jerome, Baldock replied, 'I would have had all to lose and nothing to gain by such a fight'.

When cross-examined by Mr Archer, Baldock said he first appeared at the Albert Hall under an arrangement with Mr Harry Jacobs and that he was, at the time satisfied with the contract made by Joe Morris on his behalf.

Mr Archer pointed out that the contract with the defendants for Baldock's four fights at the Albert Hall provided for a payment of £162 10s for each fight, which was more than double the highest sum he had received before.

Answering further questions, Baldock said he got £100 for his last contest in America and for his last three fights for the International Sports Syndicate, £350 for the first, £550 for the second and £400 for the third [elsewhere this was reported as £1,000 for the three fights].

After consultation it was agreed that the most sporting end to the matter would be for both parties to go their separate ways while paying their own costs. With the contract cancelled, the Judge finally ruled;

'Defendants stating that they do not wish to hold this lad to any arrangement which has been made on his behalf and having heard that he makes no charges against them, there will be a stay of all further proceedings and no order as to costs'.

Baldock, at the height of his fame, once said, 'Swank is a mistake, especially in boxers and jockeys. You may be up one year and out the next, and when you're out you're forgotten. Those who swank finish on the floor.

'I can't stand the type of man who, when he's won a few fights, goes about with a sort of 'I'll tell the world' attitude. He can't tell the world anything till it happens, and when it does happen it may not happen the way he expects. In any case, the higher you go, the less swank you find, and that's a good enough model for me.

'The Prince of Wales, the Duke of York and the Marquis of Clydesdale [known as the "Boxing Marquis"] are my ideas of what sportsmen should be. No side about them, and none about the good old-timers like Mike Honeyman and Jim Varley, who taught me all I know.

'That's why I'm afraid to feel too pleased about my own luck. I won't pretend that I am not pleased – I am – but I am pleased principally because it has cheered up my mother and my father; it seems to have carried on the family tradition – we have been boxers for almost 200 years – and, most of all, it has helped me to make a bit more money and put father and mother into a shop.'

As such, it appears that, while Teddy might well have been the retiring type, his modesty was something of a code of conduct, to paraphrase Muhammad Ali, 'A man gotta have a code.'

Joe Morris was keen for Teddy to have another trip to America and Teddy was equally keen to travel back across the Atlantic, but he would have been denied the opportunity to strengthen his claim on the title, because he was still too young for Championship matches in America. Bud Taylor had defeated Tony Canzoneri, to become the NBA's new king of the bantamweight world, and there was some effort made to get Taylor to come to London to fight Baldock, but Bud's camp declined all offers.

However, the British Champion Johnny Brown, having recovered from the illness that prevented him from meeting Baldock earlier, had started a comeback at Premierland, including a couple of knockouts, and a 15-round points victory over Liverpudlian Nel Tarleton. Now that Teddy was a World Champion, Brown was far keener to meet him.

Sir Charles B. Cochran was a theatrical manager, who had been press representative to various theatres, circuses and exhibitions in the United States. After 1917, he became responsible for the productions of the Oxford Theatre and later on showed an interest in many of the best-known English theatres either as leasee or licensee. He was planning a gigantic show at Olympia at the end of June 1927, the top-liner of which would be a world middleweight title fight between Tommy Milligan and Mickey Walker. Cochran offered Baldock a bout on the undercard with Sheffield's Johnny Cuthbert, the British Featherweight Champion, and Baldock's camp took the fight, feeling that there was nothing to lose but much to be won.

Looking back on the fight over two decades later, Baldock said that the contest was, 'a daft match if ever there was one, and it did neither Cuthbert nor myself any good, except to make us a little richer, I suppose ... At the time we thought it was money for old rope, because Johnny had to come in at 9st which meant I'd be conceding about six pounds, but the distance had been cut to six rounds to give me an opportunity to outspeed him. I was made a three-to-one favourite to knock Cuthbert out, but I never looked like doing it.'

The Sheffield man was a fine Featherweight Champion; crafty and ring-wise, he was one of the best Britain had ever produced in his division. He was not known for possessing a knockout punch and was also inclined at times to cuff with the inside of the glove, had this not been the case, Baldock might not have lasted the distance.

But Teddy found Cuthbert to be quite a different proposition from any boxer he had fought before. Baldock was able to reach him easily enough with his ubiquitous long left, but Cuthbert delivered extremely swift right counters and Teddy got caught dozens of times before he could move out of range. Johnny also knew how to use his own left, so when Baldock steamed in he would make him miss with his left lead and follow up with a jab that knocked Baldock's head back with a snap, or beat him to the punch.

Teddy decided to move inside, but Cuthbert demonstrated that his knowledge of in-fighting probably exceeded that of the Londoner; Baldock was always having to punch round his opponent's elbows, while Cuthbert secured the inside position to pound at Teddy's body. According to Baldock, 'So far as I could tell, I didn't win the first round or the second, but did better in the third, although Cuthbert got in some effective counters. Johnny took the fourth when I had an uncomfortable session.'

By now, doubt about Teddy's chances was spreading through the audience. Those who had laid wagers on him winning the contest were looking to hedge their bets. But Baldock came back at Cuthbert in the fifth and at that point things looked pretty even. In the last round Teddy went for a KO, throwing all he had at Johnny. Cuthbert was way too educated to get caught easily, but Baldock's aggression probably won him the round. Teddy was to admit that he felt he was lucky to get the draw when Sam Russell gave his decision and later in life was to confess, 'It was a scrap I should have lost.'

The fight with Cuthbert was a disappointment for Baldock and his camp, and, although he was loath to make excuses, Teddy told his manager that he had felt stale and not at all himself. It had been almost two months since the defeat of Bell, but he later speculated that his title fight may have taken more out of him than he thought. It was decided that Baldock should take a break from the ring for a couple of months. But Teddy did meet Len Oldfield (brother to Dod, whom Baldock had beaten a couple of times) at the Ilford Skating Rink. However, the fight was a brief encounter, as the Leeds man took a short right to the chin and went down for the count in the second.

While Teddy took his break, his camp looked for another big fight. With Bud Taylor reluctant to come to London, they turned their attention to South African Willie Smith, who was more than six years older than Baldock. He had recently beaten Ernie Jarvis in Johannesburg, and also had victories over both the Brown brothers to his credit.

Smith won the bantamweight gold medal at the 1924 Olympics to become the youngest ever Olympic boxing champion, and he had a perfect professional record, although at that time he had only fought about a dozen times in the paid ranks.

As Willie had defeated the British Bantamweight Champion, he had a claim on the Empire title, and unsurprisingly he wanted to meet Baldock at 8st 6lb. Teddy was comfortable with this arrangement, which meant risking his world crown in an effort to win the lesser title, but Morris did not approve, wanting Baldock to meet a good American if the stakes were going to be high. So, having made the long trip to London by arrangement with Ted Broadribb in September 1927, the slightly built and mild-mannered Smith was obliged to fight at 8st 8lb or return home empty-handed. The fight was scheduled for the Albert Hall on 6 October 1927. It would be the first boxing match covered as a live radio commentary by the BBC.

Smith's boxing career started in a Johannesburg orphanage and owed much to the first South African Flyweight Champion George Harris (who had stopped Marcus Henning in Kimberley on 12 November 1909 for the title). Twice a week Harris gave boxing lessons to orphans in the St George's Home, and 12-year-old local hoodlum Smith was among those he worked with. Willie had become acclimatised to violence but lacked the capacity to convert this into constructive aggression. Harris taught Smith a good deal about technique, but it was trainer Johnny Watson, impressed with Smith's determination, who tutored him in defensive strategies, transforming him into a boxer with style and skill.

Smith had a demanding professional debut on 25 June 1925 against South African Bantamweight Champion Scotty Frazer; the eight rounds ended in a draw. In the return fight on 26 September, which was billed as being for the South African bantamweight crown, Frazer was disqualified in the 13th round. However, the Transvaal Boxing Board of Control did not recognise the contest so Willie did not win the title.

In England, Jack Goodwin took charge of the South African, setting up their camp at Harlow in Essex. But a few days later they were in London, and Goodwin, who was known as a man with a dry sense of humour, said that if the British Government of 1815 had known that such a place as Harlow existed they would never have sent Napoleon to St Helena. Smith was then taken to Shoeburyness, accompanied by his chief sparring partner, former amateur boxer Johnny Mann.

Baldock returned once again to Hurstpierpoint with a new ally, Arthur Webb, who had been selected because he had been Smith's sparring partner in South Africa.

Before he left for Sussex, Teddy, out of the blue, contracted bronchitis. This grew so severe that his father sent for Joe Morris, who quickly summoned a doctor. However, it was agreed that as there was a month to go until the contest with Smith the problem could clear up in time for the fight. So after a few days in bed Baldock left for the training camp, still on medication.

The sea air seemed to work wonders and Teddy felt good until 10 days before the fight when he caught a chill, and the original problem reoccurred. Jack Lakey worked solidly trying to get his fighter fit by the weekend when Morris was due to visit the training camp. When he got down to Sussex, Joe was distraught at how badly out of condition the fighter looked, so much so he wanted to call off the fight, but Baldock was sure he could shake off the problem as he had previously and pleaded with his manager to let the fight go ahead.

On the day of the contest, Morris met the rest of the Baldock entourage at Victoria Station and they all made their way to The Ring at Blackfriars for the weigh-in. The match was being fought 2lb over the bantamweight limit; however, Smith was on the bantam limit while Baldock hit the scales dead on 8st 8lb.

Teddy 'was wrapped up to the eyebrows in a large overcoat, and when Joe asked how I felt I told him, "I'm OK, don't bother." '

But Morris peered into the boxer's face and said, 'You're not, you know. In fact, you look half dead.' He then had a serious conversation with Lakey about the situation.

When Baldock got to his dressing room, he took a look at himself: his skin was yellow and his eyes were dark-rimmed and sunken. However, his difficulty in breathing aside, he felt he was well enough to fight, and told the promoters that the bout was on. Morris shrugged his shoulders in an expression of his comparative helplessness and turned away hoping that maybe Teddy wasn't as ill as he looked. He had done his best to get the match postponed, but Teddy was resolute.

However, the moment Baldock shaped up to Smith, he began to wish he had gone with his manager's instinct. Willie was an awkward fighter and as speedy as Baldock at his best, which was about twice as fast as he would manage during their fight.

As usual, the people of Poplar had turned out in their droves to support their native son. On reflection Baldock was to say, 'I think it must have been the thought of disappointing all these friends and neighbours of mine that made me so obstinate about going on with the scrap. I was among these people all day and every day, and it would have been letting them down to ask for a postponement, apart from the loss to the promoters and the boxers on the bill.'

It was a real shock for Teddy that he just couldn't do what he wanted. His push to make himself work somewhere near normal, together with his loss of power, led to his making bad mistakes and missing chances. But he doggedly stuck to his path, hoping that something would click back into position and justify his decision to face Smith.

The initial round wasn't much more than a sparring session, with both boxers testing the waters, but when Baldock came out for the second his right glove was pulled up, having determined that he would need to attempt to knock Smith out while he had the strength. He sent in the piston-like left and slung a right fast and hard, but the left was not the effective piledriver he and his supporters had come to expect. It wasn't connecting and the rights were going everywhere but on Smith's chin.

The South African swerved and ducked, while coming forward to drive brutal hooks into Baldock's ribs. Teddy might have just worked hard enough to win that round by a small margin, but that was as good as it would get for him.

Smith set the agenda in the third round and he held on to the initiative for the rest of the contest. A clever fighter, he made Baldock miss continually and his counter-punching was swift and accurate. Teddy was doing the best he could, but he was being out-scored in every exchange.

The eighth almost saw the end of Baldock. As each round, each minute passed, he was feeling increasingly tired, the relentless attacks on his body taking a huge toll, but it was a left and right to the jaw that sent Baldock down.

Teddy was on his feet almost immediately but could do little more than hang on and try to keep out of trouble for what was left of the round. After that, Baldock wasn't in the fight, but took an almighty thrashing. He was to reflect later that, had Smith known what a terrible state he was in, he could have finished him on half-a-dozen occasions when he was merely stumbling round the ring. At the start of each round, Baldock would come out and throw the best of what he had and, while some blows landed well, they lacked that decisive power, so, although Smith's nose was bloodied and he also bled from the mouth a good deal in the later stages of the fight, he was never really threatened by Teddy's efforts.

Smith may have seen Baldock as being more dangerous when wounded, but his work on Teddy was meticulous, pounding away at him until there was little if anything left.

Later, Baldock was to ask himself why Joe Morris had not disregarded his insistence to see the fight to its conclusion and thrown the towel in. But Teddy had hidden the extent of his illness quite well and, like Smith, Morris probably hadn't realised just how unwell he was. Afterwards, Joe told Baldock that he was unable to watch him taking the punishment that the Smith was inflicting on him, but each time Teddy got back to his corner he demanded 'one more round'.

At the end of the fight, the verdict was clear and the awarding of the victory to Smith was just a formality. Willie went to Baldock's corner and the two men shook hands. Thereafter, as usual, Teddy slipped quietly out of the ring and made his way back to his dressing room.

Sympathy came from every direction, starting with the fans as Baldock made his way through the auditorium. One woman pressed a piece of paper into his hand, saying, 'Take this, Teddy. It's the first time I've ever lost money over you.' When he got into the dressing room, the fighter found that he had been given a £5 note.

Smith's victory was met with delight in South Africa and some weeks after the contest there were huge queues for a film of the fight that circulated the country for months.

POSTSCRIPT TO SMITH

After his win over Baldock, Willie went to the United States where he was beaten by Harlem's Dominick Petrone, a former AAU Junior National Champion at flyweight. Following a stay of five months, a disappointed Smith returned home, but in 1928 he defeated Young Johnny Brown, Sammy Tucker and Mickey Doyle and fought to a draw with Frenchman Pierre Pothier who in December 1927 had met Gustave Humery for the French featherweight title.

At the start of 1929, Smith was in Australia where, in his first fight 'down-under', he beat Archie Cowan. Then he lost against Fidel LaBarba and welterweight Jack Roberts knocked him out.

Back in South Africa, on 30 November 1929, Willie defeated Dolf du Plessis on points over 15 rounds, but, although this fight was billed as being for the South African featherweight crown, Smith was never to be recognised as such. He went on to have a couple of shots at the Empire bantamweight title, but was beaten by Dick Corbett in 1930 and Glaswegian Johnny McGrory in December 1936.

In an effort to get back into the top echelons of the fight game, Smith out-pointed Austrian Ernest Wohrer and went on to beat Maurice Holtzer, a French from Troyes, during the 1930s this tough Jewish slugger have been French, European and the IBU World Featherweight Champion.

After this good showing, the Union Sporting Club matched Willie with Cincinnati's Freddie Miller, the former World Featherweight Champion, who was more than 16 years Smith's senior. Willie was knocked out in the sixth round. Just seven weeks later, in a seemingly futile return fight, he was once more knocked out, going a round longer than he had previously managed against Miller. His rign career ended in a defeat by Glasgow fighter Johnny McGrory.

Smith worked as a salesman and commercial traveller for several years before running the Richmond Hotel on the West Rand. Following the Second World War, Willie became one of the most well-known and respected of South African referees and handled some big fights featuring Johnny Ralph and Vic Toweel, including Toweel's world title bouts against Luis Romero and Jimmy Carruthers.

Willie died of a heart attack in 1955; he was 51 years old.

Losing to Willie Smith was something of a shock for Baldock and his supporters. Teddy's confidence had been shaken and he still had a cold with the bronchial problems. As such it seemed beneficial for him to have a holiday; he went to the South of France for three weeks, where the fresh air, sunshine and change of environment did much to reinvigorate him.

When he got back to London, a challenge for a return fight with Smith was thrown down. The deal amounted to £1,000 for each fighter, but by that time Willie was on the ship bound for the US, where he had been promised a fight with Bud Taylor for the Championship (which ultimately never happened).

With defeat came numerous offers to cash in at Teddy's expense from the likes of Phil Lolosky, Mick Hill and Johnny Brown, who was still the British and European Bantamweight Champion, as well as winner outright of a Lonsdale Belt. Brown argued that Baldock could not consider himself any type of champion until he had beaten him, but as soon as the respective camps began negotiations it seemed Johnny had another engagement in mind.

For Baldock, the manner in which rival managers worked was ridiculous. Writing letters to the press and passing messages to one another via intermediaries, with the thought of meeting and getting down to business seemingly almost the last thing on their minds. Fighters were unable to be matched because one might be contracted to a certain promoter or could only box at a particular venue from which the other might be excluded.

Naturally, only one person can stand on any particular pinnacle of professional boxing; we instinctively know that there really can't be two, three or more 'Champions' in any category and the word 'undisputed' has become a necessary adjunct to denote supremacy. But efforts to literally 'claim the high ground' of the sport by way of bureaucratic splits and contending claims to the crowns of boxing are, as we have seen, nothing new, and this was not just because of differences of perspectives on either side of the Atlantic or, as today, whole regions of the world. In the last analysis it is, and always has been, not about the benefit of the sport, the fighters of the fans. For the most part, the people who make the most money out of boxing have traditionally been promoters and lawyers; in the main that has been the justification and drive of the professional game. Such is life maybe, but the result has been there have been more than a few wonderful fighters who never came near so much as a sniff of an opportunity to prove themselves the best, while at the same time there have been some truly farcical clowns dragged out of the mire to be saluted as champion.

But professional boxing is a product of late capitalist society, a society that by its very nature is exploitative. This being the case we can hardly be amazed that its stars, the men who have in effect made (if not kept) all the money are exploited. Boxing is as such a mirror and confirmation of the society it exists in; for it to be otherwise would be a contradiction on an impossible scale.

Before the 1930s, even within Britain, there were occasions when two men both claimed the Championship at the same time. New and enterprising promoters filled large stadia with contests, satisfying public demand, which brought them into conflict with the established order, the NSC. The opportunity to make vast profits overrode any concerns these promoters may have had about the legitimacy of the 'title' contests that they were staging. The public, however, voted with their feet, and the large crowds that attended these promotions gave these bouts, and the champions that emerged from them, credibility. This situation only changed as the British Boxing Board of Control gained sole authority over national championships, and this had much to do with the expanding media having to contract a named body as modern communications and their effect on mass entertainment began to dominate.

At the time when the Board of Control was in its infancy, the NSC was quickly losing its formerly autocratic power and, although the press couldn't literally make matches, the *Sporting Life* and *Boxing* tried hard to organise the complicated situation the bantamweight division found itself in.

For more than two years, Brown had failed to defend his titles and refused to make a match under 8st 10lb; Willie Smith claimed both the Empire and World Titles because he had defeated Johnny Brown and Baldock (even though the latter had been at catchweight); Kid Nicholson saw himself as a contender because he had beaten Baldock (albeit on a foul); Mick Hill had given Johnny Brown the hardest of his three Belt fights; Alf 'Kid' Pattenden had beaten Brown at catchweight and had fought a draw with Archie Bell; Phil Lolosky carried a good record and had powerful backing; and, of course, there was Baldock, who wouldn't fight anyone at 8st 6lb unless there was a title to be had.

All these claims and potential claims caused a complete deadlock, but for Teddy 'a man must fight', and eventually Morris chose to get involved with promoting with a partner and started at the Forest Gate Skating Rink then part East London/West Essex borderlands. The opening show included a 15-round fight at 8st 8lb between Baldock and Len Fowler, a clever Brummie who claimed the Midlands Bantamweight Championship.

The prospect of this encounter filled the venue, with hundreds more being turned away. Baldock was feeling good and believed he could make short work of Fowler. He started the fight working his left hand fast to the face, following up with rights to the head, but Len matched Teddy for pace in the first three rounds. In the fourth, Baldock decked him with a left and Fowler was obliged to take an eight count. Teddy had been cultivating this new, more vicious left-handed, shallow swing, deploying a slightly bent elbow, using it primarily to lower a rival's guard, making a target for a right.

Len got up only to be dropped again with a right to the jaw. This time he took nine to rise and was effectively saved by the bell. He came out surprisingly well for the fifth. With half the round done, Baldock attempted another left hook to the ribs, but this time his adversary anticipated the move and dropped his arm, catching the punch on his bony elbow.

Baldock was hit by a sudden wave of agony that radiated up his arm; his left dropped uselessly to his side. It had gone completely numb. Fowler saw that Teddy was hurt and in a split second he was on the attack with a strong onslaught. Baldock could do nothing but hold on, hoping that some feeling would return to his seemingly dead left arm. But it was still lifeless as he walked back to his stool.

Frantic massaging by his corner men had no effect. Morris instructed, 'Show him the left, but don't use it until it's all right.'

Lakey cut in, advising, 'Try and knock the geezer out with your right.'

Teddy went back into battle feeling anxious; Fowler was gunning for him and keen for a scrap. Baldock did show him the left and struck him with the right, but the Midlander kept coming. Again, Baldock was obliged to hold his rival until he could move away. The referee warned Teddy for this, so he broke away and delivered a right that floored Fowler just before the bell ended the sixth round.

As the seventh round progressed, Baldock began to feel his left arm, but he took it easy, and hardly used it apart to measure for his right. In the eighth, Teddy took a chance and screwed a hard left-handed punch under Fowler's ribs, directly in the centre of his body; Len instantly fell to his knees. He managed to get up, but was hit by a perfectly timed right that landed straight on his jaw, knocking him down for the full count.

The damage to Baldock's faithful left was a worry. It was very tender but seemed to be back to normal a few days after the fight, so quite naturally Teddy forgot all about it, although, later in life, he would wonder why he hadn't been advised to have it X-rayed.

Baldock was now basing his training at Fred Dyer's roof gymnasium in the Strand. It was relatively close to his family home but, as it was situated high above the cityscape, it was comparatively tranquil and Teddy liked the feeling of being far away from the noise and bustle of the East End.

Morris arranged for Baldock to fight at The Ring, Blackfriars, for the first time. He was set to face Frenchman Francois Biron at 8st 9lb. At this time there were more rumours that Baldock was having problems making the bantam-weight limit. There was some truth to this, as he was finding it progressively more difficult to get down to 8st 6lb, and could only make it after a push and as such risked coming in weak.

The fight with Biron never happened, as Teddy broke down in training a few days before the contest. His bronchial condition reoccurred and he was troubled by his left hand. Morris was very concerned about his fighter's health particularly as prior to the fight with Willie Smith, Baldock had always been a picture of fitness.

It was arranged for Teddy to see a specialist, who advised him to lay off for couple of months as he was suffering from 'excessive training and weight making'. Later Baldock was to wonder how the doctor had made his diagnosis and stated that he had probably come to the decision after taking a look at his fighting and training record!

Teddy Baldock – The Pride of Poplar.
The Story of Britain's Youngest Ever Boxing World Champion

12

THE CROWD EXPECTED A SHOW

1928

Teddy continued to receive a steady flow of challenges. Phil Lolosky was most persistent. Along with his tutor, the wonderfully named Taffy Isaacs (the Jewish Druid), he would press for a date almost daily. They were ready to bet on it and as such Morris consented to lay £250 to £200 at 8st 8lb.

At around the same time, the NSC offered Baldock a fight with Johnny Cuthbert for the British featherweight title, but Teddy was unable to accept because of his lack of fitness. The match was eventually made with Harry Corbett and 'H' took the title from Cuthbert, who would get his title back almost exactly a year later on the occasion of Corbett's first defence. Mick Hill was another boxer looking for a fight with Baldock. An offer of £100-a-side was made, and he was prepared to wager £50 that he would finish Teddy inside the distance.

Baldock took Lolosky on first, although not until February 1928. Teddy had been out of action for nearly 10 weeks, which was a long time in that era. The contest was staged at Forest Gate, but Teddy was unable to make the weight, and he was fortunate that Joe Morris was the promoter.

Lolosky agreed to meet Baldock regardless of his weight. He had trained hard at Alec Lambert's gym, while Teddy had been keeping himself in shape at Fred Dyer's establishment

Forest Gate was once more packed as Lolosky had a big following that were happy to take the short trip from Aldgate to support their man, and Teddy's supporters were always a loyal bunch.

The referee that evening was 'Bombardier Billy' Wells from Mile End, who was the first British heavyweight to win the Lonsdale Belt in 1911 after his knockout defeat of Iron Hague in the sixth round. He defended the title 13 times, a record that stood for many years, before losing to Joe Beckett in February 1919. Billy won the original heavyweight Lonsdale Belt, which, unlike later belts, was crafted from 22-carat gold. The BBC found the historic trophy, which is now kept at the Royal Artillery Barracks in Woolwich, Southeast London, although it is not on display to the general public.

As the fighters came together for the first time, Baldock slung a right at his opponent that missed his chin, but nearly broke his nose, and he tumbled to the ropes. Teddy was to recall, 'If I hadn't gone haywire with my right, and really measured him, I might have won the fight in the first round.'

But Teddy's timing was poor and the first time he dug Lolosky with a left he felt the familiar old ache, threatening the return of the dreaded numbness. He chose to work the hand on Phil's body, which was much more yielding than his head, but Baldock knew he couldn't overdo even this soft option.

Teddy was reliant on catching Lolosky with his right, but he also started leading with it, a move that would have made his mentors, Mike Honeyman and Jim Varley, recoil in horror. And, the following day, the press castigated the East Ender for this 'overuse' of his right: 'Where is that lightning left that Baldock once flashed so perfectly?' Of course, to answer this question honestly would have been tantamount to career suicide for Teddy.

In the second round, Baldock cut Lolosky above his left eye and opened a gash on the other in the fifth. In the seventh Lolosky was almost sent through the ropes, but Teddy was unable to find the punch to finish the tough Aldgate man.

Lolosky battled bravely, but he was very set in his punching, and Baldock knew what to expect from him most of the time. He scored well when Teddy missed; he had a good left hand and he caused Baldock's mouth to bleed, but Phil was defeated by heavy right bombs under the heart that Baldock began to get on target during the 10th. From that point on it was his best punch, and Lolosky found no way to avoid these blows. He soaked up a great deal of punishment, but refused to fall.

Teddy won the decision, but Lolosky's performance had been a crowd pleaser, and many were none too happy with the verdict. However, even many years later, Baldock was certain justice was done in that fight.

Teddy's left hand took longer to heal than when he had first sustained the injury, and he was out for five months. Every time he tested it the pain reoccurred. He told Joe Morris it was pointless trying to fight without the left jab that had underpinned his progress in the game. Even if he could have unlearned his reliance on his left hand, to box virtually one-handed would have been disastrous. So, although no one suggested that he might turn southpaw, it probably wouldn't have been a good idea.

Since the fight with Archie Bell, Baldock had been troubled by breathing problems, so taking advantage of the forced rest on account of his left hand, decided to see a specialist. On the 8 March he underwent an operation to remove a broken bone fragment from his nose. During his short stay in hospital, Teddy received many cards from friends and well-wishers. His former adversary, Phil Lolosky, who only a few weeks earlier had given him a tough fight over fifteen rounds, also paid him a surprise visit to pass on his best wishes.

Baldock had an unfulfilled contract at The Ring, so, when he thought he might be able to put on some kind of show, Teddy crossed the Thames to meet Pierre Calloir, another Frenchman, at whose request the match was made at 8st 12lb.

The Poplar fighter was grateful that his left hand held up, and, following three rounds of swift work that brought his opponent to a standstill, Teddy fired in a right, sending Calloir to his knees, gasping for air. After being counted out poor, scarcely perpendicular, Pierre had to be carried back to his corner.

In 1928, both Alf (Kid) Pattenden and Teddy Baldock saw themselves, and were regarded in different quarters, as the British Bantamweight Champion. Pattenden hailed from Bethnal Green, a neighbouring district to Baldock's native Poplar, and these two East End 'villages' managed to generate regional rivalry at any opportunity; a Baldock versus Pattenden bout to settle who was 'truly' the British Bantamweight Champion was certainly an enticing prospect in East London.

But for half a decade it was more or less unanimously agreed that the bantamweight Crown was the property of the St George's fighter Johnny Brown, who had won a Lonsdale Belt outright, had done well in the US and, in the autumn of his career, understandably looked to earn as much money as possible.

Following Brown's defeat of Mick Hill in 1925, making the Lonsdale Belt his personal property, he had gone to the US for a second time. His first trip had been very successful, but he failed to take this subsequent stay as seriously and he was defeated in all five of his fights; in the final bout he suffered a TKO in the first round.

From there Johnny travelled to Johannesburg, where he was beaten by Willie Smith on points. He returned to England and, after a longish layoff, got back into the game. Before fighting Baldock he had been involved in nine contests, winning five and drawing one, but he was defeated by Alf Pattenden and Kid Socks on points and was stopped in the 14 round by New York Jewish fighter Sammy Shack, a good featherweight and a sparring partner to Newsboy Brown.

Challenges to Brown from younger fighters were numerous, coming from the likes of Baldock and Pattenden, and there were several attempts by the NSC to persuade Johnny Brown to fight one of the youthful contenders for a new Belt. However, the club was restricted to a relatively small audience and as such, in those pre-television days, the purse they could offer was not enough to tempt the Champion, who would have had no problem getting bigger money at other venues, often without putting his title (his means of commanding a decent payday) on the line. The opportunity to win a new Belt was no incentive to Brown. He owned one and if it wasn't financially worthwhile he had no reason to seek another. But his spurning of the NSC's overtures also had a cost, and he was told he had forfeited his title. While Baldock had been out of action, the British Boxing Board of Control, which appeared to be gaining more muscle each week, had informed Johnny Brown that his British title had been withdrawn, and the IBU told Brown he was no longer the European Champion. This, of course, was predictable. But, without a named alternative champion, it almost went ignored by the boxing public. How could a mere committee take a man's Championship away from him?

Johnny himself was not too concerned; in fact, he paid so little attention to these notices that he let Morris know that he was willing to defend his now forfeited titles against Teddy if Joe made sure he got a good purse.

Alf Pattenden and Baldock were matched for the vacant Championship. However, Teddy withdrew as the purse being offered for the fight was relatively light and Alf was subsequently matched with Teddy's sparring partner Kid Nicholson for the Title at the NSC in June. The Leeds fighter lasted 12 rounds before being knocked out. But this was a hollow victory. Pattenden held a Lonsdale Belt, but Baldock was regarded by many people in Britain as the World Champion after beating Archie Bell.

However, the situation created talk and argument, rivalry and interest, which in turn generated crowds. So it was only going to be a matter of time before the two fighters would be drawn together.

In the meantime, Morris was keen to stage a big show at the Clapton Orient Football Ground with a main contest billed as the Flyweight Championship of the World between Scotland's Johnny Hill and Newsboy Brown (real name David Montrose, a Russian-born Jewish fighter from Sioux City, Iowa).

Newsboy was in Britain looking for a fight, having been brought over by a promoting syndicate that went broke before it started trading. As such, he was ready to go along with almost anything Morris might offer.

As a second top-liner, he announced a match between Johnny Brown and Baldock to be at the bantamweight limit in an attempt to legitimise a world title tag. Johnny was undefeated as British Bantam Champion, and Teddy had his claim to the World Crown. This in effect meant a second World Championship tilt for Teddy. Secretly, Baldock believed it would be remarkable if he or Johnny made the weight, as both had been nowhere near the bantamweight limit for ages.

On August Bank Holiday, Baldock travelled to Blackpool to meet one of his old sparring partners 'Bugler' Harry Lake on the local racecourse. Lake, who hailed from Plymouth, fought professionally from the age of 15 in 1917 to 1933; in his 172 fights he had been victorious 108 times. He had won the British and Commonwealth bantamweight titles after defeating Tommy Harrison in 1923. Baldock was 9st for this fight but was to claim that this was to help Bugler, who had difficulty getting down to the poundage.

Teddy was to tell how this was one of a few fights that he had been involved with where the scales were fixed: 'Lake was supposed to weigh in at 9st. Actually, when he stepped on to the scales, he must have been overweight. I don't suppose Harry knew how much overweight he was. And certainly he had nothing to do with fixing the scales. In those days anybody and everybody could get at scales. At any rate, when I got into the ring I soon saw that Harry was carrying too much weight to be able to do himself full justice. But I knew the crowd expected a show from us. What was I to do? I decided to carry Lake for a few rounds, just to give the fans their money's worth…putting on a show that certainly looked good – at least from a distance.'

However, things didn't exactly go according to plan. Teddy felt close to his old form, but it poured with rain the whole day and the expected attendance of 20,000 failed to turn up. Just 8,000 watched Lake, a shadow of his former excellent self, after the first round, totally out-boxed. He went down so often that Baldock gave up counting; he was not much more than target practice for Teddy before, in the fifth round, to Baldock's relief, the referee stopped the contest.

The fight with Johnny Brown, for which Baldock had waited more than two years, was now just three weeks away.

Morris had put together an extremely appealing programme and this was confirmed by the massive crowd of 30,000 that came to the Orient ground to see the show. This was a huge number of people, but character-fight crowds in those days were very different to the contemporary period. They would have been almost totally male and, while the venues like the Albert Hall would attract their share of dignitaries and even minor royalty, including their female escorts, the crowds were predominantly working class: factory and dock workers, miners and mill workers. Most places would attract a smattering of soldiers and other servicemen but all would be shrouded in an atmosphere of cigarette smoke and the whiff of beer would lay heavy on the air.

Individuals, communities and whole areas would identify with 'their man'. Poplar was behind Baldock as he shaped up to fight. If he was meeting a man hailing from beyond East London, then Teddy was all of the East End. Likewise, if his opponent was from Liverpool, Birmingham or Manchester, he would embody the whole of London and, when an overseas fighter was in front of him, well, then Baldock represented Britain; everyman, the first and last working-class hero.

In the bout for the Flyweight Championship, Johnny Hill fought like a tiger to beat Newsboy on points after a fabulous bout. Johnny Curley gained victory over Sammy Shack, Newsboy's sparring partner, on a foul in what turned out to be a violent contest, but Baldock's fight with Johnny Brown was a relatively brief affair.

Although Johnny had concentrated on his training as much as he had for any fight under the care of Jack Goodwin, from the start of the first round Teddy sensed that Brown was not going to put up much of a fight. He waited for Baldock to lead, and as soon as Teddy attacked Johnny retreated to the ropes where he was punched according to Baldock's choosing. Teddy withdrew to give him the opportunity to put up some kind of performance and Johnny did advance as if to make a fight of it. But Baldock countered his lead with a right cross that struck his opponent's jaw firmly, and Johnny dropped in a heap at Teddy's feet. He probably could and should have stayed down, but Brown was known to be a game fighter, and rose at eight to hold out for the bell.

However, Baldock finished the fight in the second. Launching a swift attack, he stifled Brown with blows from every direction, and soon returned the St George's man to the boards. Once more, he was on his feet as the count got to eight, but another eloquent cascade of punches sent him back to the floor, before mercifully the towel fluttered over the ropes signalling an end to the beating.

Johnny wished Teddy the best of luck in the dressing room after the fight and told him that he was pleased that he had lost his title in the ring, even though the British Boxing Board of Control had taken his crown away from him months earlier. As such, although Baldock now claimed the world, British and European Crowns, he had no agreed official recognition.

Not long after the fight with Johnny Brown, Joe Morris met with Teddy and his dad to set some plans in place for Baldock's future. From their point of view, he had a technical claim to be the British, European and World Bantam-weight Champion. However, the British Boxing Board of Control's champion was Alf Kid Pattenden, as he had won a Lonsdale Belt match. In America, Bushy Graham was seen as the holder of the world crown after defeating New York's Corporal Izzy (Isadore) Schwartz in a fight for the title vacated when

Bud Taylor moved into the featherweight ranks. As such, it was agreed among the Baldock camp that Graham had to be the main objective, probably because the 'real' Champion needed to have recognition in the United States. Teddy was now 21 and as such was able to box 15 rounds in America and, should the match be made, could fight Bushy Graham for the title. Morris organised a trip to New York as soon as possible, but in the meantime they needed to find suitable opposition closer to home.

It was very likely that the NSC would have been keen for Baldock to meet Pattenden and Teddy could probably have got a Belt match without too much difficulty. However, the financial incentives offered by the NSC were poor compared to what could be earned at the Albert Hall or through Morris's promotions. So, although a Lonsdale Belt was an alluring inducement, it was agreed that the situation also had to look good from a business perspective.

Baldock did have his own challengers; Mick Hill was keen to take him on, while Phil Lolosky and Young Johnny Brown were both looking for vengeance. But it was announced that Baldock would meet anyone in the world over 15 rounds at 8st 6lb for £500, including (and in particular) Bushy Graham, or any other bantamweight who questioned his claim to the world title. There was a quick response as two matches were immediately arranged. However, they were not at the bantamweight limit as there was no promoter able to offer a sufficiently large purse.

So, on 8 October 1928, Baldock met Mick Hill at The Ring, Blackfriars. Seventeen days after this, at the Albert Hall, Teddy was set for a rematch with Phil Lolosky. The fight with Hill was made at 8st 8lb, and the encounter with Lolosky was at 8st 10lb. The weights were fine for Teddy, although he could make bantamweight if required.

As all this was being organised, Pattenden, who like Baldock was still calling himself the British Bantamweight Champion, had his position strengthened by the NSC when they gave him a second Belt match against Young Johnny Brown. Pattenden knocked out Young Johnny in 12 rounds, so getting a second notch on the Lonsdale trophy; Baldock of course had none.

Joe Morris had been astute in persuading Hill's stable to make the match at 8st 8lb. It was the first time Mick had fought at the bantamweight limit since he took on the elder Johnny Brown for the Championship two years earlier. The Baldock camp believed Hill would struggle to make the weight.

Despite the fact it was only Teddy's second appearance at The Ring, the fans turned up in force. Hill was a South Londoner, so part of the attraction was a contest between East and South, but it was also Mick's home ground, as most of his fights had taken place at the Blackfriars venue.

Baldock was aware that Hill was a consummate body puncher, so planned to favour his usual tactic of keeping the fight at long range. But he was also keen to get the bout over with as quickly as possible. His left hand continued to trouble him, and he felt it was not going to last the distance. With this in mind, Teddy set about Mick from the start, throwing his right with greater frequency than in previous fights.

Hill was a tough fighter who believed that Baldock didn't have the arsenal to floor him, and he might not have expected Teddy to come looking for him with his big guns.

In the first minute of the bout, Baldock caught Hill with two consecutive rights, but they landed too high to trouble the South Londoner. In return he fired back a right that caught Baldock behind the ear. It shook Teddy, but he camouflaged his hurt by letting loose an assault to the body with both hands. Hill reacted in kind, and a fierce exchange ensued that had the crowd on their feet.

At the start of the second round, Baldock again came out in a rush. However, Hill, like Teddy, had a reliable straight left, and managed to fend Baldock off. In his eagerness to catch Hill with his right, Baldock was rushing in and taking unnecessary shots which he really should have slipped or blocked. He was fortunate that Hill didn't carry a heavier punch.

The third round was all-out attrition, with Hill working solid rights into Baldock's ribcage, but he paid the price of nearly having his head torn off by a perfectly timed right uppercut in the fourth, which brought blood streaming from his mouth.

Teddy was looking for a punch that had the venom to floor Hill, but he stood strong, this let Baldock know that, if he was going to knock Mick out, he would have to land the telling strike with total accurately to have any effect.

Hill was doing more than holding his own, although Teddy was on the attack for the majority of the time. The South Londoner was consistently landing an effective left jab, and seemed never to let the chance to work on Baldock 'downstairs' go by without taking advantage of the opportunity.

Teddy had put most of his labour into his straight left volleys that were followed by rights to the head. This not only kept Hill busy defending himself, but also denied him the time and concentration to work out an answering strategy. The long-range shots were picking Mick off, but when allowed to get in close Hill was able to even things up. Teddy was striking Hill's head with heavy hooks from either hand as Mick charged in with double-fisted attacks to Baldock's body.

Without warning, pain started to radiate from Teddy's armpit and drift ominously around his shoulder. He knew he would not be able to sustain his left-handed work rate, as to do so might risk permanent damage. Instead, he used the left more as a measuring device to land a knockout punch with his right.

Teddy had no way of knowing if his opponent had sensed his problems, but retrospectively he was to argue that Hill could have taken the fight if he had altered his strategy and made the bout a long-range affair, as Baldock could not call on his extended left. Hill's own left jab was a bit tasty and if he had chosen to restrict himself to that punch Teddy would have had little to answer with. However, Hill continued his attacks to the body, which suited Baldock, although he did suffer at times as Hill carried some power at short range and Teddy was the first to admit that his body was never his strongest physical attribute due to his tall lithe frame.

But the inside-work opened Mick up to a shower of hooks and uppercuts that burst on to his face and body, although he blocked some hurtful-looking rights to the head, the accumulation of blasts were having an effect.

However, Teddy took a heavy right during the 10th round, and he all but doubled up in pain. He could only hang on, for which he was admonished by the referee Sam Russell, giving him just enough time to recover.

The following round, Baldock felt Hill fading; Teddy was pulling away. Mick's punches were not carrying their former force; he was just a bit more eager in retreat and began to give ground readily as Baldock pressed forward.

In the 13th round, Hill had palpably gone, which was just as well because so had Teddy's left arm, which was all but useless as a fighting tool. Apart from this serious handicap, he felt relatively fresh. Anyone at ringside could see that Mick had fought himself to a halt and the call went up for Teddy to 'put him away'.

The subsequent round started with Baldock crashing into Hill with all the power he had left in the tank, letting go with both hands, although every left that landed was almost as excruciating for Teddy as it might have been for Hill, who did what he could to ride out the storm. However, no matter how Mick ducked, dodged or covered up, the hail of leather finally brought him to a point of exhaustion. Baldock got a glimpse of his opponent's jaw, the target he had been hunting. He flashed out a right that caught Hill flush with the back of the knuckles. Mick went down face first to lie motionless on the boards. His left arm doubled beneath his body, his right partly propping him up, he looked the epitome of a totally beaten figure.

The referee motioned for Baldock to go to a neutral corner and began his count, calling out the seconds. No one expected the man to rise after such a heavy knockdown, but, at eight, Hill was on his feet.

Mick stood, guard completely down, swaying with his knees slightly bent. He appeared stunned as Teddy moved towards him for what would have been the final assault of the fight. But it was clear to Russell that the bettered, batted and largely bewildered boxer could not stand another blow, and he stopped it there and then.

The fight fans rose to both men, acknowledging the depth of spirit they had witnessed. Most of the 14 rounds had been taken up with fast, tough fighting, and the contest provided a dramatic conclusion.

In response to this fight, the Albert Hall syndicate set up the rematch with Phil Lolosky, feeling that the close finish of the initial meeting between 'Tubby', as he was known amongst fight fans, and Teddy promised to be another thriller of a fight. When the two had come together at Forest Gate eight months earlier, many in the Lolosky camp believed he had earned a draw (or even the win) and from that point on the Aldgate man had continually challenged Baldock to a rematch; as such, he snapped up the chance to vindicate himself.

Given Baldock's continuing problems with his left hand, Joe Morris had wanted to postpone the contest with Lolosky. In the dressing room at The Ring after the Hill fight, Teddy's arm had swollen up and a lump appeared under his armpit, indicating infection. A South African surgeon, Dr Becker, took a look at the problem and advised consulting a specialist.

However, when the pain subsided and the swelling went down, Baldock told Morris he would fight Lolosky as scheduled and see a specialist after that contest. He later admitted that he knew that if he had gone to Harley Street he would have been pulled out of the bout. He also understood that he would be unable to fight for 15 rounds and would have to stop Lolosky as quickly as possible. As such Teddy asked Joe Morris to allow him to work out his fight plan on his own terms.

Phil came to the contest in a confident mood and, as such, was prepared to take risks, whereas Baldock went into the fight hoping to be allowed opportunities; Lolosky's state of mind would aid Teddy's chances of finding a quick way out.

As the fighters returned to their respective corners at the end of the first round, Baldock was well aware that, although Lolosky's work had been fast, his had been a little faster. Moreover, his punches had been more effective.

In the first part of the second round, Baldock slung a right that connected well with Lolosky's jaw. Phil staggered and before he was able to hoist his guard he had been caught twice more. Lolosky covered up and stumbled backwards but Teddy followed him and landed a telling right beneath Tubby's ribs. He crumbled, his features a picture of agony. There were a few calls of 'foul' from the ringside but the punch had been perfectly legal, and the referee never wavered.

As he got up, Lolosky held out his glove. Baldock, almost automatically, touched it, but thought it was an unnecessary gesture. However, with the niceties done, Teddy steamed in looking to finish it. Lolosky tried to rally but Teddy's rights had expelled most of the will and power he had possessed.

Back in his corner waiting for the third round to start, Baldock told Jack Lakey to pull up his right glove a bit tighter, then he came out intending to finish Lolosky.

Showing his rival a left, Teddy drew his lead and let off an arching right to Phil's waiting chin; Lolosky began to crumple, as Baldock put all his strength into a left hook to the jaw. Phil dropped to the deck while Teddy danced with pain, but he knew the Aldgate man would never beat the count.

Brave but wounded, Lolosky fought to get himself up on one knee, but as he shakily rose to his feet the referee called 'out'. There was a half-hearted protest by Phil and his supporters, claiming that he had been up before 10, but even if he had been allowed to continue it would have been futile.

However, Teddy's victory had a costly price tag. The following day, he was in Harley Street, and, following examination, his left metacarpal bone was found to be fractured in three places. (The metacarpal bones connect the wrist to the fingers and make up the arch of the hand, and a metacarpal fracture is a broken bone in the middle of the hand. One or more metacarpal bones may be fractured, and fracture of the metacarpal of the little finger is most often near the knuckle, which is commonly called a boxer's fracture.)

Disturbingly, during the operation the onset of gangrene was detected, (which would account for the swelling under the armpit). The bone was removed by Dr Becker who, it is rumoured returned to South Africa with it. The operation to treat this injury had come in the nick of time; any further delay could have resulted in very serious consequences. It left Baldock with an eight-inch scar for the rest of his life, and brought his career to a halt. It was unclear when, or even if he would box again.

13

THE CHAMPIONSHIP OF THE EAST END

1929

While Baldock was out of action, Joe Morris tried to keep the momentum of his fighter's career going, looking to negotiate for contests during 1929. This was the year the British Boxing Board of Control developed into a version of the organisation we would recognise today. Baldock was to hold on to the licence given to him by this body, the first one issued in the bantamweight division, numbered 'B.1.'

One fighter who was eager to meet Teddy in the ring was Alf Pattenden, who had two, if not three, good reasons. Firstly he wanted to be able to call himself the World Bantamweight Champion and he also needed one more notch on his Lonsdale Belt to make the coveted prize his own. But almost more importantly, Alf, like Baldock, was an East Ender (from Bethnal Green), and at that time there was a great deal of banter between Poplar and Bethnal Green boxing fans about the Championship: natives of Poplar would delight in reminding their Bethnal Green neighbours that, although Pattenden wore the Lonsdale Belt, it was Teddy who was the 'real' Champion. There was a whole set of arguments about each fighter's merits. Baldock's health permitting, a meeting between them was becoming inevitable.

However, Morris refused to be goaded into any action by even the most tempting of offers. He was negotiating with Clapton Football Ground about staging another big open-air show during the summer, when he estimated that Teddy should be fit to fight again, perhaps against Bushy Graham, recognised as the World Bantamweight Champion in New York, which would have been a huge draw and in order to bring the fight to London the Baldock camp were ready to accept a split percentage, be it 50/50, 60/40 or 75/25.

By the middle of February, Teddy's hand had healed, and following exhausting testing in the gym it appeared to have mended well. But Baldock found it appreciably less flexible and, as he put it, his most lethal tool was 'more like a prop than a snappy weapon', but he was still able to punch hard with it and could continue with his ring ambitions.

Harry Jacobs, who was back at the Albert Hall, offered Teddy a contest in March against Belgian fighter Jerome Van Paemel, officiated by Walworth's Matt Wells. (Wells had turned to refereeing after a distinguished career, during which he had defeated top-notch fighters like Owen Moran, Abe Attell and Freddie Welsh – as an amateur he won four ABA lightweight titles in succession between 1904 and 1907.)

Van Paemel could hit hard and had a particularly effective left hook, but, according to Baldock, 'when it came to real boxing he was not in the same class'. However, following nearly 21 weeks of comparative idleness, Teddy wasn't very sharp either, and he was experimenting with his revivified left, seeing how near he could get to exerting maximum power through it. After giving himself three or four rounds, he started to open up with full force and it came through fine. In the ninth, Wells deemed that the Belgian had taken enough punishment.

Both Teddy and Alf Pattenden were still claiming to be the British Bantamweight Champion and the argument was one of the premises for the NSC to stage a big show at London's huge Olympia. A week after Jacobs's offer, Morris received a letter from the NSC offering Baldock a Championship contest with Alf Pattenden, with the Lonsdale Belt at stake. Teddy's fight was to be one of no less than three Championship fights on one bill: Len Harvey was to challenge Alex Ireland (who won the welterweight silver medal at the 1920 Olympic Games in Antwerp, Belgium, for Britain and was also 1921 ABA Welterweight Champion) for the British Middleweight Championship and Sheffield's Johnny Cuthbert would attempt to take the British featherweight Crown from Bethnal Green's Harry Corbett.

The show was scheduled for the evening of 16 May, admittance would cost from 8s 6d (42½p) to 70s (£3.50). With a suitable purse and the prize of a prestigious Lonsdale Belt on offer, the Baldock camp signed up to the event and the scene was set for an East London showdown.

Teddy had more than a month to prepare for this contest and his entourage (which included Kentish Town lightweight George Davis, Arthur Bodding-ton and Sammy King as sparring partners) decamped to the Chinese Gardens at Hurstpierpoint (although he probably also travelled to the Pelham Arms in nearby Brighton for the extra training facilities it offered). Pattenden, who trained under Jack Goodwin, went to Shoeburyness, with Jack Garland, a Belfast featherweight who had a proven amateur background before turn-ing professional, as his sparring partner. In 1927, Garland had won the Army and Imperial Services Championships at bantamweight and was a quarter-finalist at the ABA Championships. During 1928, he once again took both these titles before winning the ABA bantamweight title. In August of that year, he represented Great Britain in the Olympic Games in Amsterdam but was knocked out by Vittorio Tamagnini, from Civitavecchia, Italy, who won the gold medal.

Con Lewis, from Bethnal Green, was another of Pattenden's sparring mates. Alex Ireland also trained with Pattenden, while Harvey went to Whet-stone.

It was a sell-out at Olympia and for the first time in the history of boxing the show started with a title contest. Cuthbert beat Corbett by a narrow points margin after 15 thrilling rounds.

The Baldock/Pattenden fight followed and Harvey concluded the evening in the seventh round of his bout by knocking out Alex Ireland.

However, the encounter that the crowd seemed to have been waiting for was the much disputed bantamweight title. The two fighters received huge applause as they entered the ring and it was difficult to say if Bethnal Green or Poplar was better represented when the names were announced. There were some rumours that the fight for East London supremacy might lead to a battle outside the boundaries of the rules, given the intense local rivalry that existed between 'manors'. But, for Baldock, 'although feeling may have run high among the spectators, I can assure you that we made a straight fight of it, with the rules strictly observed and true sportsmanship all the way.'

Many years on, Teddy was to recall, 'It is one of my battles I will never forget. It hadn't the grimness of the match with Bell; it wasn't like the desperate affair with Smith. This was just a fight between two youngsters, each out to prove he was the best bantam in the country and punch the hell out of the other one in the process. It was like a fight between two kids out of the same street and those pressmen who styled it as the Championship of the East End weren't far wrong. Don't think we just slogged at one another – nothing of the sort. We were both experienced fighters and the moves came natural to us. There was no restraint; we just fought freely, making openings, taking advantage of every opportunity, each trying hard to finish it off decisively.'

There had been much anticipation of a dynamic performance and the two Cockney gladiators certainly lived up to expectations. It is hard to compare these men's styles, but the clash produced a fight that ranks among the toughest and most thrilling wars seen at bantamweight. The Bethnal Green lad was a fighter from start to finish, who seemed to give little thought to defence, relying on rushing at his rival with both guns blazing until they wilted under his fire. In contrast to Pattenden, Teddy was a speedy, upstanding boxer who possessed a quicksilver left hand, with a deadly right that had prevented many an opponent from hearing the final bell.

The competitors' styles were perfect in terms of creating an entertaining and absorbing match that was a joy for any boxing aficionado to behold. The next day many newspapers classed this fight as one of the most memorable battles ever witnessed in any ring.

From what he knew and had been told, Baldock had prepared to meet a tough and durable opponent, but, as he was to complain, he was not aware that Alf had been 'carved out of rock'.

From the beginning, Teddy struck the Kid time and again flush on the jaw, but without apparent effect. During the second round Baldock picked up a cut on the cheek, but he had also drawn blood from the nose and mouth of his East End rival.

Most of those in attendance understood that Pattenden was hard, but there was general surprise at the manner in which he soaked up the harshest of Baldock's strikes, full on the chin, seemingly without registering. Teddy battered Alf's nose with lefts and twisted him round with cracking rights, but this noble foe continued to wade in with left, right, hooks and swings, pushing Baldock back to the ropes.

In fact, Pattenden took so much punishment that the ringside money was making Teddy favourite to win inside the distance. Learning of this in his corner before the third was heartening to Baldock and he determined that he would try to floor his man for the count in the next round.

Teddy came out of his corner and smothered Alf with every punch in the book, beating him back to the ropes, making Baldock's supporters wonder if he would be able to sustain the blistering offensive and scorching pace he had set himself.

Pattenden's lips were split, his mouth was cut and his face was bruising up; he was beginning to look battered. Yet he reacted by just laying out more violence and as such at the end of every round Baldock's corner showed visible signs of anxiety. Even when forced to retreat to the ropes, he took everything Teddy had to give, only to punch a way back seemingly insensible to that recent history of punishment.

Continually, throughout the fight, Baldock was up on his toes and sending crashing rights to Pattenden's head that would have surely silenced lesser men. His target would reel under the impact of these blows, lurch or step back to regain his balance, only to come marching back even more defiant, punching away as if nothing had happened. However, his advance was always met with a renewed hail of punches.

Although the action was non-stop and unremitting in its aggression, Teddy was scoring much more freely than the Kid and was pulling further ahead as each round passed. But there was always the possibility that Alf would catch him, just by the sheer number of punches he was throwing. Occasionally, Pattenden broke through Teddy's defence and hit home with a whooshing hook to the head to the accompaniment of a great roar from the Bethnal Green faithful. Baldock had to remain focused and fight back with every ounce of his strength, or Pattenden might sense he was weakening.

Teddy could not believe that Alf did not crack under the beating he was taking. But, although his face was cut and bloodied, his heart, morale and fortitude remained staunch. Each round, Baldock punched him to standstill and Pattenden returned to his corner to slump on his stool seemingly spent. However, summoned by the unforgiving chime, he would bounce back into the fray apparently reinvigorated, even if he was slowing.

With such an extent of one-way traffic, Pattenden would have understood that he was well behind on points, but remarkably this did not seem to dent his will. Baldock was to recollect that he felt at his best that evening, able to hit accurately with force and take anything his opponent had to give with minimal effect. But he believed that Alf had resolved to claim the Lonsdale Belt outright, holding on to the British title that he treasured, and could not even entertain any alternative outcome. Teddy was to tell of how he found this 'infectious' and ignored Morris's imploring him to 'Box him! Don't mix it; keep away!'

It seemed Baldock's assessment of the Kid was correct when Alf began to throw back punch for punch; he would take a spectacular left hook only to return it in kind. Baldock would score with a right, and Alf would throw over an immediate reply. But over the duration of the bout he had not connected with the regularity that Teddy had achieved, while he had also managed to parry, block and duck the majority of Pattenden's efforts.

Very occasionally, Baldock would be beaten to the punch with a Pattenden lead, or he would thump in a counter that came over too quick for Teddy to avoid. These were hard, cruel blasts and during the ninth round one sortie sent Baldock tumbling through the ropes, drawing celebratory shouts from the Bethnal Green section of the crowd, but it was more the result of a scrum than the consequence of the Kid's diminishing punching power.

Having clambered back up, Baldock caught Pat with a right to the chin. This led to a furious trading of hostility, with minimal clinches or backward steps, roared on by the crowd. When the men were in their respective corners, the crowd had gradually become hushed awaiting the bell to begin the next round, when the volume would grow again as the two warriors entered the fray once more.

From the 10th round on, it appeared that Teddy was getting desperate to end proceedings. He would rise up on his toes to smash a right into Pattenden's jaw, shooting sizzling jabs to his head, before slamming in the right, and driving at his opponent's body with two fists. The Kid answered once more with hooks and swings, but Baldock's science was overcoming Pattenden's brute force.

Teddy was aware that all he had to do was to stay upright for the last round to take the decision, but he was tiring. Could he last until the final bell? It was the question being asked in the minds of all the fans watching the epic encounter.

The final round was fought with an even fiercer passion. Both men realised they would need to labour until the last gasp. The noise from the huge arena, almost equally divided in terms of support, was deafening each time Baldock landed a seemingly telling blow, or whenever Pattenden shook Teddy.

Baldock started the round with two hard rights to Pattenden's jaw; with all the power he could muster behind both superbly placed shots. Instead of going down, Alf leaped at Teddy with a non-stop bombardment, each hand looking for his demise with hunger, purpose and the rashness of despair. The sheer fury of this counter-attack sent the bewildered Baldock back to and through the ropes where he lay contorted on the ring apron, his authority apparently shattered. Alf was obliged to step back while Teddy recovered to his feet, his eyes blazing at the indignity; the man who would be king met his tormentor head on. This is just what Alf wanted and they stood toe-to-toe, asking profound fistic questions of each other but no quarter and giving none.

Pattenden had the edge in terms of strength and a shattering blow to Baldock's ribs had the Poplar man through the ropes again, but this time Teddy was hurt. Getting back into the ring, he tumbled on his hands and knees and on to his side, his shoulder on the lower rope. When he was finally on his feet, Teddy desperately sought to grab hold of Pattenden, who strove to wrench himself free to finish his man off.

Having regained something of his composure, Baldock was on the retreat, using the ring and his left to fend off his adversary. But perhaps out of exhaustion or maybe as a product of pride (probably a bit of both) Baldock decided to make a stand. Squaring himself, he turned on his flailing hunter, lashing back with a quick-fire flurry of punches before going into an all-out, on-the-cobbles, East End slugging match. The long, unforgiving seconds ticked by as the fans rose to cheer this brave last-stand encounter. When the final bell rang the fighters fell into each other's arms, both completely spent, as the great arena shook under the massive boom of appreciation from the assembled masses. Teddy had fought brilliantly, and Pattenden, fighting like a demon, had coaxed the very best out of him.

The Master of Ceremonies entered the ring and immediately awarded Baldock the decision as the winner and new 'official' British Bantamweight Champion, but the announcement was completely drowned out by the roar of the frenzied crowd that continued their raucous applause for many minutes after the fight had ended.

History was made, for the first time during the belt's twenty-year existence, it was presented in the ring by none other than Lord Lonsdale himself. As Baldock was handed the prestigious trophy, another awesome cheer resounded into the night. But even that was eclipsed when Teddy lifted Pattenden's hand.

Baldock would never match his performance against Pattenden. It was probably his greatest fight. It was not known at the time but in truth that contest might have finished both men; it took so much out of them that neither fighter was quite the same again. Of course, for Teddy, it was the second time he had undergone such an intense battle; retrospectively, it seems remarkable that he had been able to find such a fight in himself after the rigours of his previous endeavours.

In his dressing room, Pattenden, with just a few of those close to him, broke down. A hero had fallen; despite one of the greatest examples of determination in the bantam class, his Belt, the source of enormous pride to him, had gone. Teddy was to name him 'the gamest loser I ever met'.

About five weeks after their fight, the two men bumped into each other by chance; Pattenden, his face still bruised and swollen, told Baldock that he had been confined to bed for almost a fortnight following their clash at Olympia.

Baldock's dressing room, in contrast to that of the man he had vanquished, was jubilant and full to bursting as he looked towards a world title fight in America. Winning the Lonsdale Belt, in what many would argue was the best fight of his entire career, brought Baldock recognition as the Bantamweight Champion, and the manager of the NSC was impressed enough with his performance to promise him a match with a leading American later in the year.

Oddly, a piece appeared in the *Evening Standard* on 10 June 1929 that seemed to begrudge Teddy his acclaim. It was entitled 'Poplar Address for Teddy Baldock. Ministry Say it Should Not be Paid for from Rates'.

Poplar Council's Finance Committee annual report for the year ended March 31 has led to a complaint from the Ministry of Health concerning an Item of £13.13s for an illuminated address 'to a local boxer named Edward Baldock.'

The Ministry state that expenditure of this kind should not be levied out of the rates.

Teddy Baldock is the British bantamweight boxing champion. He regained his title by defeating Kid Pattenden at Olympia last month.

He was born in Poplar, and began his boxing career there at the age of 10.

The illuminated address was presented to him by the people of Poplar on July 7 1927. It recorded that 'The inhabitants of the borough cordially congratulate young Baldock on his wonderful success, and hope that he may enjoy physical fitness, and add many notable victories to his wonderful present record.'

The Mayor (Alderman Goodway) made the presentation. Most of the Poplar city fathers and many ratepayers were present.

In New York, the NYSAC had suspended Bushy Graham and the NBA quickly cited Panama Al Brown as its 8st. 6lb. title holder. At the time it was of no great importance for Baldock who the Americans named as their Champion; he just wanted the opportunity to make the crown his for a decent purse. But Brown (born in Colon, Panama, on 5 July 1902) was known to carry a powerful punch and Teddy wondered if this tall thin man could match his own hammer-hard blows.

It was while he was working as a clerk for the United States Shipping Board in the Panama Canal Zone that Alfonso Teofilo Brown took to watching US military personnel box. The sport captured his imagination to the extent that he chose to have a go at it himself. He was talented enough to become the Panama Isthmus Champion and catch the eye of Tom Fahy, an American boxing manager who took him to New York City.

Brown was liked by the boxing crowds of the time. Nearly 6ft tall, with a massive 76in reach; Al was one of the tallest and rangiest fighters in bantamweight history. In May 1929, new manager Dave Lumiansky told the New York press that Brown held the IBU Bantamweight World Title, having defeated Domenico Bernasconi at the Comunidad de Madrid, late in March 1929.

Guided by Lumiansky, he won the vacant NYSAC World Bantamweight Crown on 18 June 1929 in New York, defeating the Spaniard Vidal Gregorio (born Gregorio Vidal, the name he used in Europe; he was also known as Young Marty) with a unanimous points decision, which made him the first Panamanian and Latin American to be officially recognised as the globally dominant figure in a category of boxing.

The Baldock camp had been disappointed when the news came that the Panamanian had been matched with the 25-year-old Gregorio (who fought out of Marseille, France) for the world title. Morris complained, and the British Boxing Board of Control, which had recently developed some real muscle, agreed with Baldock's claim to the crown and sent a letter to the US protesting in Teddy's favour. The Americans responded with the proposal that Baldock should meet the winner of the fight between Brown and Gregorio for the undisputed World Championship.

Following this recognition by the NYSAC, American promoters started to show an interest in Baldock. Jess McMahon, who had been closely associated with Tex Rickard, was one of the first to get in touch. He cabled an offer of a fight with Brown or Gregorio for £2,000 or 17½ per cent of any gate (whichever was more) on 17 September 1929 at Ebbets Field, the famous open-air venue, home of the Brooklyn Dodgers that at the time could host 25,000 spectators off the field alone.

These terms suited the Baldock camp, with Morris having also negotiated three round-trip tickets as part of the deal (for Morris and Lakey to accompany Teddy) and plans were made for the trip before Baldock's annual engagement in Blackpool. On August Bank Holiday, Teddy met Belgian Gideon Potteau, who proved himself to be no pushover. A crowd of 10,000 gathered at Bloomfield Road, Blackpool Football Club's home ground.

When Potteau was dropped with a right to the chin and fell between the bottom and second ropes, it looked as though the crowd would be in for an early finish. But he got up almost straight away and fought back fiercely. Teddy was to remember, 'Like most continentals he was very fit, but being short in the arm was at a disadvantage in reach, and had to take plenty of punishment while he tried to get to close range.'

Baldock found Potteau something of a sitting duck with his left, but harder to catch with the right because of his bobbing and dipping style of fighting. However, when the Belgian moved inside, Baldock was to teach him a few lessons when it came to evading punches and the Poplar man soon beat his attacker off with lively two-fisted counter-attacks.

During the 10th, Potteau expended a great deal of energy in his attempts to get to Baldock, and by the end of the round he had tired considerably. As the fighters faced the first seconds of the 11th round, Teddy drew the exhausted man's lead and whipped in a left hook to the Belgian's body. This blow brought Potteau's head forward, and, in Baldock's words, 'timing a short right to a nicety, I caught him flush on the chin. He came down with a crash and I trotted off to my corner thinking that was that.'

To the consternation of most people present, the Low Country man was on his feet as the referee called out 'five'. But he was out on his feet and pitched towards his corner, grasping the ropes with both gloves to save himself from falling. Teddy hurtled across the ring looking to put an end to the fight, but the referee beat him to it, calling on Potteau's corner men to look after the defeated man.

Not long after this convincing win, arrangements for the trip to the US were finalised, and Baldock was looking forward to another successful expedition 'across the pond', that also included the promise of a good payday. However, it seemed as if the journey was doomed from the start. Morris and Lakey got themselves safely aboard the *Mauretania* at Southampton but without Teddy. As Baldock was later to explain, 'The geezer at the barrier wanted to see my passport, and, when I felt in my pocket, it wasn't there.'

As trainer and manager rummaged through their man's luggage, the customs official and Teddy searched the suit he was wearing, the fighter recalled that at home he had taken his papers from the pocket of another jacket and placed them on the mantelshelf. He had changed his clothes and left with the passport still sitting where he had put it.

Teddy's dad was immediately wired London with instructions to find his son's documents and get them to Southampton as quickly as possible and a speedboat was put on standby to tear after the liner if the passport arrived soon after the *Mauretania* left port. But the car didn't make it (by hours) and Baldock literally missed the boat. All he could do was watch as Lakey and Morris shook their fists at him from the rail of the ship.

Teddy stayed in port for a couple of days and fortunately was able to board the *Leviathan*. He had wired his manager informing him that he was on his way and got to New York two days after the *Mauretania*. During the passage Baldock met the great sporting philanthropist and tea millionaire Sir Thomas Lipton. Between 1899 and 1930, Lipton had challenged the American holders of the Americas Cup via the Royal Ulster Yacht Club on five occasions with his yachts, all named *Shamrock* (I to V). His efforts to take the trophy were rewarded with a specially designed cup for 'the best of all losers'.

As luck would have it, Packey O'Gatty, a well-known American bantamweight contender, was employed as the liner's gym instructor. He relished the idea of assisting the British champion with his training and on several occasions the pair put on sparring sessions for the entertainment of their fellow passengers.

During the trip it was reported by *The New York Times*, 'The British Boxing Board of Control has decided to send Charles F. Donmall, its secretary, to the United States to look after the interests of the board and of Baldock on the occasion of the match between Teddy Baldock, English titleholder, and Al Brown, Panama bantamweight.'

The German family from Woodhaven, who Teddy had stayed with during his first visit to New York, were waiting for him as he docked. They were keen for him to take up residence with them once more, but Morris had made other arrangements. Baldock was upset about disappointing these people, as they had previously shown him such kindness and hospitality.

Following a stay of a day or two in New York, Joe Morris finalised details of the fight contract with the Boxing Commission and the promoter, before taking Teddy to Gus Wilson's renowned training camp in Orangeburg, New Jersey. Wilson had looked after the legendary French light-heavyweight

Georges Carpentier and a stable of fine fighters. It was in the camp that Baldock met Argentine Vittorio Campolo (El Gigante de Quilmes), the tallest and biggest heavyweight he had ever seen in real life. He had been born in Reggio, Calabria, Italy in 1902, and he stood 6ft 9½in, had a 32½in reach and weighed over 17st. He was training to fight with Leicester's Phil Scott (who for a very short time, held the British Heavyweight Championship in the spring of 1926) scheduled to be on the same bill as the Baldock's bout with Al Brown.

Campolo felt confident that he would beat the British Champion and at the start of that fight few would have given Scott much of a chance, as was reported in the press: 'The blond British giant had hardly had time to make a few preliminary gestures last night when he was in full retreat, doubled up and badly punished by a crushing succession of short pile-driving rights to the body. The shaggy-haired, towering Argentine was on his foe like a tiger, delivering body blows that made shuffling Phil wince and become a distinct shade paler.'

However, Scott's confidence returned in the second round and with neat footwork and a good straight left, he started controlling the fight. Some believed that the outcome of the contest was decided by the last round, it was certainly close. In the final three minutes, Phil caught Campolo with a left, followed by a smashing right, which had Vittorio rocking; a knock out seemed possible but the Argentine was strong. The fight ended with a toe-to-toe rally in the centre of the ring with Phil Scott being awarded a close points decision.

Jack Sharkey, later to become World Heavyweight Champion, was also in the camp, preparing for a contest with Tommy Loughran. Teddy was to remark that he had never met 'a more temperamental bloke'. According to Baldock, Jack was Lithuanian by birth, but seemingly didn't like to be associated with the idea that he had Eastern European heritage, and became angry on seeing a newspaper headline that read 'LITH-LOUGHRAN GO TO-NIGHT', promising to get even with the journalist responsible (who was little bigger than Baldock). The hack was petrified as Sharkey lifted him off his feet, threatening to snap him in half. According to Teddy, 'He scared me stiff an' all. With two days to go for our fights his manager came over to me and said he was having a lot of trouble with him.' The handler told Baldock, 'He's rarin' to go, and I can't do anything' with the basket…What d'you know? He wants to take a car out on the "no-limit" road, and he's goin' crazy 'cause I won't let him…He's a lot of time for you…Ever since you bin here, Red. Will you have a talk with him?'

But Teddy asked, 'Why not let him take the car? He's keyed like we all get towards the end of training. Tell you what, I'll go with him if you like.'

So Sharkey and Baldock got out on the nearby no-limit road, on which drivers could travel as fast as they liked. Teddy recollected that the man nicknamed 'the Boston Gob', due to his outspoken confidence in his own abilities, 'drove that car as if he was a stunt man in a film'. The two fighters raced down the wide road, swerving from one side to the other, evading cars coming towards them 'by a coat of cellulose'. Teddy watched their speed edge close to 100mph and was as scared as he could remember being and thought if Joe Morris could have seen him 'he'd throw a fit'.

When Baldock eventually talked Jack into returning to the camp, as he exited the car his legs were like jelly.

The following day, Morris received a wire from Jess McMahon (who was promoting the fight) requesting an urgent meeting with him at his office. When the two men met, Morris was told that Brown had just got back from Paris and felt that he had insufficient time to prepare for the scheduled fight.

This was both frustrating and annoying for the Baldock camp. Teddy's training schedule had been planned to within a few hours of the fight and as such Morris and Lakey had to put together a revised training programme for Baldock's preparation. Joe fought hard against accepting a postponement, but he eventually conceded, accepting $200 compensation for extra training expenses, and the fight was rescheduled for 2 October.

Teddy stopped training for a week and then resumed his strict regime to ensure he would be ready for the new date. Within a few days of the fight, Morris was instructed to visit the NYSAC. Baldock went with Joe to their offices where they met Al Brown and his manager Dave Lumiansky. Jess McMahon, Bill Muldoon and Jim Parley (senior representatives of the NYSAC) were also in attendance, along with other major officials of New York boxing. Brown demanded yet another two-week postponement due to his suffering from 'neuritis and stomach trouble'.

Morris lodged a vehement protest, telling the assembly that his people were not going to be messed around anymore. The commissioners appeared supportive to the Baldock camp, but Joe and Teddy started to sense this was a ploy by his opponent's management team to wear him down both physically and psychologically. Joe Morris finally agreed to a further two-week postponement but only on the condition of receiving another $200 expenses, plus a guarantee of £500 from Brown that he would forfeit should he not be able to meet with Baldock on 16 October. This was accepted in principle but then came a snag: Brown's party wanted the same £500 assurance that Teddy would be in the ring on that day. Morris was having none of it, stating that, should Baldock become unwell or suffer an injury during training, he would be £500 out of pocket, having twice been ready for the engagement. At this point the title fight was called off.

It was a sad ending to what Teddy had seen as a journey of destiny but which had turned out to be something of a wild goose chase.

On 16 December, the NBA announced the completion of a working agreement with the British Boxing Board of Control for mutual recognition of fines, suspensions, contracts between managers, contestants and regulation of World Championship titles.

Stanley M. Issacs, Cincinnati, and John W. Driskill, President and Secretary, respectively, of the NBA, and the Right Honourable Earl of Lonsdale and Colonel R.E. Myddleton, president and Chairman of the British Boxing Board of Control, negotiated an agreement as part of a working relationship with the British Board that a recent ruling of the NBA would be reversed concerning the former world ranking of Al Brown as World Bantamweight Champion. It was changed to the extent of declaring the World Title open. Brown would be recognised as the American Champion and Teddy was announced as Brown's leading contender.

14

FIGHTING, FIGHTING, FIGHTING

1930

The international promoter Jeff Dickson, who had set up shop in London, was putting on shows at the Albert Hall and he wanted Baldock involved. The Cuban, Kid Chocolate, Dick Corbett, Willie Smith, Kid Pattenden and Frenchman Kid Francis were suggested as potential opponents, before Emile 'Spider' Pladner was selected. Pladner, born in Clermont-Ferrand, France, in 1902, had been a successful sculptor in Paris before he turned professional after winning the European amateur flyweight title in 1925, and taking up with manager Louis de Ponthieu (known as the 'one-armed' manager – as a fighter himself he had injured his left forearm in a bout versus Tancy Lee in December 1919; the problem worsened and in January 1920 he had to have it amputated). Pladner had been accredited as World Flyweight Champion, but had been over the weight limit when he defeated Izzy Schwartz in Paris during 1928. By the time he was put forward as an opponent for Baldock, Pladner was fighting at bantamweight.

Dickson planned to match the victor of the Baldock/Pladner clash with the winner of a contest he was looking to stage in Paris, pitting Kid Francis against Al Brown. Dickson's terms were generous, and the 8st 8lb weight made the match with Pladner beneficial to Teddy. The Frenchman trained at Fred Dyer's gym, while Baldock adopted new quarters in Brighton, using an expansive room above the bar at Jolly Jumbo's pub; Jim Briley and Sid Raiteri were employed as Baldock's sparring partners. On this occasion, fight trainer Alec Goodman was given the job of overseeing Teddy's training, as his long-term trainer Jack Lakey was ill.

Pladner's style was considered typically continental. He emerged from his corner, hands high, chin tucked behind his shoulder. His single tactic was to get in close with two-fisted hooks and uppercuts, and, as such, he was perfect for Baldock's usual game plan – a long-range strategy, allowing Pladner to come forward and make the attacking moves, when he could then be countered with the straight left, or right hand to stop him in his tracks.

The Parisian turned out to be as hard as the stone, and skilled at working with what assets he had. He took Teddy's best blows almost without flinching and he had his successes. He specialised in forcing his man on to the ropes, then, leaning on his opponent, letting loose with both fists.

Baldock decided early on not to attempt to out-punch the Parisian on the inside. The Londoner had the reach advantage, so it would have been foolish to get involved close in. Instead, he focused on nullifying Pladner's work by shrewd defence and keeping him on the end of the jab.

The fight followed the same pattern for six rounds. Baldock was content with this, waiting for his rival to tire, at which point he intended to increase the pressure and take the fight to the Frenchman. However, Pladner once more forced his opponent into the ropes, predictably swinging hard at his ribs. This assault was followed by two heavy digs, which sank into the pit of Baldock's stomach, next came a low left that had Teddy writhing in pain around the canvas. He had never suffered agony like it; even though he was wearing a protector, it had not afforded a suitable barrier.

Matt Wells, the referee, swiftly directed the Parisian to his corner, where the Frenchman's back-up team shouted and gestured their protest, but most of the crowd had seen the foul. It was the first and only time Teddy got a decision on a disqualification in Britain (although a bout in the US had gone the same way).

The fight was to provide Teddy with a purse of £3,000, the biggest he would ever be paid. But, after deductions for sparring partners, etc., the amount was reduced to just £1,000.

Jeff Dickson was unhappy with Baldock and accused him of acting, for which he was sued for libel. He lost the case and had to pay the costs, added to which he was required to announce a humiliating apology in print. He informed Morris that he wanted no further involvement with the Pride of Poplar, and Teddy never again fought at the Albert Hall. Subsequently, Dickson matched the Frenchman with Dick Corbett for what was called an eliminator for the Championship; although they boxed at 8st 8lb, Corbett was a clear points winner over the dozen rounds and as a result challenged Baldock for his Lonsdale Belt.

However, the British Boxing Board of Control nominated Alf Pattenden as Teddy's challenger, but the fight only attracted a bid of £1,000, which Morris believed Baldock should demand for his end alone, so the stewards rejected it and agreed to recognise a contest putting Teddy in with Willie Smith for the Empire title; that bout also did not materialise as the South African postponed his sailing for a number of months.

But, when the news arrived that Al Brown had been matched with Johnny Erickson for the NBA and NYSAC vacant bantamweight title, there was anger in the Baldock camp, as three years previously Teddy had decisively defeated Erickson in New York. Baldock believed he had more right than Erickson to be nominated as the leading contender for the American version of the World Championship and was sure that there were plenty of people who would support this claim. Morris lodged a stern protest with the British Boxing Board of Control and they passed this on to the NYSAC, although this turned out to be a futile effort.

Panama Al Brown beat Erickson who was disqualified in the fourth round by the referee Jack Dorman. Brown had easily evaded Erickson's rushes and had built up a healthy lead before being fouled. The Brooklyn fighter had already been warned several times for hitting low before he floored Brown in the fourth and the referee had no choice but to disqualify him.

Baldock had been prepared to travel to New York – in fact, he had refused matches in the hope that his challenge would be upheld – but the Americans rejected the claim which seemed to make a mockery of the meeting between the representatives of the NBA and British Boxing Board of Control in December the previous year. Baldock thought it might have had something to do with the run of 11 wins and one draw he had achieved during his previous visit to America.

Jeff Dickson matched Pattenden with Dick Corbett, and declared that the winner should be understood as a contender for the British title, although it was clear he would also be in line for a World Championship fight. Once more Corbett claimed a points victory, and he was instantly hailed by the media as Baldock's number-one challenger.

When Willie Smith arrived in England, the NSC decided that he would fight Teddy for the Empire Bantamweight Crown as part of a big tournament to be staged at Olympia (similar to the event a year earlier). It was envisaged that Len Harvey would defend his middleweight title against Steve McCall, the Scottish Middleweight Champion: Johnny Cuthbert, the featherweight title holder, would meet the challenge of Dom Volante, while heavyweights Don Shortland and Charlie Smith would contest an eliminator for a challenge for Phil Scott's title.

However, from Teddy's point of view, if Smith could repeat his victory, it would mean that his claim to the British version of the World Championship would be completely undermined. This of course warranted a better payday for Baldock, but the NSC didn't see things quite the same way, so Teddy was replaced by Dick Corbett who comfortably disposed of Smith, who looked a pale imitation of the man who had faced Baldock more than two years before. This seemed to make it inevitable that Teddy would have to fight Corbett sooner rather than later.

Bill Glass had taken over promotions at the Ilford Skating Rink, and he asked Teddy to open a run of shows at the venue. First up was a 15-rounder at 8st 10lb against the clever Charlie Rowbotham, one of two fighting brothers from Birmingham. Rowbotham had recently beaten and been defeated by Pattenden within a month, so he had the public attention and a good crowd turned up for the contest.

Both fighters received a rousing reception as they ducked through the ropes. The match began at a swift pace, Rowbotham dashing forward attacking with both hands. In response, Baldock attempted to hold him at a distance with the familiar straight left. Teddy felt strong and was hitting hard with accuracy, but his opponent carried a handy sting of his own which he found out when the West Midlander got through his defence.

In the second round, Teddy tagged his man with a firm right but Rowbotham absorbed it well and fought back with greater ferocity. Baldock changed his tactics in the third and made Charlie's body his objective. A couple of telling rights under the heart caused Rowbotham to hang on, and the referee had to step in to separate the two fighters.

In the fourth, a fast, cutting right opened a gash close to the Brummie's left eye, which started to shut almost immediately. Rowbotham was severely hampered in terms of his options and was forced to try to bludgeon his rival out of the fight; at one point he nearly shoved Teddy out of the ring. Charlie's persistent attacks gave Baldock little room or time to work out a means of launching an assault of his own, so he resolved to allow Rowbotham to tire himself out and then take the fight to him.

Rowbotham's eye was practically useless by the seventh when Baldock went on the offensive. A powerful right connected sweetly with his jaw, causing him to stagger but he refused to go down.

The rest of the bout was very one-sided despite valiant attempts by Rowbotham to make a fight of it. By the 11th round, his position was hopeless and the referee stopped the contest deciding that the brave fighter had taken enough.

The moment Teddy's victory was made official; Mickey Doyle and Lew Pinkus charged into the ring and challenged Baldock.

Pinkus, from Mile End, was selected as Teddy's next test; this was to be a demanding 15-rounder. The fight was made at 8st 12lb, showing that Baldock was finding it increasingly difficult to make the bantamweight limit. With an extended training regime and a stricter diet, he could probably have made the weight, but it would need a title fight with a decent payday to motivate him.

Although Pinkus hadn't won over a dozen fights since defeating Johnny Brown on a disqualification in November 1928 (he lost 26 of his 36 recorded contests), he was an awkwardly persistent customer and, given his recent record, was desperate to better Baldock. Teddy weighed in at 8st 10lb, while his opponent was all but on the limit of the agreed poundage. Although feeling good himself, Baldock couldn't help but notice that Lew looked strong at the weight.

With Teddy finding it hard to keep Pinkus at arm's length, the crowd certainly got their money's worth. The Mile Ender was fast and able to get close and work at Baldock's body with two fists. No one punch felt damaging to Teddy, but it was the accumulation of blows his opponent was able to throw that had the potential to make dangerous demands on his resources of strength and endurance. Teddy needed to tie Pinkus up, but he was less than easy to corral and hard to catch with long-range shots. However, Baldock managed to land some telling punches of his own and built up a decent points lead; with a dozen rounds fought, Teddy was well ahead.

However, with time running out, Pinkus came back and seemed to be evening things up. He came at Teddy so fast that the Poplar man began to think he would be outpaced (a rare experience for Baldock). Lew was also putting together some heavy-duty work that was starting to bring results. Nevertheless, Teddy's skill was certainly of a higher order, allowing him to hold on to his lead, and claim the eventual points victory.

In July 1930, Teddy had his only contest in the Eastern Counties vs. Scotland's Johnny Docherty. The 15-round fight was staged on what was then the Norwich Football Club's ground, The Nest (in Newmarket Road, to the north of the city centre). However, a couple of days before the match, the British Boxing Board of Control vetoed the fight, seeing it as a mismatch. Teddy was ignorant of this decision, only finding out about it when he got to Norwich. He immediately travelled to the offices of the local paper the *Eastern Evening News* in the hope of reassuring the public that the fight would definitely be taking place, stating, 'I have to keep faith with the public.' Unfortunately the damage had already been done and ticket sales suffered as a consequence of the rumours.

The promoter Captain Prince-Cox described the intentions of the British Boxing Board of Control as unwarranted interference: 'Surely it is realised by everyone who follows boxing that for Baldock to fight a class performer or champion he must receive remuneration of a very high sum and this of course cannot be done in Norwich. I have therefore done the next best thing in endeavouring to show the Norfolk public Baldock in a serious contest with a real good boy.'

Baldock was determined to deal with Docherty as quickly as possible to avoid any accusations of carrying the Scot. But the Caledonian elected to go on the defensive for most of the initial round; however, just before the bell he let loose a right hook that struck Teddy directly on the jaw. It was a lesson learned and he didn't let the Scot repeat this success.

The subsequent two rounds were a story of an exchange of powerful punching. However, a short right to the chin from Baldock consigned Docherty to the canvas for a count of five.

Teddy worked hard to finish the fight in the fourth but Docherty resisted and appeared to be gathering strength as the rounds passed. However, flurries of thrashing lefts under his ribs caused him to drop his arms and, with his favoured 'one-two', Baldock ended it in the sixth; a left to the body, then a looping right to the jaw ensured Docherty went down for the full count after which he was carried back to his corner.

New York and a meet with Al Brown was once again a topic for the Baldock camp. Morris was asked what he wanted and a figure of £2,000, plus £300 expenses, was put forward (the same as had been previously offered). There was also the insistence that Panama Al put up £500 appearance money.

There was no reply and the next news that reached the Baldock camp was that Jeff Dickson had arranged for the French Champion Eugene Huat (Chat-Tigre) to take on Brown in Paris for the world title.

Baldock had only three fights in eight months and, as a boxer who was prone to ring rust, felt this was harming his career.

Joe Morris arranged a fight in Newcastle with Benny Sharkey over 15 rounds at the New St James' Hall. Coming from a Jewish family of boxers (along with his father Tom and brother Willie), Benny was speedy on his toes and a fast puncher with both fists. There wasn't much known about Sharkey in the South, so Teddy underestimated him, failing to regard him as a potential threat; he later said, 'I'd met dozens like him and knew just how to cope with them.'

But on that night he was to be proved wrong. Boxing before his home crowd Sharkey was brimming with confidence, and foolishly Teddy allowed him to build up a useful lead. Having allowed Benny to make the pace, Teddy learned that, for a short fighter, Sharkey had a fine, straight left, as well as an impressive right to follow up with.

Midway through the bout, Baldock started to open up, but the Geordie based Scot stayed with him and the pair looked well matched in terms of firepower. Facing the forceful and brutal fighter, Teddy was hard pressed by this tough, durable combatant. Although Baldock came back with a grand-stand finish in an attempt to snatch the verdict, Sharkey fought back fiercely and it seemed anyone's fight at the final bell. The venue was in uproar when the local man got the decision. Both men agreed on a return in East London, but it was never to happen.

Sharkey's win created further interest in the bantamweight division. Benny, understandably, felt entitled to a shot at the title, but he was to meet Dick Corbett at a pound or so over the Championship weight. Corbett won and the NSC matched him with Baldock in a Lonsdale Belt contest in December 1930 at Olympia. But with Morris continuing to insist on Teddy getting £1,000 (and the promoters only offering that amount to be divided between the boxers) meant the fight didn't happen. The asking price Morris was demanding was not excessive, given that Teddy had claims on three Championships, but, in place of the proposed Baldock/Corbett bout, Al Foreman met Johnny Cuthbert in a lightweight title battle, which concluded in a draw.

POSTSCRIPT TO SHARKEY

From the start of his career in 1928 to its conclusion in 1940, Sharkey (who passed away in 1975) was to defeat three World Champions (Emile Pladner, Teddy Baldock and Baltazar Sangchili). He also beat five British Champions (Jimmy Walsh, Johnny McGrory, Dave Crowley, Johnny King and Johnny Cusick) and a South American Champion (Simon Chavez, who was the Featherweight Champion of Venezuela and a consistent contender for the featherweight title). Benny also got the better of three Bantamweight Champions of Wales (Phineas John, Cuthbert Taylor and Stan Jehu) and a Scottish Featherweight Champion (Johnny McMillan). Yet another mark of his quality was a draw with Maurice Holtzer, who made a claim to the World Featherweight Crown.

Benny was ranked in *The Ring* among the top 10 as a bantamweight during 1931 and placed ninth in the world by the NBA in 1931. In February 1938, *The Ring* had him as their seventh best featherweight in the world. Sharkey was a fine boxer and was unlucky not to have more in the way of titles from his dozen years in the professional ring. In his 196 fights, he won 128 (54 by knockout) but, having fought over nearly 2,000 rounds, he never won a major title.

ALF'S BACK

The Ring management at Blackfriars signed Alf Pattenden and Teddy to fight a return match. Since Baldock had won the Belt from Pat, he had yearned for a rematch. The 15-round fight at 8st 12lb would not be for a title, but victory for Alf would win him a definite shot at the Championship.

The second meeting of 'the two Alfs' took place on a Sunday afternoon. An exodus of East End fight fans headed across Blackfriars Bridge to watch the rematch and were easily equal in numbers to the South London fight fraternity who had turned up to cheer their man. The result was that the old fight hall was packed to overflowing.

From his corner Teddy could see that the management had brought in boxes and other forms of seating from the dressing room and offices, placing them in gangways for latecomers. There was not an inch of space throughout the venue and both boxers received a glorious welcome as they were introduced.

As the referee uttered the usual formalities to the combatants, Baldock noted that his opponent appeared to be in fine shape, but Teddy had worked hard on his stamina and felt fairly confident. As the bell rang, Alf was on Baldock like a shot, starting the relentless attack that would continue throughout the fight. Likewise, Teddy began the contest stabbing Alf with the left, finding his face an easy target. Pattenden was kept at a distance for most of the opening round and, when he did come close, he didn't find much more than Baldock's elbows, which he kept close to the side of his body (a valuable lesson taught to him by his old mentor Mike Honeyman). After getting away, he used the ring again, scoring with the left and dealing with Pattenden's repeated charges, either by making him miss or halting his progress with a stiff left, sometimes letting go with a right to the head. Pattenden was tough and took it all while still pressing forward his attacks. One good right did shake him noticeably, stopping him in his tracks, a reassuring sign that he wasn't completely invulnerable.

In the third Teddy got caught with a couple of right hooks as Pattenden let loose with a whirlwind assault. For Baldock, it was a case of respond or be defeated, he stood his ground and launched a fierce counter-attack with both hands which drove Alf across the ring.

Pattenden absorbed a great deal of punishment throughout rounds four, five and six, but, although he flinched, he did not wilt. Teddy expected him to retire on his stool but each time he was out of his corner ready for more.

In the seventh, Pattenden surprised Baldock by increasing his tempo; Teddy needed to use the full extent of the ring to keep clear of trouble. However, from the eighth round, while the pace of the bout was maintained, the fight grew increasingly one-sided. Alf became an easier target, but Teddy sensed that he would not be stopped before the final bell (over his career few fighters were able to stop the tough fighter from Bethnal Green). Pattenden continued to move forward, shooting straight lefts, followed by hooks and swings with both gloves; he took Baldock's best punches on his nose and forehead as he continued to bob and weave, attempting to get inside Teddy's defences to attack the body. As such, he remained a threat, so Baldock stayed on his toes in order to hold on to his advantage. When Alf did get through, Teddy shortened his punches, sometimes letting go with a frantic two-handed response to beat off the danger. Pattenden resorted to wild runs at his rival and in the 10th rushed in so fiercely that he knocked Teddy to the floor. Both boxers rolled untidily on the canvas. However, no damage was done and they were quickly up on their feet to resume the battle.

Baldock's snappier and more precise punching won him the last five rounds, while Pattenden began to show signs of tiring.

Teddy was hardly marked at the end, although he sustained an unintentional eye injury from Pattenden's thumb. This troubled him for quite some time after the fight and only really got back to normal after he retired from boxing.

In truth, this return fight between Pattenden and Baldock could not compare to their previous battle. Pattenden had shown the same fighting spirit but there was little left of the supreme battler who had lost his title at Olympia. Winner Baldock was also comparatively lacklustre; comparatively the victory was not dramatic and the fight was not notable. Perhaps the two men just had too much respect for each other.

Pattenden was forced to retire with eye trouble at the end of 1931, a few months after Baldock had walked away from the ring.

It was not long after meeting Pattenden at The Ring that Baldock had to admit to himself that the 8st 6lb limit was beyond him. This meant he had to inform the British Boxing Board of Control that he would abandon any ambitions in the bantamweight division and as a result was required to hand back his cherished Lonsdale Belt.

Shortly afterwards, he challenged Johnny Cuthbert for his featherweight crown, on the grounds that he had previously held him to a draw. The British Boxing Board of Control approved the match, although the NSC wanted Teddy to meet Al Brown, who was making a tour of Britain.

Perhaps it was fortunate for Baldock but the great fighter from Panama suggested that the fight be made at 9st, which was happily agreed upon by Joe Morris.

The match was agreed but it would be half a year before it was staged.

Teddy Baldock – The Pride of Poplar.

The Story of Britain's Youngest Ever Boxing World Champion

15

FOR THE LOVE OF MAISIE

Away from the ring, on 12 February 1931, Teddy got married to blue-eyed, auburn-haired 22-year-old, Miss Maisie McRae (the youngest daughter of former farrier Don McRae) from Morden, Essex (where her father ran The Cricketers' Arms pub) at All Saints Church, Poplar. The couple first met at a party when Teddy was 13 and the two had been 'sweethearts' ever since. Thousands turned out to see the bride and groom, and, in fact, traffic was held up for an hour as people climbed lampposts and trees and got on to roofs for a view of the happy couple. The crowds had gathered hours before the ceremony ready with coloured streamers and confetti. Such was the size of the assembled throng that mounted police were in attendance to keep order.

Rev. F.R. Shields conducted the service that was packed with Teddy's relatives and friends long before the service was due to start and the atmosphere was more like a music hall than a church at times. When the bride arrived, people clambered on to the pews, clung to pillars and hung perilously over the gallery rails trying to get a glimpse of her as she moved up the aisle. She wore a gown of oyster-tinted satin, trimmed with pearls and her long, pink tulle veil was fastened with a 'dainty headdress' of silver and orange blossom, again trimmed with pearls which matched her shoes; Maisie's bouquet consisted of pink and white carnations.

The wedding breakfast was held at The Guild Hall, Poplar, after which there was a reception at Woodgrange Hall, Forest Gate, with over 200 guests. The two groomsmen were Sonny Provost (best man and lifelong friend of Teddy) and Thomas Hardy. The two bridesmaids were named as Miss Rose Baldock (Teddy's sister) and Miss Florence Provost. They both wore black and white dresses, with hats to match. Among the guests were the jockey Charles Lane, referee Sam Russell and Joe Morris. Sir Harry Preston (the hotel entrepreneur and a leading figure in making Brighton into a holiday resort) attended the reception but was unable to be present at the church.

The Baldocks had an enormous wedding cake decorated as a huge boxing ring, with stools and towels all ready for the match. Although Maisie had never witnessed Teddy box before they were married – as it was reported he had old-fashioned views concerning women and did not 'think boxing matches the sort of sights a girl should be allowed to see' – after the wedding it was said that Maisie would be allowed to see one, with Teddy quoted as saying, 'After they're married women – well, it's different.'

The police horses had a hard job clearing a way through the crowd as the new Mr and Mrs Baldock tried to drive away from the church. The great numbers of people that turned up for the 'event' demonstrates the level of Baldock's popularity at the time.

The *Daily Express* reported that,
On the way up the aisle one of the bridesmaids inadvertently trod on the bride's veil, and the incident was greeted with such audible mirth that the parson was compelled to utter a reproof.

'This is not a place of entertainment,' he said, 'but the House of God.'
The rector again admonished the congregation when he saw some of them had climbed on the seats. 'Get off the seats please,' he said. 'I won't continue till you do.'

Afterwards the best man, Mr Provost, was heard to express his regret at the noise which disturbed the ceremony throughout, and a great many guests deplored the unrestrained behaviour of the public in the gallery, who kept up a murmur of conversation, punctuated with the wailing of infants and the thumps and bangs of overturned pews.

When the ceremony was ended the din broke out again.

'Good luck, Maisie,' cried the bride's friends as Teddy led her to the vestry to sign the register, while the bridegroom's friends shouted 'God bless you, Teddy!'

When the couple left the church Baldock had probably the most enthusiastic welcome he had ever received. As he stood on the steps in his immaculate morning suit and silk hat, he was greeted by great cheering and waving of handkerchiefs.

The enthusiasm was extraordinary as he led his bride to the waiting motorcar, which was surrounded by an excited mob.

The couple bought a house in East Ham (423 Katherine Road) where 'brand new furniture wrapped in brown paper was placed on a brand new carpet' and there were 'brand new aluminium cooking utensils' that 'gleamed in a brand new kitchen'. Maisie commented, 'I don't know how we shall get straight.'

By now Teddy's social standing appeared to have changed and, while it seems certain he never forgot his roots, he had moved on; it would perhaps have been hard not to, as knights of the realm, top sportsman and leading entrepreneurs were calling him a friend, and he spent time with some very influential and powerful people. Some of his family thought he had become a bit of a 'snob', but perhaps he may have found it difficult to acclimatise to his newly acquired social status. Nevertheless, he bought his mum and dad an East London sweet shop, located in Cotton Street, and set up some of his other brothers in business, all of which lifted the family away from the financial challenges of their some relatives and former neighbours. In 1935, his dad would invest in a pub, The Ship, in Poplar High Street, which proved something of a goldmine, and was packed out seven days a week (as it was opposite the Queens Theatre), which passed to Louisa Rose when her husband died.

Teddy Baldock – The Pride of Poplar.
The Story of Britain's Youngest Ever Boxing World Champion

16

PANAMA AL AT LAST

1931

It was a disappointment to Teddy that he had been obliged to go on something of a fool's errand to the US chasing Al Brown for a crack at the World title, only for him to come to Britain to meet him at catchweight, but he, Lakey and Morris realised that they had to work with what they had and started to prepare for the contest with a fight at the East Ham Skating Rink against Baldock's old rival Gideon Potteau (the man he had stopped in Blackpool in 11 rounds almost two years earlier).

Some had wondered if Baldock's marriage might have an effect on his dedication or fitness but, about six weeks after his wedding, Teddy scaled 8st 9lb for the meeting with the Belgian, probably the lightest he could have expected to be at that point. Potteau was three pounds heavier, but Baldock didn't see that as placing him at a disadvantage.

Hundreds were turned away from the packed venue, but one spectator that did get a good seat was Al Brown, who had come along to take a look at what he would be up against in Baldock. Shrewdly, Teddy decided he would be careful not to give too much away.

Baldock began with a left to the face, and Potteau responded by charging him into the ropes, hooking with a left and right to the Londoner's head. It was a frantic start to the round and the fans watched in anticipation of an early finish. The Belgian rushed in again and was caught with a left hook to the body, dropping him for a count of five. No sooner had he risen to his feet than another left hook returned him to the boards, this time for nine. He got up but grasped the bottom rope and crouched. Teddy hesitated, unsure if he should finish his opponent in this position. Even as he rose to the middle rope, still Baldock waited, despite pleas from his crowd and his corner to 'Get him!'

The referee instructed Potteau to stand; the fighter did as he was told and was instantly hit with a merciless right from Baldock that laid him flat. The count reached nine as the bell sounded and the Belgian was helped back to his corner.

Remarkably, Potteau answered the bell for the second round, but was rocked by two straight lefts before a no-nonsense right landed smack on his chin, and he fell heavily; it was a devastating knockdown, and there was no chance that the bell would save him this time. As Teddy left the ring, Potteau remained where he fell while the crowd called for Al Brown to get in the ring to fight Baldock there and then.

Almost obediently, the freakishly tall bantam from Panama jumped up into the ring and received a big cheer from the fight fans. It was good publicity for the forthcoming fight but in the back of his mind Al must have been quietly impressed by Teddy's clinical finish of the Belgian.

Just under five weeks later, Teddy returned to The Ring for a meeting with Terence Morgan. The contest with the clever Welsh fighter was a 15-rounder made at 9st. The Baldock camp wanted to use this fight as a warm-up but also to test Teddy at the weight he intended to be for the contest with Al Brown. Although Morgan had experienced only a single win in his last five outings in April 1928, he had claimed the Welsh Flyweight Championship after defeating Ginger Williams.

Morgan was fast and smart, although not exactly in the same class as Baldock. However, he was seen as a fighter who would make for an examination of Teddy's pace and stamina over the 15-round distance. With the Brown fight now just three weeks away, the plan was to perfect Baldock's timing and get a good workout before going away to train.

Teddy allowed the Welshman to do most of the work as he picked up the points by scoring with the straight left. In the 12th, the East Ender put an end to the exhibition, sending Morgan to the boards with a heavy straight right. This was designed to finish the fight but was caught on the left glove, partially blocking the punch. The Welshman beat the count and defended well enough to get himself to the end of the round. Baldock took it relatively easy for the rest of the bout, not willing to take any unnecessary chances before his what might be the biggest bout of his life, and won by a comfortable points margin.

Teddy felt so confident he had the beating of Brown that he instructed Morris to put up a £250 side-stake, although Brown's camp were not keen to take up the offer.

It was annoying for Baldock that the fight was not for the world bantamweight title, which both boxers had claimed as their rightful crown. But Teddy later recalled that he felt that he had been 'a lot luckier than most boys who take up fighting for a career, and couldn't expect everything to come my way. Quite a lot I'd received, and for that I was satisfied.'

Baldock changed his training quarters to the Star and Garter at Windsor. Many fighters used that venue and the preparation went well, but everyone, including Baldock, understood that he was facing the most serious fistic trial of his life. Teddy would not have his usual physical advantages. Al Brown was 6ft, about five inches taller than Teddy at 5ft 61/2in, he had a longer reach and, as Baldock was to relate, 'he had the shoulders of a lightweight'. Baldock had never faced an opponent with such physical superiorities, but Brown was five years older than Teddy, and Baldock had been fighting seriously since he was 14, while the Panamanian hadn't started until he was about 20. Brown was a bright man who had command of four languages (English, French, Spanish and Italian) and had boxed all over the world. Teddy was of course no fool, but his experience had been confined to Britain (mostly London) and his comparatively brief sojourn in New York.

Just before the meeting with Brown the *Daily Sketch* of 11 May 1931 reported, 'Baldock Knocks Out Sparring Partner': 'Teddy Baldock is an earnest young man these days. Realising the stiff fight he has before him with Al Brown at Olympia on 21 May, he is putting his best into training at Windsor.

'Yesterday, Baldock had a field day among his sparring partners. Wearing big gymnasium gloves, he knocked out Jimmy Wheeler, of Bermondsey, in the first few seconds of his opening sparring bout. Afterwards he gave Jimmy Boulger a gruelling time, punching hard and at great speed.'

The Baldock versus Brown fight topped a strong bill at Olympia, organised by the NSC. Teddy came in at 8st 12¼lb; Brown was 8st 9½lb. 'The Fearless' Owen Moran, the well-known Birmingham bantam and featherweight (who had retired 10 years previously), was the referee.

The contest started relatively quietly, each fighter feeling the other out. Baldock knew he was up against the most formidable opposition he had ever encountered. During the opening rounds he was content to stay on the defensive, waiting for Brown to make a mistake that he could exploit to his advantage. Initially the Panamanian seemed nervous, unwilling to lead, although occasionally he would flick out his left like a lizard's tongue. Baldock was able to duck under one or two of these but the rest found their target. Teddy was finding himself beaten for speed, his timing was off and without the reach advantage was finding his own left repeatedly falling short.

The third opened with a lot of sparring, at which point Owen Moran called both boxers together and demanded more action. Brown at once jumped in with a right swing to the head, driving Baldock to the ropes where he caught him with lefts to the face. This salvo was followed by double-handed blows to the body. It was during this exchange that Teddy suffered a graze to his left eyeball, the same place that had been damaged during the Pattenden fight.

The eye became flooded until streams rolled down Baldock's cheek, and for the rest of the round he fought with the left eye tightly closed.

At the time both Teddy and his corner believed something had got in his eye. Between the rounds, desperate attempts were made to clear the problem. But this probably did more harm than good, the eyeball itself was damaged, and there was nothing that could be done in the ring to change that. Baldock came out for the fifth half-blind, blinking repeatedly in a vain attempt to clear his vision.

From then on Brown found it an easy task to score with his rangy left; again and again Teddy failed to see it coming. He knew that the Central American was starting to dictate the rhythm of the fight. Attempting to break his confidence, Teddy fought back, catching Brown with a straight left, followed by a left and right hook to the head, earning him loud applause from the crowd.

The fight followed this pattern until the 10th when it was clear to Teddy and everyone else that he was well behind on points. His eye was worsening and so he had to take more chances and hope for a 'pay-off punch' to turn things around.

The Londoner made a desperate attack to the head but was driven back to the ropes and in the midst of an exchange fell to his knees; his gloves touching the resin. 'One, two' and he was up. He went to his corner to have his gloves wiped. Brown watched his target, seemingly surprised that Teddy had effectively declined to make use of the possible damaging effect a resin-covered glove could have on an opponent, but after the fight Baldock was to declare, 'I never wanted to win a fight that way.' However, as Teddy later reflected, 'The coloured man might have been impressed, but was not going to show any appreciation. As I turned from my seconds he rushed me back into the corner and handed out a two-fisted assault to the head and body. For the first time he really let his punches go.'

Now Baldock was in more trouble than he had ever been in the ring. He came out for the 11th 'to have a bundle'. Brown was up for this and the two men punched away at each other, the whole time being urged on by the now roaring crowd. It was 'a fighting round', but Brown was by far the faster with his punching, although towards the end of the three minutes Teddy landed two flashing rights on Brown's chin that caught the Panamanian by surprise.

Baldock's corner instructed their man to take it easy; there were still four more rounds to fight, so Teddy could go all out for the last two and maybe snatch the decision. His left eye was still very painful, so he had to more or less rely on his right eye to guide him. His left arm was swelling up but the 12th beckoned, and out he went to face the seemingly endless seconds, half- blind, almost one-handed. Brown met him and smashed Teddy to the ropes with a simultaneous and repeated left/right attack. Baldock was stretched back over the ropes, preventing him from contracting his abdominal muscles. His solar plexus was totally exposed to Brown's left hook. In a moment Teddy found himself on his knees, forehead on the canvas. He crawled round trying to catch his breath; he could hear the count and managed to rise as the referee bellowed 'Eight!' But Brown was on him, showering spiteful hooks into his body before going for the jaw with left and right hooks; Teddy fell again. 'Eight!' He was up! Too fatigued to defend himself, he was hit with a hail of blows, which sent him once more crashing back to the boards. 'Nine!' Baldock stood yet again. Brown dipped down to deliver a deep, aching left hook. Although both corner and crowd all but felt the blow, Baldock was past pain. Flat on his face, head pressing hard into the canvas, he wanted to rise but his legs would not support him. Trying to push himself up, the beaten fighter merely rolled through 180 degrees on to his back. Moran got to 'Three!' but abandoned the count; he then threw up his hands and beckoned to Teddy's seconds to pick him up and assist him back to the corner.

Sitting on his stool, Baldock thought he was going out for another round and for a moment struggled to break free as his corner restrained him, but then it hit home; the hardest blow of all, he was the loser. Brown had already been proclaimed the victor and as the Panamanian approached the Baldock corner, Teddy raised his weary body from the stool that supported him. The two adversaries embraced and the Londoner congratulated his opponent, everyone of his sentiments suffused with admiration..

Having recovered the best he could and changed, the defeated boxer was ready to go home but decided to make his way to Brown's dressing room. He told Al, 'So we've settled our three-year quarrel and you've won…Good luck, Al, but you caught me on my left eye in the fourth round and I was troubled by it afterwards. Still, I don't want to make excuses, I just want to say you are a clean fighter and a true sportsman.'

The Panamanian wished Baldock luck, and told him it wasn't his fault they had failed to meet sooner. He showed Teddy his badly swollen right hand. It later transpired that he had broken five small bones and probably would not have been able to continue the fight much beyond the 11th round.

POSTSCRIPT TO BROWN

Over the years after his fight with Teddy Baldock, Al Brown would defend various versions of the World Bantamweight Title throughout the world before losing what was considered the generally recognised bantamweight title to

Spain's Baltazar Sangchili (who was named as the 'worst bantamweight champion of all time' by *The Ring* in May 1981) in Valencia. Brown then decided to retire from boxing.

Two years later, in September 1937, Al made a comeback, achieving five straight wins before defeating his former nemesis, the IBU Champion Sangchili (although the first Puerto Rican to win a world title, 'El Gallito' Sixto Escobar, was considered the World Bantam Champion by most other boxing commissions), on 4 March 1938, in Paris. Based on this result, the IBU proclaimed that Brown was once more the World Bantamweight Champion. Al successfully defended his crown against Frenchman Valentin Angelmann (one-time holder of the IBU flyweight World Championship) but then, unable to make the bantamweight limit, gave up his title. Brown finally hung up his gloves in 1942; in his long career he had never been stopped in the ring.

Sadly, after fronting an orchestra on the French Riviera for a while, Brown was finally stopped by cocaine. Panama and Latin America's first boxing Champion was arrested in New York for using the drug; the judge ordered his deportation for one year, a relatively light punishment.

He was just 48 when he died penniless of tuberculosis in New York City, where he was buried, although his remains were later interred at Amador Guerrero Cemetery in Panama City, Panama.

17

THE GOLDEN ROAD HAD TURNED TO DUST

As Baldock left Olympia after his defeat by Al Brown, he felt it was time to step away from the ring; he had relinquished the British title, and Johnny Cuthbert had not responded to his challenge. But his father and Joe Morris persuaded him to meet Dick Corbett in an open-air fight at Clapton Stadium at the start of September. At this point, Teddy rated Corbett as probably the best bantamweight in Britain (he had lost just one of his previous 15 contests, the one before he met Baldock, versus Willie Smith). Dick was a smart fighter, but Teddy believed he lacked a 'finisher's punch' (although he did knock out 31 men in his 184-fight career). Baldock certainly believed Corbett would be unable to stop him but feared the Bethnal Green man might be too fast as he was conscious he had slowed up of late. Teddy's main concern though was his eye; obviously he didn't want to risk losing his sight.

The bout was set at 12 rounds at 9st, but both men were well inside the weight, with Baldock a pound or so heavier than his opponent with his usual advantage in height and reach. More than 30,000 people travelled to the Clapton Stadium, the majority from either Poplar or Bethnal Green, where there was naturally enormous interest in the fight.

Teddy knew from the opening bell that he would have a tough task ahead of him, and he had only thrown a few punches when his left arm began to swell. By the end of the second round, it was hardly good for anything other than ineffective defence. Corbett took no chances and was satisfied to box his way to a points win. Baldock was getting caught with Corbett's left with monotonous regularity.

Without a left to measure with, Baldock's right became useless as the formidable weapon it has once been; Teddy had never missed as much and started to believe he'd be better fighting with his eyes shut, scoring better by chance than by flawed judgement. Nevertheless, he persevered in the face of Corbett's predictable, orthodox style. By the end of 10 rounds, it was doubtful if Baldock had won a single one.

With two to go, Teddy decided to throw caution to the wind and came out firing rights, hoping to land a lucky shot, while occasionally pushing out a left in an attempt to beat Dick to the punch. Baldock's supporters appreciated what their man was trying to do, but Corbett got the decision, in what would turn out to be Teddy's last fight; a defeat, but he left the fight game carrying the shield.

POSTSCRIPT TO CORBETT

Tragically, Corbett (born Richard Coleman) was one of 173 men, women and children who met their deaths in a matter of minutes in what could be considered as Britain's worst civilian disaster of the Second World War. The tragedy took place close to where Teddy Baldock was born. A plaque above one of the three entrances to Bethnal Green Underground Station, at the junction of Roman Road and Cambridge Heath Road, on the corner opposite the Church of St John on Bethnal Green, continues to commemorate the calamity. This was the only entrance in use at the time of the disaster. On Wednesday, 3 March 1943, the station had yet to be completed (it wasn't to be opened as an underground station until 4 December 1946) but during those years of war it was used as an air-raid shelter for 9,000 people, holding 5,000 bunk beds.

The Times of 5 March 1943 reported the catastrophe:
'About 178 people were killed and 60 were injured when the crowd entering a London tube shelter after the alert of Wednesday evening tripped up and fell on one another, blocking the stairway.

'When a middle-aged woman with a bundle and a baby tripped near the foot of a flight of 19 steps.

'The woman fell down the last two or three steps and lay on the landing. Her fall tripped an elderly man behind her, and he fell similarly, and their bodies again tripped up those behind them. So that within minutes there were hundreds of people crushed together and lying on top of one another, covering the landing and the lower steps.

'Dick Corbett, former Bantamweight Champion boxer, was killed in the shelter disaster. He had gone to the shelter to find his wife and children who were unharmed.'

The plaque at the station concludes 'Not Forgotten'.

I WAS A GHOST OF WHAT I WAS

The day after the fight with Corbett, feeling he had let his fans down and that as a boxer he was 'through', Teddy announced his retirement from the ring. Retrospectively, it is hard to think it wasn't the right thing to do. His left arm was practically disabled and over his career a range of bones in his right hand had been broken; his weapons were worn out as he was to reflect, 'As hands for ordinary purposes they were still all right, but as efficient tools for a fighter they were useless and broken.'

Considering the persistency with which Corbett had punched Teddy with his fine left, Baldock was surprisingly little the worse for wear. There was the telltale puffiness about his normally thin lips, and his eye too told that he had been in a fight, but otherwise he was seized by weariness and conscious that he had failed.

As the *Daily Mail* reported,
'Baldock took his beating as a champion should. Punched from pillar to post, outboxed and outclassed, his lips swollen from punishment, his eyes and mouth reddened and battered, he fought bravely on in a lost cause, shirking nothing and always striving to make a fight of it.'

Teddy told the press, 'I have no excuse for my defeat by Dick Corbett, except this, I was a ghost of what I was. I could not do the right thing. I would take no credit from Corbett. He well won his victory, and he fought a clean, good and sportsmanlike fight. And I am left without a complaint.

'But it hurts to be made to realise that I must now leave boxing to others. I am through: at least at the moment I am quite decided that I will not enter the ring again.

'I regret the going, but though I had every confidence that I would win last night, for I had thrived on my training, I found when no more than four rounds had gone that there was something fatally wrong.

'I was not hurt to any great extent. If I seemed to be in distress my appearance lied. Corbett has a great left hand and no man could have made freer or greater use of it. But he has not a hard punch. My trouble was that I was so often out of distance, I cannot explain why, but it was a fact from which I could not escape. But now, when I come to look back, I feel that I have never been the same since I had my left hand, the bones of which were broken, operated upon. That was some three years ago; and, besides, I have had serious trouble with my nose. And my ailments, together with the many 15 round fights I had when I was a growing boy must have taken a deal out of me. It is possible, so intent was I on winning, that I took too much weight off and too hurriedly. While I was training I never felt fitter in my life until last Friday night, when I grew tired and I began to doubt myself. When I took to the ring belief that I would win returned; but somehow my arms went back on me. I could punch with neither accuracy nor power; and I was well and deservedly beaten.

'I do not despair of the future. I have other interests outside the ring. For my age I have perhaps had all the fighting a man need wish for. How many? It is impossible to say; more than 200; and now, when I am through, I have the sureness that I was a credit to the ring.

'That which happened to me last night sooner or later is the fate of all fighters. I have had my fling. I have done well. Now I am finished.'

Since the operation on his left forearm, after the fight with Mick Hill, Teddy had certainly been suffering with it. He had kept quiet about it not wanting to upset the plans and the hopes that his manager, trainer and father had for him. Of course, if he had continued to fight, he would also have risked further damage to his left eye.

Baldock's memories of his final fight were tinged by the fickleness of the boxing public. He recollected, 'When you're on top, they're with you all the way. But when you're on the slide…they're not averse to turning hostile…My fight with Dicky Corbett…taught me that. Early on, the crowd had been rooting for me. The women around the ringside were yelling, "Teddy, Teddy, come on, sweetheart." Then the tide of the fighting turned against me. So did the fans. I came out for the last round to shouts of "Sock him, Dick! You've got him groggy." The referee's points verdict was just a formality. Teddy Baldock was at the end of his reign. The golden road had turned to dust.'

Tens of thousands had witnessed Baldock's fall from the heights of boxing fame, the game that probably ranked as the most popular of all sports in that era, but, although there has never been much room for tears around the 'magic square', many hard-bitten faces were dampened by the spectacle of the once great fighter defeated and bewildered.

The boxing scribe Ben Bennison summed up the situation: 'Remembering the proud position that was his, the display Baldock gave was incredible, so inept, so utterly foreign to his former self. Only was his heart as stout, as unbreakable, as it was when, little more than a child, he made a habit of flattening out full-grown men.

'Not a single round did he score the most points; always was he fighting a losing battle. His defence had so many gaps in it that it was no defence at all.

'That Baldock was sorely worried and perplexed from the moment that Corbett landed the first blow I have not the least doubt, but so did he mask his face – a face that might have been hewn out of a slab of marble for all the emotion it denoted – that he spread a belief among his army of supporters that sooner or later he would send ripping to the jaw of Corbett a punch that would turn the tide in his favour.

'As the curtain was about to be lowered upon the tragedy of Baldock and the conquest of his neighbour the two embraced. There was a queer curl in the battered face of Baldock, but though he must have realised that he had lost he forced himself to smile as Corbett patted him on his cruelly tired arms that hung loosely about his hips.'

Teddy Baldock had won three titles, held the Lonsdale Belt and was still being called the 'Pride of Poplar' long after he finished fighting. He was to ask, 'What more could I want?' Immediately after his fighting career he had some money and felt he had 'done my parents and brothers and sisters some good turns'.

Yes, his eye, hand and arm were hurt, but the reality of the situation was that Teddy's boxing heart had perhaps been broken (like many before him) by what might have been. Baldock's life was changed by Al Brown ducking him at a time when Teddy was close to his peak. Then, full of enthusiasm in the American milieu by which he was so motivated, he might have had the beating of the Panamanian he had gone gunning for all the way to the US. However, by the time the two finally met, Al was physically in better shape than Baldock. In his final years Teddy would tell how he was unable to get close to Brown because of the Panamanian's height, and recalled how Al 'punched like the kick of a horse'.

18

LIFE OUTSIDE THE RING

Teddy was 24 years old and he had retired. He now had to choose what to do with the rest of his life. Aside from a short period working on the docks and running bets for his dad, the fight game was all he had known in terms of making a living and much of his education, after all he had been a top liner at the Albert Hall by 17. In those days, there was no recognised second career in commentating and merely being a boxing celebrity would not earn him a living.

During his first years of ring life, Baldock was known to fight twice in one day and on occasions two or three days a week. After the routine of training and boxing, which had had an impact on everything he ate and even the time he would go to sleep and wake up in the morning, Baldock was anchorless; his stringent self-discipline evaporated and it seemed that the leash that had held his taste for the excess in check had been removed. Sadly, Teddy would go on to succumb to the temptations of both drink and gambling.

The ex-pro would tell how, shortly after retiring, he was approached by the famous Paris-based American promoter Jeff Dickson, who told him that if he returned to the ring he would pay him £5,000 for three fights: 'the first crooked, in England; the second, in France, also crooked, and the third wherever I decided – but straight. I told Mr Dickson that I'd never fought crooked in my life.'

For a short period, Baldock went into partnership as a boxing promoter and made a bit of money on a couple of shows at Lea Bridge. He recalled he lost all he had on the Walter Neusel and Jack Pettifer heavyweight clash in June 1933 (the German knocked out Pettifer in the eighth round).

Teddy's social life continued to escalate apace. The *Evening News* on 25 February 1936 reported that Baldock had been involved in a car crash in Marylebone Road in the early hours of that morning and had been taken to Middlesex Hospital with a 'severely cut forehead' and 'very slight concussion', where his condition was said to be 'quite satisfactory'. At that point he was detailed as still living in Katherine Road, Forest Gate. It was reported that a passenger, a 'Miss Winifred Knight of Eastcheap', had suffered a broken leg. It appears the car had skidded 'after colliding with street refuse' and then hit 'a motor van'. Winifred was the wife of the Californian Jewish comic, actor, singer and producer Bert Le Blanc (Bertram Leon Cohen) who established his early career in the US as an actor and variety performer and toured as a member of the American Burlesque Company before eventually settling in Australia.

Baldock came from a family of street bookies (at a time when off-track gambling was illegal) and perhaps from this culture he acquired a weakness for the horses, and greyhound racing. After he retired from fighting, he ran a book for a time in partnership with his brother Stan, but they were both gamblers (in fact, of the Baldock brothers, only Bob and Alec weren't). Like all the Baldocks, they were relatively intelligent, but they did not have a gift for the trade and lost much more than they won. As with most unsuccessful gamblers, Baldock's ambitions were based on a few lucky incidents. One such happened at Epsom when a jockey told him to get on 'Punch', an outsider for the 1937 Cesarewitch. It seemed an appropriate nag, given Teddy's former profession, and he backed it at 50–1. When it came home he won £5,000, but those winnings were soon spent and much more besides. Baldock guessed that his bookmaking venture and his own bets cost him 'the thick end of £10,000' – a sizable fortune in the late-1930s – a comparable sum today would be approximately £630,000 (at that time 85 per cent of new houses sold for less than £750 – that would be around £45,000 today. Terraced houses in the London area could be bought for £395 in the mid-1930s when average earnings were about £165 per year).

At the time of this good win Teddy was still something of a celebrity. A headline in the East London newspaper, the *Stratford Express*, in September 1937 named him (and an old friend) among a host of famous names who had come together for a Pageant of Sport for Charity on the 24th of that month;

FAMOUS ARTISTE SINGS AT STADIUM - 30,000 CHEER MISS GRACIE FIELDS

Thirty thousand people cheered Miss Gracie Fields, the famous artiste and film star when in the company of the Mayor of West Ham, and the Mayoress, she walked out onto the greyhound track of the West Ham Stadium on Friday night. She had visited the stadium to give her support to the pageant of sport organised to inaugurate a fund for the rebuilding of the out patients department of St Mary's Hospital.

'Can you hear me mother?' she asked as she picked up the portable microphone and then to the bandsmen of the 6th Battalion the East Surrey Regiment T.A. who provided the music for the evening, 'Come on lads play summat'. They played 'Laugh Your Troubles Away' and Miss Fields sang it to the delight of the crowd. Then she gave them 'Sally' and afterwards at her invitation to 'get a bit matey' they sang it with her. When she walked round the speedway track with the Mayor and Mayoress there was a rush from the enclosures on to the greyhound track to get a 'close-up'.

'The famous star was certainly a great attraction and by her presence largely helped the venture of rebuilding, for which approximately £23,000 is required. Many others also gave their aid in staging what was a unique entertainment, including as it did speedway and cycle racing, boxing and a parade of famous greyhounds, including a firework display. Another celebrity in the world of entertainment also helped. She was Miss Pat Hyde of Plaistow, the well-known radio entertainer who played her accordion and sang into the microphone in the boxing ring, which was erected in the centre of the arena. Eric Chitty, the West Ham Speedway rider, also crooned a few choruses from this ring, where previously two famous local boxing champions of the past Teddy Baldock, the ex-bantamweight champion, and Mike Honeyman ex-featherweight champion, had given an exhibition bout, and a comedy bout had been provided by Billy Robins of Bethnal Green and Jack Maynard of Kent.

'There was also cycle racing in which two teams of riders representing

West Ham and Herne Hill contested a match of nine heats on the same lines as speedway racing.

'The speedway challenge match was between a team of West Ham reserve riders and Norwich.

'The celebrated Mick the Miller led the parade of famous greyhounds followed by other well known performers in Flying Wedge, Avion Balerino and Wattle Mark, and a string from the West Ham kennels. Altogether the event was highly successful as well as entertaining and all those associated with its organisation and carrying out duties are deserving of congratulation.

'The Mayoress of West Ham, who was the chairman of the committee, over the microphone voiced her thanks to all who had joined in helping the cause. She said they were particularly grateful to Miss Gracie Fields for her generosity in attending, to Miss Pat Hyde, and to all those who had given their services in providing their entertainment.

* * *

While researching this book I came across a photograph of Oswald Mosley in his brown shirt days sitting at a table with two or three other men. Two men stood either side of those seated and one was Teddy. Ted Kid Lewis had been recruited by Mosley at one point to train young people in his movement, but after Lewis had found out the nature of Mosley's intentions he walked out on the fascist leader, dropping two minders as he went.

I don't believe that Teddy was a political man, or that he was in any way in sympathy with the type of anti-Semitism Mosley and his followers espoused, certainly given his close friendship and associations with many Jewish people (including Joe Morris, his manager). Although Teddy might just have been looking for something to believe in, I suspect payment and hope of some publicity might have been his main motivation and I am confident that, like Lewis, when he became fully aware of what the brown shirts stood for, a man like Baldock would not have wanted anything to do with the organisation. Indeed, he actively identified himself as an enemy of fascism when he was quick to sign up for the RAF during the early stages of the Second World War. All the Baldock brothers volunteered for service early in the War, but Ernie (who joined the Royal Marines) and Teddy were the first, not wanting 'somebody else to do the fighting for you'. There was a big party organised to mark their leaving to serve King and country, but they were back the very next day, having to await posting.

Teddy began his service career on the 16 December 1940 when he enlisted at No 2 Recruitment Centre, RAF Cardington, Bedfordshire, as an Aircraft Hand (ACH)/Physical Training Instructor (P.T.I). In 1941 he was posted to RAF Bridgenorth at Stanmore, Shropshire. Originally designated as No 4 Recruitment centre, in 1940 it was briefly a transit camp to deal with many nationalities of troops etc returning from France. Here Teddy was attached to the School of Physical Training. Finally in 1943 he ended up at 52 Operational Training Unit (OTU) Aston Down, Gloucestershire from where he was discharged from the RAF on 10 August 1943. His record stating that he was physically unfit for Air Force service although fit for employment in civil life. On occasions during his time in the service he would be sent to Scotland to box exhibitions for the entertainment of the troops, but he cracked a bone in his left arm, which required surgery. The injury ended this role and may have had a part in his discharge.

Puzzlingly, given his discipline during his boxing years, Teddy found it hard to be governed by the strict rules and regulations of military life. His service record is littered with references to going AWOL, sometimes for weeks at a time, despite his brothers loading him on to the trains returning him to his squadron, that he would otherwise do all he could to avoid getting on.

But it seems his membership of the Masons might have lightened the consequences of his actions as his punishments were hardly ever severe. On the 22 January 1929 Teddy had been initiated into the Freemasons, Cosmopolitan Lodge No. 917, Mark Masons Hall, 86 St James St, London SW1. His entry no doubt facilitated by some of the powerful connections he had made throughout his boxing career. In some photographs Baldock is wearing a tiepin depicting the 'Eye of Providence' demonstrating this affiliation.

It seemed Teddy had inherited his father's lack of financial discipline. The nest-egg which he thought his father had saved for him from his boxing earnings had all but disappeared. For Baldock, 'The trouble was that the old man, who handled all my money, was like me. He just couldn't say "No" to people who asked for money – *my* money.'

Teddy recalled the moment when he asked his father for what remained of his savings, wanting £250 to buy himself a pub; he found that there was hardly anything left, a few hundred instead of the thousands his fists had earned. But he got the pub, The Earl of Derby, in Forest Gate, and for a time did well enough and, at least, he was making a living instead of drawing on capital. However, Teddy had no real idea of how to run a business and he and Maisie were never going to make the best of the trade. His mother had to take time off from her own responsibilities at The Ship to sort out her son's accounts.

But when the bombing started, custom vanished overnight and Baldock was glad to hand the pub back to the brewery. What money he had was soon gone after losing as much as £200 a week on the dogs and horses.

He owned a house in Barking, Essex, which was destroyed during the blitz. He recieved £3,000 from the War Damage Commission for this loss, getting the cheque about the time of his divorce. This was around the same time as he lost contact with his daughter Pam. He recalled that the money 'went through my pockets as quickly, as if it were acid burning holes in the lining. It was all gone in four months. Racing took a packet. At this time I thought nothing of being £100 a day down.

'Drinks swallowed up a lot. Drinks for myself and others. For though I never drank at all while I was fighting, I certainly began to make up for it when my marriage went wrong. And the inevitable unsecured loans to the inevitable insecure pals ran away with the rest.'

According to Teddy as long as he 'had the dough' he was content to spend it. 'The quicker I could get rid of it the happier I was. I was that bitter about my broken marriage.'

But what probably really caused Teddy to finally crash was his excessive drinking. He had never touched alcohol until his father had died while pulling pints at The Ship in 1944. Ted had to be lifted over the bar after he collapsed.

His last words were 'I'm sorry'. It was difficult to see what he was apologising for until it was discovered he had used up all the family's cash on gambling. Baldock Sr had always been Teddy's guiding light and the most constant figure in his life, certainly a big part of the reason he boxed was to please and impress his dad. Discipline and control had, in terms of Teddy's life, always been placed outside himself, either in the hands of Joe Morris (who passed away in Weston-super-Mare) or Jack Lakey, but most enduringly Ted. Teddy was apparently totally disoriented by his father's passing.

There was a second chance after his mother died in 1951 (in a nursing home in Redbridge) and he got his share of her will, much coming from the sale of The Ship, which she had taken over when Ted died. Louisa Rose had remarried Arthur Austin, who owned a couple of pubs, in 1947. He had died around a year later a wealthy man, leaving all his worldly goods to his new wife. But she passed everything from her second husband's estate on to the Austin family.

It seems the Baldock family sold The Ship in 1951 as the licence changed from L.R. Austin (Louisa's married name) to Mr Stephen Magee and the Baldock siblings inherited a fair amount; however, Teddy booked himself into a hotel and in record time blew the lot. Baldock had got used to the high-life during his time in the ring and even then it seemed that it was a priority over his home life. Maisie once went out in search of her husband to one of the big West End clubs and caught him chatting up other girls. Infuriated she dampened his ardour by spraying him thoroughly with a soda siphon.

Having run a pub while continuing to enjoy a heavy standard in socialising, seemed to be a path Baldock could not leave. He lived a life with something of the playboy flavour about it up to his late forties/early fifties, but had no clear fixed abode. He would turn up at the homes of his relatives and after two or three weeks inform his hosts that he was going out for an hour and didn't come back for three weeks. It was rumoured that he would stay with a former high-ranking military officer on occasion and maybe his Masonic connections would have been supportive too; however, Baldock's demise was steady but sure and he reached some desperate levels. He once turned up at Sammy King's billiard hall; his former sparring partner saw that his clothes were crawling with lice. Teddy asked to put his head down on the premises overnight, but

Sammy could not allow that and gave him a few bob to find himself somewhere to stay.

However, Teddy was never to lose his fascination for the ring and whenever it was possible he would watch a fight. For years he hoped to find another East End boy to work with, develop and make a champion. In the early 1950s, Baldock worked with Tommy Newton, acting as a sort of scout for youthful talent and adviser to young boxers. Newton, a former lightweight boxer and then a licensed British Boxing Board of Control manager, ran a gym at 25 Rhodeswell Road, E14. But Teddy's boxing dreams were to fade and die long before he did; possibly his own personality got in the way as much as anything else.

He had a job as a physical training instructor at a Butlin's Holiday Camp and a messenger in Fleet Street. However, as Baldock got older, when he had to look for a job there was nothing he could do. It seems his contacts, family, Masonic and otherwise, had run dry. He got work labouring as a steel erector and other odd jobs before getting a temporary card on the docks. As a 14-year-old, he had worked in the docks for a short period as a rivet-boy and at 16 he used to run round 'Dog Island' for training, but by the mid-1950s Teddy was something of a sorry sight. The man who once had a wardrobe full of suits (and a couple of cars) then had just the one shabby outfit. At that time he estimated he had made £20,000 from boxing before reaching 24 (around £250,000 today). In 1956, he confessed that he was 'almost in the gutter. I'm the living ghost of a man whose right hand the Prince of Wales once shook as he said: "Ted, I'm pleased to meet you. I've wanted to for a long time." '

He had not yet reached his 50th birthday when he told the world, 'I'm right down on my luck, down to my knees, very nearly. Yes, that's what Teddy Baldock has come to…winner of more than 200 fights…one-time Golden Boy of English Boxing. A kiddies' cot is named after me in Poplar Hospital. That cot was endowed by pennies dropped into tins by people in the streets of London's East End. People who bought flags with my face on them, the face of a local, almost a national hero.

'I lived in the oyster bars and plush restaurants of the West End. Dukes and Earls and their ladies and lady friends rubbed shoulders with me in the big clubs. Today, I don't even own pyjamas.'

By then Teddy knew what it was to be obliged to sleep on a couple of boards and considered himself lucky to get a place in 'common lodging houses'. He called himself 'the biggest fool ever born' and 'the world's champion sucker'.

He recalled, 'All sorts of people used to come round to my dressing-room or go to Dad, who minded all my money for me, on the borrowing stakes. No one ever got "No" for an answer.'

He told how the actor Sid Fields (cited as an influence by the likes of Cary Grant, Laurence Olivier, Eric Morecambe and Tommy Cooper, among many others, and described by Bob Hope as being 'probably the best comedian of them all') was 'one of my regulars. He'd touch me for £2 every week. Sid was broke till he became famous but I'll say this for him. He was a great pal, and he'd pay back just as regularly, as soon as he got his wages.'

Baldock advised others not to follow his example: 'My advice to all present-day fighters is not to listen to any of their stories. Think of yourself first, last, and all the time … for me there was no one around to talk advice into my ears, even if I would have listened to it.'

The way Teddy chose to live his life had a great cost, not least on his marriage. In 1956, he told how often, on a Sunday, he would leave his one room in a London boarding house to go to Woodford, in Essex, to see a pretty, blonde 19-year-old woman ride by on a horse. Hiding from her behind a tree or lamp-post, he would watch her as she cantered by. Within an instant she had ridden out of sight, into and out of his life and Teddy would make his way to a pub, if he had the price of a pint in his ragged coat pocket. That girl on horseback was Teddy's daughter, his only child, Pam, and he didn't want her to see what he, 'the Daddy she once worshipped', had become. As often as he could, he would make the journey to Essex just for that minute or two; the hope that Pam would be taking her usual weekly ride and that he would be able to glimpse her face again. And always he would tell himself that, the next weekend, he would pluck up enough courage to speak to his child. But when next week came he would argue with himself that 'it wouldn't be courage at all to speak to her; it would be weakness. Pam, God bless her, must go her way along life's road. I must go mine.'

But Pam often detected her father watching while she was out riding and admits she had the option to stop. But as a teenage girl, who had lost touch with her dad, she saw him as an embarrassment in his dishevelled state. In hindsight, she wished she had possessed the courage to stop and speak with him; who knows, maybe this would have altered the course of the final chapter of his life. It is only now that Pam recognises her father's greatness in the boxing ring but still feels that, as a dad, he had let her down. Her most lasting memories of his presence in her life were his 'comings and goings' with constant arguments behind closed doors with her mother.

For her birthday he once bought a brand-new Hercules bike, which was quite a treat that most youngsters from a working-class background could only dream of. But it was much too big for her, showing that her father was out of touch with her needs.

After her parents' divorce, living above her uncle's greengrocers shop with her mother was not always easy for Pam. As well as an absent father, her mother went to work in an office to earn enough money to keep them going, but unfortunately also started to drink heavily to drown her sorrows. This in turn made life very difficult for Pam as, although she wanted her mum to see her in school plays/sports etc, she would never know if her mother would arrive the worse for alcohol.

At the first opportunity Pam left school at 14 and went to work at Dorothy Perkins to train as a window dresser, but when they found out her age she was sent back to finish her schooling. She eventually trained as a secretary and worked for an insurance company in the City. When Pam got married at St John's Church, Leytonstone on 23 September 1957, a member of her immediate family spotted a lone figure across the road from the church; he was later to be identified as Teddy. The father who had appeared to have walked out of her life years before was still taking an interest, albeit from a distance.

However, Teddy was a 'gentle man' in all respects and not totally uncaring. In fact, under different circumstances, he would probably have spoiled her. Indeed, there is no evidence to suggest that he was a violent man outside the ring; although he was once banned from The Ship, there is nothing to suggest this was because of his temper. In fact, Kate Baldock told how her uncle Teddy wouldn't tolerate swearing in the house and when her own dad came home drunk he was a calming influence; for her Teddy was a gentle, generous person who bought her first pair of ballet shoes and gave out half-crown pieces (2s 6p/12½p) to kids.

Baldock's avoidance of violence is perhaps best illustrated by an incident that took place while the family were involved in the licence trade. Pam, still very young, was caught pulling the family cat's tail. She recalls that her punishment, being made to stand on a table in the bar, was worse than any smack, having to explain to curious customers that she was standing on the table because of her cruelty to the house moggy.

Baldock would say he didn't know whose fault it was his marriage broke up but he was 'prepared now to say it was mine. But when the break did come I didn't care. I was long past caring about anything. The skids were under Baldock, the ex-champ, fast by then. And I was content to let them go.'

But Teddy never blamed his plight on his boxing career; he believed that 'there was nothing else I could have been but a boxer. With a background like mine, it was almost predestined that I should fight for a living. My old grand-dad had been a bare-knuckle champ. A great-uncle had been pretty useful too. Dad himself wasn't exactly a slouch with his mitts, until one evening he came home with a couple of black eyes, and Ma made him give up boxing.'

Twenty-eight years after announcing his retirement from the ring, Teddy's name and achievements had not been forgotten. On 6 October 1959, he was asked by the BBC to appear as a guest on the programme *It Happened to Me* (other guests included Jock McAvoy, the former British and Commonwealth Champion, and Len Harvey, former British Middleweight, Light-Heavy and Heavyweight Champion and British Empire Light-Heavy and Heavyweight Champion).

The central figure was the Liverpudlian featherweight Dom Volante who had been a great favourite in British rings during the 1920s and 1930s. His career spanned the years 1923–35, during which time he fought 131 professional contests, winning 95, a fine record by anyone's standards. Unfortunately, he was one of boxing's 'nearly men' who today would probably have won a British title and may have been a contender for world honours. However, he fought in an era flooded with talented featherweights such as Johnny Curley, Johnny Cuthbert and fellow Liverpool figher Nel Tarleton, to name but a few.

Although he held decisions against both Cuthbert and Tarleton, Volante was to fail in his attempt to win the British featherweight title on 22 May 1930 when he dropped a 15-round points decision against Cuthbert.

Dom at this time was the physical training instructor on the Cunard liner the *Britannic*. Interviewed by the television personality Hywel Davies, Dom discussed how he had hitchhiked from Liverpool to Manchester to take part in his first boxing competition and how his brother, a bookie, had lost all the money he had made and even sold the car he had once owned. As Dom recalled, 'So I hit him, Sir, on the impulse. I'd never done anything like it before. My sister was crying, my mum was crying, even my old dad was crying.'

Like Baldock, Dom had nothing to show for all the blood, sweat and tears from his distinguished ring career apart from the flattened nose and scar tissue around the eyes that still glistened when recalling his stories from the ring. Even a scrapbook charting his ring records had gone missing after he loaned it to a friend who had subsequently died. But in a philosophical manner, as Teddy himself was to profess in a later BBC programme, he had no regrets and would do it all again tomorrow.

During the programme, the former fighters went on to discuss televised fights such as Ernie Roderick vs. Eric Boon, Len Harvey vs. Jock McAvoy and Freddie Mills vs. Johnny Ralph.

Coincidentally, in January 1957, the *Britannic* was returning from New York to Liverpool on its final voyage. Dom was working in the gym as usual and got chatting to a young man determined to lose weight for his forthcoming marriage. The topic of Dom's boxing career came up, at which point the young man introduced himself as Theo Sax who at the time was second mate with the Prince Line shipping company, trading out in the Far East on a cargo ship, the *British Prince*. As the ship would not be returning to Britain, the company had paid for Theo to return to the UK via New York as a passenger on the *Britannic* to marry his sweetheart, none other than Teddy's daughter Pam.

In the last days of 1963, Baldock was a square little man, broad in the beam with his flattened nose, scar tissue round his eyes and mostly grey and thinning hair, he had the look of what used to be called an 'Old Pug'. But at 56 he proclaimed himself to be 'as a fit as a fiddle' and 'never ill because I can't afford to be'. However he confessed, 'Things have been a bit rough lately. Nobody wants to know when you're broke and out of a job...I thought I was set for a Post Office job this Christmas, but I've lost that.' By this time he hadn't seen his daughter at all for 16 years.

But Baldock was not the only boxer to fall from grace. The BBC documentary programme *Man Alive*, featuring Baldock, in 1965, showed that, of the then 10 living Bantamweight and Flyweight Champions from the years between the wars, two had been convicted of acts of violence, five (including Harry Lake and the great Jimmy Wilde) were in mental hospitals, six had broken marriages and most of them were comparatively poor. Baldock's great rival, Alf Pattenden, by then virtually unknown, was living on what was then called national assistance after severe health problems.

However, when asked about his career, Pattenden responded by saying it had broadened his outlook, done him good and told how he had nothing against the sport, seeing it as having given him opportunity 'to get on'.

Given all this, it may not be surprising that Teddy, who at the time was working as a messenger, told the cameras that he had 'no worries' and had 'nothing to worry about at all'. The documentary told how he saw himself as living a 'quiet life', wanting little more than his 'beloved glass of bitter' and to 'go to Southend now and then for a bit of fun'. Teddy told how many of the men he fought were dead and as such he saw himself as lucky, he said, with a faint flicker of a smile, 'They'd like to be in my position.'

But, according to *Man Alive*, Baldock was almost blind in one eye following a car crash and at 58 (he looked much, much older) a former hero of British sport who was no more than a familiar figure in London pubs. The voice-over declared that Teddy had 'declined to a humdrum corner of some blousy pub'. He was depicted in the grainy black and white of the time cutting a sad figure. In a bulky, blanket-like black overcoat, he gave a rendition of the melancholic 'Glad Rag Doll', perhaps in the hope of being bought a drink, to a half-listening audience with the accompaniment of a honky-tonk piano (all the Baldock kids liked to sing).

Not long after this Terry Murphy, who would become the legendary landlord of The Bridge House in Canning Town, one of East London's most famous music venues, would often pass a few bob on to Teddy. He would come down to Billingsgate, where Terry was working at the time, to ask the porters for handouts. Formerly a fine fighter himself (he twice fought for Southern Area titles and an eliminator for the British light heavyweight crown vs. Alex Buxton in 1956 at Earls Court), Terry recalled it was hard to see him having come to that.

Later Teddy moved to Southend, a place he and his family had visited when he was a boy, like many East Enders, as a 'day-out' treat. He didn't appear to have any permanent address in the area, but it seemed he found a bed where he could. As a successful sportsman, he had taken longer holidays there, at the more expensive Westcliffe hotels, but he always associated the estuary town with good times and respite. However, his lodgings in the last part of his life were much more humble than they might have been in the 1920s and 1930s; at one point he was living in the boiler room of a seafront pub called the Borough Hotel. The landlord, Ron Bently, and his wife Kay, provided him with a bed and meals. He could be often found there, in the Ivy House or the Criterion (three pubs almost next to each other on the seafront), where, in return for a drink, he would talk about his fights and unsuccessful business ventures, including how one of his brothers cheated him out of a fortune. He would recall how the renowned Gutteridge twins, Dick (the father of the famous boxing commentator Reg, who passed away in 2009, 14 years after being awarded an OBE) and Jack, would be his corner men and at times, in the summer season, when many more mature trippers would be around, he could command quite an audience.

Without exception, those who met Teddy at that time found him to be a polite, nice man, who had managed to hold on to at least some of his dignity, and many deemed it a privilege to have heard his recollections.

He was later taken into a local old people's home where he said he was happy because he got his meals, a clean bed and the occasional visit to local pubs.

On 18 March 1971, East London newspaper, the *Newham Recorder* reported, 'Teddy "Lightning Fists" Baldock, the pre-war king of East London boxing and one of the highest-paid fighters of his time, has died penniless at the age of 63.'

His brother Ernest told how, 'Teddy was one of the greatest bantamweights the world has ever seen. He was terrifically fast and that was in the days when a fighter would be in the ring every week...In the old days they were hungry fighters. You really had to be good to make a go of it. I can remember Teddy fighting two or three times in one night, on some occasions.

'When bombs fell on some houses near his pub in Forest Gate he gave all his spare clothes to the homeless people…He did lots of people favours, but he finished up broke. Then it was the old story – suddenly many of those old pals were missing.'

Teddy passed away in Rochford Infirmary in Essex on 8 March, 1971, with literally nothing, not so much as a pair of pyjamas. To the end he was very articulate, bright and ready with a dry wit – even when his sister Rose came to visit him in his last days he was able to say, in gentle jest, 'things must be bad. My sister is here!' And he was persuading the nurses to place his bets for him. However, not a single national newspaper recorded his passing. One of Britain's landmark boxers and a great sportsman of his era, the country's only boxer to win a World Championship during the 1920s (he remains, to the time of writing, Britain's youngest World Title holder) who had excited packed boxing arenas, crowds of tens of thousands for the best part of a decade was completely forgotten.

Teddy Baldock's story is one of the sadder sides of boxing. It confirms how the hangers-on are there when a man is at his best; yet disappear when the cash runs low. Hence the biography of the 'Pride of Poplar' may be seen as much a morality tale as a record of boxing achievement.

I was informed that Teddy donated his brain to Runwell Neurological Hospital. If that is true, it means he continues to contribute to the knowledge of boxing even after his death; this is a fitting legacy for the man and emphasises his altruism, the quality that both made him exceptional and played a part in his downfall.

Teddy's funeral was held 10 days after his death, the once great champion was laid to rest at Southend, and his ashes were interred in the Garden of Remembrance at Southend-on-Sea Crematorium (he was cremated with his Mason's apron draped over his coffin).

His view of life seemed surprisingly generous, he claimed he wasn't bitter and passed his more negative experiences off with 'Well, that's life' and only a hint of a sigh. He spent years sleeping rough and in his late fifties the best he could hope for was a shared room. At that time he remarked, 'I still don't know where I went wrong. I never drank or smoked in those days; I lived for my boxing.'

Teddy lived life his way; never a moment, even his last, had been infected by the fear of living that seems to pull so many of us down from time to time. At the height of his career he once said, 'I'm proud of Poplar. It made me.' It is my hope that Poplar and all of East London will be proud of him, he lived his own way; an imperfect man but who was, after all, the Pride of Poplar.

TEDDY BALDOCK CAREER TIMELINE

The following record has been compiled from fight programmes and most reliable journalistic texts in particular boxing historians Harold Alderman MBE and Miles Templeton who provided most of the undercard results. However, it should be noted that before the Second World War it was not unusual for boxers to fight under more than one name or variations of the same name (sometimes fighters assumed several names during a career), nicknames or different appendages to their titles. Often the same boxer would be accredited as coming from a number of places over their time in the ring. This was due to mistakes, poor geography, alternating place of birth with place of residence or sometimes just to suit a venue (looking to pull the maximum audience).

At the same time, records were not kept as diligently as they are today. It is likely that Baldock had many more fights than those listed here, but it is also the case that other records of his career are not identical to that detailed below. There is any number of reasons for this. Sometimes records are reproductions or compilations of previously produced records. This means that mistakes can be replicated but also that errors can occur in the process of duplication. On occasion, data has been drawn from limited sources (one or two particular newspapers) because they were the only publications that published the information.

With all this in mind, where apparent anomalies have been identified, the most straightforward interpretation has been used.

23 MAY 1907

Teddy Baldock born in Poplar, London

EARLY YEARS (EXACT DATES NOT KNOWN)

Won, East End Boys Championship at 5st

Trained by Jim Varley, at the Port of London Authority Club at Custom House

Sparring partner: Len George-Featherweight

Apprenticed as a Jockey to a Mr Weedon, at Epsom

1921

14 MARCH

Teddy Baldock vs. Young Makepeace (Custom House)

Won, 6 rounds on points

Location: The Public Baths East Street, Barking, London

Promoter: Mr Ray England

On the same bill

Mark Swan (Plaistow) beat Alf Craig (Aldgate)

15 rounds on points

Bob Jackson (Tilbury) beat Jack Walker (Bermondsey)

10 rounds on points

15 DECEMBER

Teddy Baldock vs. Young Makepeace (Custom House)

Won, 6 rounds on points

On the same bill

Tom Berry (Custom House) beat Alf Bright (Kingsland)

15 rounds on points

Johnny Gibbons (Bermondsey) beat Charlie Williams (Kings Cross)

10 rounds on points

Teddy Affleck (Shepherds Bush) beat Jack Crowley (Stratford)

10 rounds on points

1922

16 FEBRUARY

Teddy Baldock vs. Johnny O'Brien (St George's)

Won, 6 rounds on points

Location: St Michael's Hall, Poplar

On the same bill

Bert Harris (Stepney) beat Arthur Partridge (St George's)

10 rounds on points

Fred Newberry beat Mark Swan

Retired 5 round, towel thrown in

Guardsman Clark (Scots Guards) beat Guardsman Watson (Scots Guards)

Retired 5 round, on stool

Wally Schofield (Bermondsey) drew with George Kelly (Canning Town)

10 rounds

John Stephenson (Poplar) beat Alf Milton (Custom House)

6th round stoppage

29 JUNE

Teddy Baldock vs. Johnny O'Brien (St George's)

Won, 8 rounds on points

Location: Premierland, London

On the same bill

Andrew Newton beat Billy Quinn (Bethnal Green)

Retired 10th round, on stool

Albert Danahar (Bethnal Green) beat Jack Allen (Canning Town)

KO 4th round

Sid Franks (Aldgate) beat Len Oldfield (Leeds)

15 rounds on points

Bill Deeble (Bow) beat Jim King (Poplar)

6 rounds on points

Alf Simmons (Hackney) beat Arthur Abbott (St George's)

Retired 5th round, towel thrown in

1923

8 JANUARY

Teddy Baldock vs. Johnny O'Brien (St George's)

Won, 3rd round, referee stopped fight

Location: NSC, London

Annual Stable lads Tournament in aid of St Dunstan's

13 FEBRUARY

Teddy Baldock vs. Young Stoneham (Hoxton)

Won, 4th round retired

Location: Central Finsbury Radical Club, Finsbury, London

On the same bill

Charlie Evans (Bethnal Green) beat Bert Hicks (Walthamstow)

5th round stoppage

Charlie Wye (Hoxton) beat Dan Trainer (Hoxton)

Retired 6th round, on stool

Joe Casbolt (Islington) drew with Bill Duckworth (Hoxton)

10 rounds

Harry Burke (Stepney) beat Joe Barrett (Clerkenwell)

6 rounds on points

Sam Steward (Clerkenwell) beat Ted Smith (Finsbury Park)

6 rounds on points

24 MARCH

Teddy Baldock vs. Arthur Webb (Deptford)

Won, 10 rounds on points

Location: Industrial Hall, Edinburgh, Scotland

In aid of the Scottish branch of the British Legion

On the same bill

Tom Berry (Custom House) beat Jim Rideout (Ipswich)

10th round stoppage

Fred Davies (Llanelly) beat Fred Newberry (London)

20 rounds on points

Billy Housego (London) beat Billy Pinn (London)

10 rounds on points

Tom Cherry (London) beat Jimmy Corp (London)

10 rounds on points

Exhibition by Wally Pickard and Joe Bowker

24 APRIL

Teddy Baldock vs. Arthur Webb (Deptford)

Won, 10 rounds on points

Location: Hoxton Baths, London

Benefit for Tom Pedlar Palmer

On the same bill

Harold Jones (Ferndale) beat Bert Marsh (Clerkenwell)

15 rounds on points

Teddy Murton (Plymouth) beat Barney O'Malley (Poplar)

Retired 11th round, on stool

Fred Richmond (Barnsbury) beat Jim Rideout (Ipswich)

10 rounds on points

Willie Lincoln (Hoxton) beat Young Makepeace (Custom House)

6 rounds on points

SEPTEMBER

Teddy Baldock vs. Young Faithful

Won, KO 2nd round

Location: Addlestone

14 OCTOBER

Teddy Baldock vs. Young Riley (Stepney)

Won, 10 rounds on points

Location: Premierland, London

(Teddy gave away a stone)

On the same bill

Billy Palmer (St George's) beat Fred Bullions (Deptford)

15 rounds on points

Con Hollingsworth (Stepney) beat Sonny Doke (Battersea)

10 rounds on points

Jim Walsh (Bethnal Green) beat Chris Scales (Poplar)

6 rounds on points

Jack Stravell (Stratford) beat Mike Savage (Stepney)

6 rounds on points

8 NOVEMBER

Teddy Baldock vs. Kid Roberts (Bethnal Green)

Won, 3rd round retired

Location: Premierland, London

Referee: Dick Smith

On the same bill

Ted Kid Lewis (St George's) beat Fred Archer (Hucknall, Nottinghamshire)

20 rounds on points

Harry Corbett (Bethnal Green) beat Mike Branstone (Spitalfields)

10 rounds on points

Len Jay (St George's) drew with Mick Hill (Wandsworth)

10 rounds

13 DECEMBER

Teddy Baldock vs. Percy Faithfull (Addlestone)

Won, 10 rounds on points

Location: Premierland, London

On the same bill

Bill Handley (Hackney) beat Billy Moore (Penygraig)

15 rounds on points

Mike Honeyman (Woolwich) beat Jim Carroll (Liverpool)

15 rounds on points

Joe Bloomfield (Islington) drew with Joe Green (Aldgate)

15 rounds

Arthur Cameron (Fulham) beat Bob Brown (Stepney)

10 rounds on points

17 DECEMBER

Teddy Baldock vs. Joe Goddard (Brixton)

Won, 3rd round retired

Location: Hoxton Baths, London

(Mike Honeyman worked as Baldock's corner man)

On the same bill

Ted Harper (Hoxton) drew with Sid Franks (Aldgate)

10 rounds

Bill Carlisle beat Ernie Mills (Clapham)

on points

Ernie Jarvis (Millwall) beat Young Farnham (Hackney)

Retired 3rd round, on stool

Gunner Bennett (RFA) beat Bill Mannering (Chatham)

10 rounds on points

Tom Humphreys beat Charlie Webb (Bow)

10 rounds on points

Tom Clifford (Wandsworth) beat Battling Saker (USA)

KO 1st round

1924

Teddy Baldock vs. Young Bill Lewis (Bethnal Green)

Won, (the fight is mentioned by Lewis's manager but is not shown on Teddy's Official Record)

Won, 10 rounds on points

Location: Pier Pavillion, Southend, Essex

10 JANUARY

Teddy Baldock vs. Arthur Cowley (St George's)

Won, 2nd round retired

Location: Premierland, London

On the same bill

Tommy Morgan (Blaenavon) beat Mike Honeyman (Woolwich)

15 rounds on points

Ted White (St George's) beat Luther Thomas (Swansea)

15 rounds on points

Kid Nicholson (Leeds) beat Harry Corbett (Bethnal Green)

15 rounds on points

24 JANUARY

Teddy Baldock vs. Young Bowler (Bethnal Green)

Won, KO 1st round

Location: Premierland, London

On the same bill

Mike Honeyman (Woolwich) beat Billy Moore (Penygraig)

15 rounds on points

Ted White (St George's) beat Joe Davis (Hoxton)

Retired 10th round, on stool

17 FEBRUARY

Teddy Baldock vs. Young Bill Lewis (Bethnal Green)

Won, 10 rounds on points

Location: Premierland, London

On the same bill

Harry Salkind (Stepney) beat Ted White (St George's)

Disqualification, 7th round

Albert Jacks (Mile End) beat Sid Cannons (Spitalfields)

10 rounds on points

Note: Teddy was now training at Silvertown with Mike Honeyman in a garden shed converted into a gym

24 MARCH

Teddy Baldock vs. George Kid Socks (Bethnal Green)

Draw 10 rounds

Location: NSC, London

On the same bill

Harry Corbett (Hackney) beat Len Fowler (Birmingham)

KO 12th round

Fred Brown (Birmingham) beat Billy Hobbs (Chepstow)

10 rounds on points

B Blyth (Croydon) beat A Mason (Borough)

1st round stoppage

Joe Lee (Marylebone) beat Bill Saker (Marylebone)

3 rounds on points

Signaller A James (RCS) beat Mike Russell (Paddington)

3 rounds on points

T. Langridge (Croydon) beat Sid Freeman (St Pancras)

3rd round stoppage

Signaller A James (RCS) beat George Bough (Kensington)

3 rounds on points

Mike Russell (Paddington) beat George Thomas (Finsbury Park)

Disqualification, 2nd round

F Honeywood (Bermondsey) beat George Newton (Barnes)

3 rounds on points

Johnny Williams (St George's) beat Harry Morris (Bethnal Green)

2nd round stoppage

D. Feldman (Spitalfields) beat G. Swinbourne (Maidstone)

3 rounds on points

J. Boulston (Finsbury Park) beat Joseph Morgan (Kennington)

3 rounds on points

17 JULY

Teddy Baldock vs. Young Bill Lewis (Bethnal Green)

Won, 15 rounds on points

Location: Premierland, London

On the same bill

Mark Lesnick (Stepney) beat Tommy Davies (Treherbert)

Retired 11th round, towel thrown in

Mike Honeyman (Woolwich) beat Billy Landeg (Aberavon)

15 rounds on points

Charlie Wright (Stoke Newington) beat Tom Newcombe (Bethnal Green)

Retired 1st round

Ted Vickers (St George's) beat Dick Talbot (Wales)

6 rounds on points

20 JULY

Teddy Baldock vs. Dod Oldfield (Leeds)

Won, 10 rounds on points

Location: Leeds

On the same bill

Mike Honeyman (Woolwich) beat Nipper Moore (Sheffield)

15 rounds on points

Tracey Howard (Leeds) drew with Young Darkie (Sheffield)

8 rounds

Young Ingham beat Nipper Peacock

6 rounds on points

7 AUGUST

Teddy Baldock vs. Dod Oldfield (Leeds)

Won, 15 rounds on points

Location: Premierland, London

On the same bill

Len Johnson (Manchester) drew with Frankie Burns (Australia)

15 rounds

Harry Corbett (Bethnal Green) beat Mick Hill (Tooting)

15 rounds on points

Charlie Bretton (Bowes Hill) beat Jack Allen (Aldgate)

Retired 2nd round, on stool

Dan Dando (Bermondsey) beat Tom Huxley (Putney)

1st round stoppage

Jim Skinner (Bermondsey) beat Fred Gains (Custom House)

1st round stoppage

Joe Godfrey (Hounslow) beat Joe Howe (Islington)

KO 1st round

Teddy Pullen (Blackfriars) beat Young Coote (Islington)

1st round stoppage

8 SEPTEMBER

Teddy Baldock vs. Kid Hughes (Maesteg)

Won, 7th round – retired, towel thrown in

Location: Premierland, London

On the same bill

Harry Leach (Doncaster) drew with Johnny Curley (Lambeth)

15 rounds

Len George (Custom House) drew with Sid Cannons (Spitalfields)

10 rounds

Kid Lewis (Manchester) beat Charlie Evans (Bow)

Retired 3rd round, on stool

George Green (Bethnal Green) beat Johnny Banks (St George's)

6 rounds on points

25 SEPTEMBER

Teddy Baldock vs. Vic Wakefield (Manchester)

Won, 10th round, referee stopped fight

Location: Premierland, London

On the same bill

Mark Lesnick (Stepney) beat Jim Smethhurst (Oldham)

4th round stoppage

Len Jay (St George's) beat Sam Blacker (Aldgate)

Disqualification, 5th round

Harry Burnstone (St George's) drew with Kid Lewis (Aldgate)

15 rounds

George Green (Bethnal Green) beat Battling Clark (Poplar)

10 rounds on points

6 NOVEMBER

Teddy Baldock vs. Harry Hill (Birmingham)

Won, 15 rounds on points

Location: Premierland, London

On the same bill

Kid Kelly (Plymouth) beat Billy Colbourne (Leeds)

15 rounds on points

Sam Blacker (St George's) beat Harry Fenn (Poplar)
15 rounds on points
Len Davies (Aldgate) beat Harry Ascott (St George's)
KO 1st round
Jim Nelson (St George's) beat Charlie Packer (Clerkenwell)
3 rounds on points
Jack Bull (Barking) beat Alf Ray (Spitalfields)
Retired 1st round, on stool
Young Bull (Bermondsey) beat Teddy Lowe (Brixton)
3 rounds on points
Frank Kilbane (Islington) beat Barney Joel (Stepney)
Retired 1st round, on stool

1925

15 JANUARY
Teddy Baldock vs. Fred Hinton (Forest Gate)
Won, 8th round retired

Teddy joined a training camp at Billericay, Essex, where Tom Berry was training for his fight with Syd Pape and Ted Kid Lewis for his return match with Frenchman Francis Charles

On the same bill
Mark Lesnick (Stepney) beat Alf Thornhill (Leeds)
Retired 4th round, towel thrown in
Phil Richards (St George's) beat Kid Lewis (Manchester)
15 rounds on points

1 FEBRUARY
Teddy Baldock vs. Willie Evans (Port Talbot)
Won, 5th round, referee stopped fight
Location: Premierland, London
Referee: Sam Russell

On the same bill

Phil Richards (St George's) beat Kid Lewis (Manchester)

5 rounds on points

George Nolan (Kings Cross) beat Sam Blacker (St George's)

12 rounds on points

Tom Daly (Bermondsey) beat Young Osborne (Lee)

3 rounds on points

Joe Siebler (Hayes) beat Bill Thompson (Wandsworth)

3 rounds on points

Harry Reed (Islington) beat Joe Howe (Finsbury)

3 rounds on points

Jack Drake (St George's) beat Len Ashdown (Bow)

1st round

25 MARCH

Teddy Baldock vs. Fred Hinton (Forest Gate)

Won, 5th round, referee stopped fight

Location: East Ham, London

On the same bill

Len George (Custom House) beat Kid Booth (East Ham)

15 rounds on points

Nobby Clark (Sheffield) beat C Higgs (Woolwich)

10 rounds on points

George Kelly (Canning Town) beat Harry West (Silvertown)

Retired 7th round, towel thrown in

Jim Bailey (Walthamstow) beat Alf Sharp (Leytonstone)

Retired 2nd round, on stool

Jim Summers (Canning Town) beat Jerry McCarthy (Limehouse)

3 rounds on points

6 APRIL

Teddy Baldock vs. Willie Evans (Port Talbot)

Won, 12th round, referee stopped fight

Location: Premierland, London

On the same bill

Jack Kid Berg (Stepney) beat Sid Carter (Deptford)

15 rounds on points

Mark Lesnick (Stepney) beat Sonny Parker (Dewsbury)

12th round stoppage

Fred Smith (St George's) beat Dan Trainer (Hoxton)

6 rounds on points

Billy Young (Bethnal Green) beat Alf Conn (St George's)

KO 5th round

27 APRIL

Exhibition: Teddy Baldock vs. Charlie Trainer (Hoxton)

Location: New Gaiety Cinema, East Twickenham, London for three nights

21 MAY

Teddy Baldock vs. Ernie Jarvis (Millwall)

Won, 15 rounds on points

Location: Premierland, London

Referee: Jack Goodwin

On the same bill

Jack Kid Berg (Whitechapel) beat Kid Lewis (Manchester)

10th round RET

Dod Oldfield (Birkenhead) beat Mark Lesnick (Stepney)

15 rounds on points

7 JUNE

Teddy Baldock vs. Johnny Haydn (Wales)

Won, 7th round, referee stopped fight

Location: Premierland, London

On the same bill
Jack Kid Berg (Whitechapel) beat Billy Shepherd (Sheffield)
KO 7th round
Young Jack Brown (St George's) beat Eddie Pinn (Marylebone)
12 rounds on points
Young Stanley (St George's) beat Harry Hill (Birmingham)
12 rounds on points

24 JUNE
Teddy Baldock vs. Johnny Murton (Plymouth)
Won, KO 2nd round
Location: The Dome, Brighton
Referees: Sam Russell, Moss Deyong and Joe Wilson
Promoted by Messrs Dorras & Hymans
Matchmaker: Joe Morris

On the same bill
Alf Barber (Brighton) beat Frankie Ash (Plymouth)
15 rounds on points
Billy Bird (Chelsea) beat Mike Honeyman (Woolwich)
Retired 7th round, towel thrown in
Bob Hutman (Brighton) beat Sam Lawrence (Brighton)
3 rounds on points

9 JULY
Teddy Baldock vs. Frankie Kestrell (Cardiff)
Won, 3rd round retired
Location: Premierland, London

On the same bill
George Green (Bethnal Green) beat Franco Vitalle (Italy)
15 rounds on points
Young Jack Brown (St George's) beat Jim Baylis (Euston)
Retired 1st round, on stool

Young Stanley (Battersea) beat Young Bill Lewis (Bethnal Green)
12 rounds on points

30 JULY

Teddy Baldock vs. Frankie Ash (Plymouth)
Won, 15 rounds on points (debut at 3-minute rounds)
Location: Premierland, London
Referee: Sam Russell

On the same bill
Les Tarrant (Coventry) beat Young Stanley (Battersea)
12 rounds on points
Young Jackie Brown (St George's) beat Tommy Mitchell (Tottenham)
12 rounds on points
Billy Boulger (Poplar) beat Pat Daly (Marylebone)
6 rounds on points

3 SEPTEMBER

Teddy Baldock vs. Tiny Smith (Sheffield)
Won, 15 rounds on points
Location: Premierland, London
Referee: Mr Saville

On the same bill
Billy Adair (Bethnal Green) beat Bill Softley (Poplar)
10 rounds on points
Nobby Clarke (Poplar) drew with Mark Wemborne (Poplar)
10 rounds
Nipper Pat Daly (Marylebone) beat Jim Hocking (Camden Town)
6 rounds on points

1 OCTOBER

Teddy Baldock vs. Jim Haddon (Birmingham)

Won, 5th round, referee stopped fight

Location: Premierland, London

On the same bill

Nobby Clarke (Poplar) drew with Kid Williamson (Manchester)

10 rounds

Johnny Edwards (Bermondsey) drew with Bert Laws (Islington)

10 rounds

Mark Wemborne (Poplar) beat Barney O'Malley (Poplar)

9th round stoppage

Young Palace (Old Ford) beat Bill Squires (Poplar)

6 rounds on points

25 OCTOBER

Teddy Baldock vs. Billy Shaw (Leeds)

Won, 1st round, referee stopped fight

Location: Premierland, London

Referee: Sam Russell

On the same bill

Pete Howard (Stepney) beat Billy Clark (Poplar)

10 rounds on points

Albert Jacks (Mile End) beat Phil Conn (Stepney)

10 rounds on points

23 NOVEMBER

Teddy Baldock vs. Ernie Veitch (Lemington)

Won, 7th round, referee stopped fight

Location: Premierland, London

(In aid of the Mayor of Poplar's Children's Fund)

On the same bill
Harry Venn (Poplar) beat Billy Spiers (Bow)
6th round retired
Con Hollingsworth (Stepney) beat Johnny Stephenson (Poplar)
10 rounds on points

17 DECEMBER
Teddy Baldock vs. Antoine Merlo (France)
Won, 15 rounds on points
Location: Albert Hall, London
Referee: Sam Russell

Trained at the Chinese Gardens, Hurstpierpoint, run by Mr H.L.V. Pearn

On the same bill
Hamilton Johnny Brown (Scotland) beat Emile Romerio (France)
15 rounds on points
Bert Laws (Islington) beat Young Jackie Brown (St George's)
5th round stoppage
Harry Corbett (Bethnal Green) beat Jack Dando (Manchester)
10 rounds on points
Alf Mancini (Notting Hill) beat Laurie Raiteri (Stratford)
5th-round stoppage

1926

11 FEBRUARY
Teddy Baldock vs. Frankie Ash (Plymouth)
Won, 15 rounds on points
Location: Albert Hall, London

Trained at Hurstpierpoint with Johnny Curley

On the same bill

Harry Mason (Leeds) beat Ernie Rice (Hounslow)

Disqualification, 5th round (Lightweight Championship Fight)

Harry Corbett (Bethnal Green) beat Jackie Kid Berg (Whitechapel)

15 rounds on points

Charlie Smith (Deptford) beat Louis Wilms (Belgium)

10 rounds on points

Jackie Brown (St George's) beat Teddy Tompkins (Deptford)

Retired 9th round, on stool

18 MARCH

Teddy Baldock vs. Alf Barber (Brighton)

Won, 5th round, referee stopped fight

Location: Albert Hall, London

On the same bill

Johnny Brown (St George's) beat Antoine Merlo (France)

15 rounds on points

Phil Scott (Marylebone) beat Frank Goddard (Clapham)

KO 3rd round

Tom Heeney (New Zealand) beat Charlie Smith (Deptford)

Disqualification, 5th round

Jackie Kid Berg (Whitechapel) beat Andre Routis (France)

15 rounds on points

29 APRIL

Teddy Baldock vs. François Moracchini (France)

Won, 15 rounds on points

Location: Albert Hall, London

On the same bill

Len Harvey drew with Harry Mason

20 rounds

Kid Froggy (Stepney) beat Nobby Clark (Poplar)

10 rounds on points

Harry Hammond (Acton) beat A Boddington (Wellingborough)

10 rounds on points

Young Marty (Spain) beat George Kent (Bethnal Green)

10 rounds on points

10 JUNE

Teddy Baldock vs. Tiny Smith (Sheffield)

Won, 5th round, referee stopped fight

Location: Premierland, London

Referee: Sam Russell

On the same bill

Bill Huntley (St George's) beat Billy Boulger (Plaistow)

10 rounds on points

George Gogay (Poplar) beat Harry Stone (The Borough)

10 rounds on points

15 JULY

Teddy Baldock vs. George Kid Nicholson (Leeds)

Lost on a foul (Baldock's first defeat)

Location: Premierland, London

Referee: Sam Russell

On the same bill

Mark Wemborne (Stepney) beat Johnny Gordon (Mile End)

7th round stoppage

Kid Herman (Aldgate) beat Bert Gilbert (Aldgate)

4th round stoppage

31 JULY

Departed England for America with Ted Broadribb, Jack Hood and Alf Mancini on board the *Berengaria*

27 AUGUST

Teddy Baldock vs. Mickey Gill

Won, 6 rounds on points

Location: Steeplechase Arena at Rockaway Beach

Trained at the St Nicholas gym

On the same bill

Jackie Pilkington (Yorkville, NY) beat Phil Richards

6 rounds on points

Danny Smith (Brooklyn, NY) beat Nick De Salvo (Corona, NY)

6 rounds on points

Joe Lockhart (Evansville, IN) beat Art Brouse

6 rounds on points

Joe Santiago beat Willie Greenspan (New York)

KO 1st round

Willie Feldman (Brooklyn, NY) beat George Rafferty (New York)

KO 1st round

22 SEPTEMBER

Teddy Baldock vs. Tommy Abobo (Philippines)

Won, 6 rounds on points

Location: Mitchel Field, Mineola, New York

On the same bill

Jimmy Lanning (Wichita, Kansas) beat Harry Duer (Brooklyn, NY)

6 rounds on points

George Herman (Moline, IL) drew with Freddie White (Newark, New Jersey)

4 rounds

Buck Westhouse beat Bobby Mack (Mineola, NY)

KO 1st round

Joe Lenz (Oceanside, NY) beat Lou Trimacera

4 rounds on points

Joe Lynch (New York) beat Frankie Murray (Toronto)
KO 3rd round

30 SEPTEMBER
Teddy Baldock vs. Arthur de Champlaine (Canada)
Won, KO 1st round
Location: Madison Square Garden, New York

On the same bill
World junior lightweight title
Tod Morgan (Seattle, Washington) beat Joe Glick (Brooklyn, NY)
15 rounds on points
Frankie Fink (Dallas) beat Al Tripoli (New York)
10 rounds on points
Young Harry Wills (Panama) beat Bobby Robideau (Pennsylvania)
4 rounds on points
Hilario Martinez (Spain) beat Harry Wallach (Brownsville, NY)
KO round on points

6 OCTOBER
Teddy Baldock vs. Johnny Erickson
Won, 8 rounds on points
Location: Mitchel Field, New York

On the same bill
Alf Mancini (Notting Hill) beat Milton Jampole (Bronx, NY)
10 rounds on points
Harry Sankey beat Connie Holmes (New Jersey)
6 rounds on points
Jimmy Abbot (New York) beat Eddie Bowe (Harlem, NY)
6 rounds on points
Chuck Fitzsimmons beat Eddie Barton (New Jersey)
4 rounds on points

Sammy Sober (New York) beat Eddie Parson
4 rounds on points

19 OCTOBER
Teddy Baldock vs. San Sanchez
Won, 6 rounds on points
Location: Pioneer AC New York

On the same bill
Sammy Dorfman (New York) beat Lew Hurley (Harlem, NY)
Disqualification, 3rd round
Lou Kersch (New York) beat Jose Lombardo (Panama)
6 rounds on points
Eddie Guida (Harlem, NY) beat Georgie O'Mara
KO 3rd round
Mickey Durano (Harlem, NY) beat Frankie Trepia (Syracuse, NY)
6 rounds on points
Willie Feldman (Brooklyn, NY) beat George Lunden (Harlem, NY)
4 rounds on points

25 OCTOBER
Teddy Baldock vs. Jackie Cohen (Brooklyn)
Draw, 6 rounds
Location: New Broadway Arena, New York

On the same bill
Jackie Bernstein (Yonkers, NY) beat Charley Rosen (New York)
10 rounds on points
Andre Routis (France) beat Johnny Leonard (Pennsylvania)
10 rounds on points
Frankie Fink (Dallas) beat Joe Malone (Bronx, NY)
10 rounds on points
Frankie McKenna (Scotland) beat Nate Cohen (New Jersey)
4 rounds on points

4 NOVEMBER

Teddy Baldock vs. Billy Marlow (New York)

Won, on a foul 1st round

Location: Mitchel Field Arena, Mineola, New York

12 NOVEMBER

Teddy Baldock vs. Tommy Lorenzo (New York)

Won, 6 rounds on points

Location: Pioneer A C New York

On the same bill

Lew Kersch (New York) beat Bud Dempsey (Illinois)

KO 3rd round

Alf Mancini (Notting Hill) beat Paul Gulotta (Brooklyn, NY)

6 rounds on points

James J. Braddock (New Jersey) beat Lou Barba (New York)

6 rounds on points

Willie Siegel (New York) beat Irving Shapiro (Brooklyn, NY)

KO 5th round

Eddie Goldberg (New York) beat Al Dewitt (Croton, NY)

KO 2nd round

Max Dempsey (Bronx, NY) beat Abe Rosenberg (New York)

4 rounds on points

17 NOVEMBER

Teddy Baldock vs. Billy Reynolds

Won, 6 rounds on points

Location: New Manhattan Sporting Club, New York

On the same bill

Al Goldberg (Harlem) drew with Murray Fuchs (East Side)

6 rounds

Joe Marino (Bronx) drew with Joey Knapp (Harlem)

6 rounds

Bob Nelson (Harlem) beat Willie Singer (East Side)

KO 3rd round

Charlie Sewell (East Side) beat Charlie Fleischman (Bronx)

4 rounds on points

Mickey Polo (Harlem) beat Eddie Vartas (East Side)

4 rounds on points

22 NOVEMBER

Teddy Baldock vs. Ralph Nischo (Brooklyn)

Won, 6 rounds on points

Location: New Broadway Arena, Brooklyn, New York

On the same bill

Tony Canzoneri beat Andre Routis (France)

12 rounds on points

Nat Kawler (East Side) beat Benny Gould (Canada)

10 rounds on points

Marty Shapiro (Brooklyn) beat Jimmy Sullivan (East Side)

KO 3rd round

Lou Barba (Greenwich) beat Willie Brown (Harlem)

KO 2nd round

6 DECEMBER

Teddy Baldock vs. Pierre De Caluwe

Won, 6 rounds on points

Location: New Broadway Arena, Brooklyn, New York

On the same bill

Billy Petrolle (Fargo) drew with Cuddy De Marco (Pittsburgh)

6 rounds

Eddie O'Dowd (Ohio) beat Dominick Petrone (Harlem)

6 rounds on points

Freddy Anderson (Norway) beat Frankie McKenna (East Side)
6 rounds on points
Jimmy Mendoza (Brooklyn) beat Jimmy Clayton (Brooklyn)
KO 1st round
Eddie Goldberg (East Side) beat Steve Angell (East NY)
4 rounds on points
Bobby Bolin (Bronx) beat Sammy Rosenfeld (East NY)
4 rounds on points

13 DECEMBER

Teddy Baldock vs. Joe Clifford (West Side)
Won, 2nd round, referee stopped fight
Location: Madison Square Gardens, New York

On the same bill
Maxey Rosenbloom (Harlem) beat Phil Kaplan (Harlem)
10 rounds on points
Alf Mancini drew with Farmer Joe Cooper (Indiana)
10 rounds
Babe Herman (NY) beat Eddie Anderson (Wyoming)
10 rounds on points
Johnny Philipps (Toronto) beat Sammy Morgan (NY)
4 rounds on points
Jack Bernstein (NY) beat Ray Miller (Chicago)
on points

15 DECEMBER

Teddy Baldock left America to return to England in time for Christmas

22 DECEMBER

Teddy Baldock arrived back from America to be greeted by a crowd of relatives and friends.

1927

16 FEBRUARY

Teddy Baldock vs. Young Johnny Brown (St George's)

Won, KO 3rd round

Location: Albert Hall, London

Referee: J.W.H.T. Douglas

(Jimmy Wilde at ringside along with Prince of Wales)

Weigh in at a hotel in Leicester Square

Trained at Hurstpierpoint

Sparring partner: Fred Patten

On the same bill

Frank Moody (A. Pontypridd) beat Roland Todd (Doncaster)

15 rounds on points

Johnny Hill (Edinburgh) beat Phil Lolosky (Aldgate)

Retired, 15th round

Alf Mancini (Notting Hill) beat Emile Romerio

12 rounds on points

Archie Sexton (Bethnal Green) beat Reggie Caswell (Mitcham)

8 rounds on points

Don Shortland (Sheffield) beat Fred Young (Marylebone)

Disqualification, 2nd round

28 FEBRUARY

Billiard match with Sydney Lee (boy amateur champion of London)

Location: Camden Terminus Club

30 MARCH

Teddy Baldock vs. Felix Friedmann (Germany)

Won, KO 2nd round

Location: Albert Hall, London

On the same bill

Johnny Hill (Fife) beat Petit Biquet (Flyweight Champion of Belgium)

Disqualification, 11th round

Barthelemey Molina (Middleweight Champion of France) beat Harry Collins (Australia)

KO 2nd round

Herman Herse (Welterweight Champ Germany) beat Frankie Burns (Australia)

KO 4th round

Con O'Kelly (Hull) drew with Ted Sandwina (Germany)

15 rounds

Walter White (Leith) beat Harry Fenn (Poplar)

6 rounds on points

Con O'Kelly (Hull) drew with Ted Sandwina (Germany)

15 rounds

11 APRIL

Teddy Baldock entertained by admirers at a Holborn restaurant

13 APRIL

Teddy Baldock and Archie Bell sign contracts at Frascatis restaurant

22 APRIL

Teddy Baldock vs. Len George (Custom House)

3 round exhibition in aid of the New General Hospital for Southend and District

Location: The Kursaal, Southend-on-Sea

Referees: Jimmy Wilde and Eugene Corri

5 MAY

Vacant World Bantamweight Title

Teddy Baldock vs. Archie Bell (Brooklyn, NY, USA)

Won, 15 rounds on points

Location: Albert Hall, London

Referee: Sam Russell

Reception at the Lido Club

Weigh-in: The Ring, Blackfriars/Fred Dyer's gym in the Strand

Trained at Hurstpierpoint

Sparring partners: Johnny Curley, Harry Bugler Lake, Billy Boulger, George Davies (Camden Town), Len George (Custom House)

On the same bill

Alf Mancini (Notting Hill) beat Johnny Brown (Hamilton)

KO 6th round

Con O'Kelly (Hull) beat Gunner Bennett

4th round stoppage

Alex Ireland (Edinburgh) beat Bart Molina (USA)

15 rounds on points

Johnny McMillan (Glasgow) beat Kid Nicholson (Leeds)

12 rounds on points

10 MAY

Charity Boxing Tournament in aid of the Notting Hill Branch of the Norwood Orphanage.

Exhibition

Teddy Baldock vs Kid Nicholson

Location: National Sporting Club, Covent Garden, London

23 MAY

Court Case with Harry Jacobs

31 MAY

Teddy Baldock vs Johnny Curley

Three round exhibition, Derby eve ball in aid of the Great Northern Hospital

Location: The Albert Hall, London

31 MAY – 4 JUNE
Teddy Baldock vs Johnny Curley
Three round exhibition, appearing daily 3.20pm and 9.20pm before the showing of the boxing film comedy **"IS ZAT SO"**
Location: The Astoria, Charing Cross Rd, London

30 JUNE
Teddy Baldock vs. Johnny Cuthbert (Sheffield)
Draw, 6 rounds
Location: Olympia, London

On the same bill
Mickey Walker (USA) beat Tommy Milligan (Shieldmuir)
KO 10th round
Archie Bell (Brooklyn, NY, USA) beat Alf Kid Pattenden (Mile End)
10 rounds on points
George Cook (New Zealand) beat Ted Sandwina (Germany)
3rd round stoppage

7 JULY
Teddy Baldock presented the illuminated address by the Mayor of Poplar

21 JULY
Teddy Baldock vs. Len Oldfield (Leeds)
Won, KO 2nd round
Location: Ilford Skating Rink, London

On the same bill
Billy Streets (Portsmouth) beat Len George (Custom House)
Disqualification, 7th round
Leslie Polaine (Bow) beat Willie Wood (Upton Park)
Retired, 2nd round
Harry Reeve (Plaistow) beat John Strand (Sweden)

15 rounds on points
Charlie Thomas (Hammersmith) beat Jim Hocking (Plaistow)
Retired, 10th round

6 OCTOBER
Teddy Baldock vs. Willie Smith (Johannesburg, Transvaal, South Africa)
Lost 15 rounds on points
Location: Albert Hall, London
Referee: J.W.H.T. Douglas
Weigh-in: The Ring, Blackfriars

Trained at The Pelham Arms, Brighton
Sparring partners: Arthur Webb (Deptford), Kid Pattenden and Bob Wise (Lambeth)

On the same bill
Jack Hood (Birmingham) beat Jack Etienne (Belgium)
10 rounds on points
Billy Brown beat George Rose (Bristol)
10 rounds on points
Harry Corbett (Bethnal Green) beat Henri Scillie (Belgium)
Disqualification, 8th round
Tommy McGrath (Manchester) beat Ted Miller (Becontree)
6 rounds on points

After this defeat, Teddy took a break for three weeks in the South of France

16 NOVEMBER
Teddy Baldock vs. Billy Boulger
Three round exhibition
Location: Winter Gardens, Margate.

19 NOVEMBER
Teddy Baldock vs Billy Baldwin (London)
Three round exhibition in aid of the local branch of the British Legion
Location: The Drill Hall, Neath, South Wales

5 DECEMBER
Teddy Baldock vs. Len Fowler (Birmingham)
Won, KO 8th round
Location: Forest Gate Skating Rink, London

Trained at Hurstpierpoint
Sparring partner: Arthur Webb

On the same bill
Dod Oldfield (Leeds) beat Mark Lesnick (Mile End)
15 rounds on points
Jim Hocking (Canning Town) drew with Jimmy Thornton (Bethnal Green)
10 rounds

1928

16 JANUARY
Teddy Baldock vs. Francois Biron
Fight cancelled due to Baldock suffering from acute bronchitis
Location: The Ring, Blackfriars, London

Training at the RAF Depot Henlow, with Mike Honeyman, Kid Nicholson,
Jack Watts and Sammy King; also at Fred Dyer's gym, the Strand, London, with
George Rose

13 FEBRUARY
Teddy Baldock vs. Phil Lolosky (Aldgate)
Won, 15 rounds on points
Location: Forest Gate, London
Referee: Bombardier Billy Wells

Trained at Fred Dyer's gym, the Strand, London

On the same bill
Dod Oldfield (Leeds) beat Mark Lesnick (Mile End)
15 rounds on points
Tom Berry (Custom House) beat Harry Reeve (Plaistow)
15 rounds on points

Note: Baldock out of the ring due to trouble with his left hand damaged in the Fowler contest and also an operation to remove a piece of broken bone from the nose

8 MARCH
Daily Mirror reports Teddy Baldock underwent an operation on his nose to correct an injury sustained during the World title contest against Archie Bell

15 JULY
Teddy Baldock vs. Pierre Calloir (France)
Won, KO 4th round
Location: The Ring, Blackfriars, London

On the same bill
Jack Whitmore (Tottenham) beat Stan Edwards (Watford)
4th round stoppage
Donald Jones (Penygraig) beat George Peck (Stepney)
8th round stoppage
Seaman Badman (Chatham) beat Tony Palino (Spain)
KO 3rd round
Billy Reynolds (Dalston) beat Joe Young (Bethnal Green)
6 rounds on points
Billy Walker (Bethnal Green) beat Jerry Brunt (Welling)
12 rounds on points

6 AUGUST
Teddy Baldock vs. Bugler Harry Lake (Plymouth)
Won, 5th round, referee stopped fight
Location: Blackpool

On the same bill
Harry Crossley (Mexborough) beat Harry Robinson (Manchester)
15 rounds on points
Dod Oldfield beat Johnny Doherty
15 rounds on points

29 AUGUST
Teddy Baldock vs. Johnny Brown (St George's)
Won, 2nd round retired
Location: Clapton, London
Referee: Eugene Corri

Trained at Fox and Hound, Carshalton, also mentioned the Ex-Servicemen's Hut

Sparring partners: Billy Boulger (Canning Town), Nobby Clark (Poplar), Albert Jeal and Arthur Lloyd

On the same bill
Johnny Hill (Scotland) beat Newsboy Brown (Muscatine, IA, USA)
15 rounds on points
Johnny Curley (Lambeth) beat Sammy Shack (IA, USA)
Disqualification, 7th round
Alec Brooman (Camden Town) beat Bob Walker (Stratford)
KO 1st round
Sammy King (Poplar) beat Kid Baker (Bow)
6th round on points

8 OCTOBER

Teddy Baldock vs. Mick Hill (Tooting)
Won, 14th round, referee stopped fight
Location: The Ring, Blackfriars, London
Referee: Sam Russell

On the same bill
Billy Mack (Camberwell) beat Harry Vaughan (Croydon)
15th round stoppage
Jack Greenland (Chelsea) beat Jack Stratton (Holloway)
6 rounds on points
George Clarke (Kings Cross) drew with Bert Burrows (Camberwell)
6 rounds

25 OCTOBER

Teddy Baldock vs. Phil Lolosky (Aldgate)
Won, KO 3rd round
Location: Albert Hall, London
Referee: Matt Wells

On the same bill
Jack Hood (Birmingham) beat Bruno Frattini (Milan, Italy)
3rd round, retired by corner
Nel Tarleton (Liverpool) drew with Julian Verbist (Belgium)
10 rounds
Fred Webster (St Pancras) beat Charles Ernst (Paris, France)
12 rounds on points
Petit Biquet (Belgium) beat Bert Kirby (Birmingham)
8 rounds on points
Dod Oldfield (Birkenhead) beat Johnny Gibson (Bermondsey)
8 rounds on points
Jack Hyams (Stepney) drew with Francois Sybille (Belgium)
6 rounds

26 OCTOBER

Teddy Baldock was taken to Harley Street and after an examination was told that his left metacarpal was fractured in three places. The bone was removed by Dr Becker who returned to South Africa with it

1929

22 JANUARY

Teddy Baldock Initiated into the Freemasons, Cosmopolitan Lodge No. 917, Mark Masons Hall, 86 St James St, London SW1.

FEBRUARY

Teddy Baldock returned to the gym after the operation on his hand

30 JANUARY

Teddy Baldock vs. Billy Boulger

Three round Exhibition

Location: Corn Exchange, Cambridge.

21 MARCH

Teddy Baldock vs. Jerome Van Paemel (Belgium)

Won, 9th round, referee stopped fight

Location: Albert Hall, London

Referee: Matt Wells

On the same bill

Johnny Hill (Leith) beat Ernie Jarvis (Millwall)

15 rounds on points

Nipper Pat Daly (Marylebone) beat Nicholas Petit-Biquet (Belgium)

10 rounds on points

Fred Webster (St Pancras) drew with Jack Hyams (Stepney)

10 rounds

Jack Kirby (Birmingham) beat Kid Nicholson (Leeds)

6 rounds on points

Jack Negal (Bethnal Green) beat Kid Silver (St George's)

6 rounds on points

Charlie Smith (Deptford) beat Ted Sandwina (Sioux City, Iowa, USA)

Disqualification, 7th round

16 MAY

Teddy Baldock vs. Alf Kid Pattenden (Bethnal Green)

Won, 15 rounds on points

Location: Olympia, London

Trained at The Pelham Arms, Brighton, and Chinese Gardens with Harry Corbett, Fred Green (Blackfriars), Alf Mancini and Nel Tarleton

Sparring partners: George Davies (Kentish Town), Arthur Boddington (Wellingborough), Sammy King (Poplar)

Referee: P.J. Moss

On the same bill

Johnny Cuthbert (Sheffield) beat Harry Corbett (Bethnal Green)

15 rounds on points

Len Harvey (Plymouth) beat Alex Ireland (Leith)

KO 7th round

10 JUNE

Teddy Baldock vs. Sammy King

Three round exhibition

Location: National Sporting Club, London

18 JUNE

Teddy Baldock at Carshalton assisting Harry Fenn in his training for his contest with Fred Webster (British lightweight champion)

6 JULY

Teddy Baldock vs Jim Hocking

Exhibition at the annual Pinner Fete.

Also present were Phil Scott, Dick Smith and Pat O'Keefe

5 AUGUST

Teddy Baldock vs. Gideon Potteau (Belgium)

Won, 11th round retired

Location: Blackpool Football Ground

On the same bill

Jack Ellis (Todmorden) beat Sammy King (Poplar)

15 rounds on points

Nipper Pat Daly (Marylebone) beat Tommy Rose (Bolton)

KO 3rd round

Fred Cookson (Oldham) beat Fred Chandler (London)

12 rounds on points

6 AUGUST

Teddy Baldock vs. Sammy King

Six Round Exhibition

Location: New Market Boxing Stadium, Market Street, Burnley

27 AUGUST

Teddy Baldock left Southampton on the *Leviathan* for New York after forgetting his passport. Other passengers included: boxer Archie Sexton (father of Dave, former West Ham United player and Manchester United and Chelsea manager) Jack Harris, Packey O'Gatty and Sir Thomas Lipton

2 SEPTEMBER

Teddy Baldock arrived in America on the *Leviathan* to fight Al Brown

Trained at Gus Wilson's training camp, Orangeburg, New Jersey; also in the camp were Vittorio Campolo, who was training to fight Phil Scott, and Jack Sharkey, preparing for his fight with Tommy Loughran

25 SEPTEMBER
Teddy Baldock departed America on the *Mauretania* after his World title contest with Al Brown falls through.

1 OCTOBER
Teddy Baldock arrives in Plymouth on the *Mauretania*

1930

22 JANUARY
Teddy Baldock vs. Emile Pladner (Clermont-Ferrand, France)
Won, on a foul 6th round
Location: Albert Hall, London
Referee: Matt Wells

Trained at Jolly Jumbo's pub, Brighton
Sparring partners: Sid Raiteri and Jim Briley; Jack Lakey was ill so Alec Goodman superintended training

On the same bill
Dick Corbett (Bethnal Green) beat Wyndham Blake (Wales)
Retired 7th round, towel thrown in
Roberto Roberti (Sorbano del Giudice, Italy) beat Maurice Griselle (France)
12 rounds on points
Young Bill Lewis (Bethnal Green) beat Kid Socks (Bethnal Green)
6 rounds on points
Jack Walters (Eltham) beat Jack Greenland (Chelsea)
4 rounds on points
Harry Droy (Islington) beat Bobby Jones (Hoxton)
3rd-round stoppage

Jerry Daley (Penycraig) drew with Stan Waller (Cambridge)
4 rounds

1 FEBRUARY
Teddy Baldock vs. Harry Mason
Three round exhibition
Location Alexandra Palace, Musswell Hill

20 FEBRUARY
Teddy Baldock vs. Jim Briley
Three round exhibition
Location: Manor Place Baths, Walworth

6 MARCH
Teddy Baldock vs. Charlie Rowbotham (Birmingham)
Won, 11th round, referee stopped fight
Location: Ilford Skating Rink, London
Promoter: Bill Glass

Mickey Doyle and Lew Pinkus both challenged Baldock from the ring

On the same bill
Young Franks (Stepney) beat Charlie Webb (Bow)
15 rounds on points
Joe Gavin (Bethnal Green) beat Billy Lowe (Custom House)
10 rounds on points

3 APRIL
Teddy Baldock vs. Lew Pinkus (Mile End)
15 rounds on points
Location: Ilford, London

On the same bill

Moe Mizler (St George's) drew with Dod Oldfield (Leeds)

15 rounds

Charlie Webb (Bow) beat Steve Merritt (Silvertown)

Retired 13th round, towel thrown in

Curly Merritt (Silvertown) beat Fred Chandler (Canning Town)

Retired 8th round

Jimmy Taylor (St James) beat Fred Patten (Canning Town)

10 rounds on points

5 JULY

Teddy Baldock vs. Jimmy Docherty (Scotland)

Won, KO 6th round

Location: Norwich Football Club's ground

MC: Patsy Hagate

Promoter: Capt A.J. Prince-Cox

On the same bill

Billy Edmunds (Coventry) beat Ernie Bicknell (Doncaster)

15 rounds on points

Jack Scott (Derby) beat Johnny Allen (Bermondsey)

11th round cut, referee stopped fight

Young Hawes (Norwich) drew with Bobby Jones (London)

8 rounds

Nipper Fred Morris (London) beat Nipper Joe Winch (Dagenham)

2nd round, referee stopped fight

1 SEPTEMBER

Teddy Baldock vs. Benny Sharkey (Newcastle)

Lost, 15 rounds on points

Location: New St James's Hall, Newcastle

Referee: Harry Jennings (Bradford)

Weigh-in: New St James's Hall

On the same bill
Billy Graham (Teams) drew with Walter Wright (Huddersfield)
15 rounds, referee stopped fight
Bob Lamb (Sunderland) beat George Meakin (Newcastle)
10 rounds
Eddie O'Keefe beat Billy Lyle (Swalwell)
6 rounds on points

26 NOVEMBER
Teddy Baldock vs. Harry Wragg (Jockey)
Three round exhibition
Location: The Stadium Club, Holborn, London

7 DECEMBER
Teddy Baldock vs. Alf Kid Pattenden (Bethnal Green)
Won, 15 rounds on points
Location: The Ring, Blackfriars, London

On the same bill
Jack Stone (Deptford) drew with Jack Stratton (Highbury)
12 rounds
Willie Baker (Paddington) beat Joe Blake (Hammersmith)
12 rounds on points
Jim Lawrence (Bermondsey) beat Sid Lloyd (Camberwell)
6 rounds on points

1931

12 FEBRUARY
Teddy Baldock and Miss Maisie McCrae were married at All Saints Church, Poplar

26 MARCH
Teddy Baldock vs. Gideon Potteau (Belgium)
Won, KO 2nd round
Location: East Ham Skating Rink, London
(Al Brown present at ringside)

Trained in Poplar
Sparring partners: Alf McBride and Harry Daniels (Stepney)

On the same bill
Pat Bransfield (Ireland) beat Jerry Sands (Lambeth)
12 rounds on points
Roy Robbins (Bethnal Green) beat Sid Lloyd (Camberwell)
12 rounds on points
Dave Lee (Camberwell) beat Dave Morbin (Walworth)
6 rounds on points
Nipper Fred Morris (Stepney) beat Charley Shorey (Islington)
6 rounds on points

28 APRIL
Teddy Baldock heads for his training camp at the Star and Garter Hotel, Windsor; Len Harvey also there for his fight with Rene Devos at the Albert Hall, 1st June

30 APRIL
Teddy Baldock vs. Terence Morgan (Newport)
Won, 15 rounds on points

Location: The Ring, Blackfriars, London
Referee: Matt Wells

On the same bill
Jimmy Lindsey (Fulham) beat Glen Jones (Bishop's Stortford)
Retired 10th round
Alf Noble (Bermondsey) beat Jim Monk (Wormley)
KO 1st round
Nipper Morris (St George's) beat Bertie Brooks (Stratford)
6 rounds on points,
Dick Pinder (Canning Town) beat Tommy Daniels (Stepney)
6 rounds on points

10 MAY
Teddy Baldock knocked out his sparring partner Jimmy Wheeler (Bermondsey)

11 MAY
Teddy Baldock vs. Jimmy Wheeler
One round exhibition
Teddy Baldock vs. Les Burns
Two round exhibition
Location: National Sporting Club, London

13 MAY
Teddy Baldock in training at Windsor boxed four rounds with Billy Boulger (Canning Town) and Les Burns (Bowes Park) and two rounds with Terence Morgan (Wales)

20 MAY
Teddy Baldock vs. Al Brown (Panama)
Lost, 12th round, referee stopped fight
Location: Olympia, London
Referee: Owen Moran
Weigh-in: NSC

Trained at the Star and Garter, Windsor

Sparring partners: Terence Morgan, Jimmy Wheeler, Les Burns and Billy Boulger

On the same bill

Nel Tarleton (Liverpool) beat Jack Garland (Ireland)

12 rounds on points

Eddie Phillips (Mile End) beat Tony Arpino (Bedford)

KO 4th round

Tommy Toner (Newcastle) beat Don Shortland (Sheffield)

12 rounds on points

Jack Pettifer (Kings Cross) beat Desmond Jeans (Mayfair)

5th round stoppage

Harry Connolly (Highbury) beat Moe Mizler (St George's)

6 rounds on points

Teddy Berg (Stepney) beat Charlie Jordan (Brixton)

6 rounds on points

Note: Baldock visited a specialist for treatment to his left eye damaged during the fight

7 SEPTEMBER

Teddy Baldock vs. Dick Corbett (Bethnal Green)

Lost, 12 rounds on points

Location: Clapton, London

Referee: Moss Deyong

Trained at The Packhorse, Staines

Sparring partners: Billy Boulger and Les Burns

On the same bill

Dave Crowley (Clerkenwell) beat George Marsden (Nottingham)

4th round stoppage

Tommy Hyams (Kings Cross) drew with Kid Farlo (Mile End)
8 rounds on points
Tommy John (Pentre) beat Seaman Barry (Chatham)
8 rounds on points
Nipper Morris (St George's) beat Kid Glass
4 rounds on points
Harry Fox beat Young Kirkland (Bethnal Green)
6 rounds on points

8 SEPTEMBER

Teddy Baldock announces his retirement from the ring

1933

---

28 MAY

Teddy Baldock v Billy Reynolds
Four round exhibition Speedway Stadium, Lea Bridge
On the same bill
Jack Kid Berg beat Louis Saerens
KO 4th round
Charlie Baxter beat Moe Moss
10th round referee stopped fight
Reg Perkins beat Leo Wax
6 rounds on points
Kid Farlo beat Peter Nolan
4th round disqualified
Fred Nipper Morris beat Harry Paulding
6 rounds on points

8 MARCH 1971

Teddy Baldock died at Rochford Infirmary, Southend

BIBLIOGRAPHY

Batchelor, D. (1953) *Best Boxing Stories* Faber

Batchelor, D. (1964) *The Boxing Companion* Eyre & Spottiswoode

Butler, F. (1972) *History of Boxing in Britain* A. Barker

Corri, E. (1928) *Gloves & the Man: The Romance of the Ring* Hutchinson

Goleworthy, M. (1960) *The Encyclopaedia of Boxing* Robert Hale & Company

Hails, J. (1989) *Classic Moments of Boxing* Moorland Publishing Company

Harding, J. (1998) *Lonsdale's Belt: Story of Boxing's Greatest Prize* Robson Books Ltd

Hauser, T. & Brunt, S. (2004) *The Italian Stallions: Heroes of Boxing's Glory Days* Sport Media Publishing

Leigh-Lye, T. (1971) *Century of Great Boxing Drama* Mayflower

McGhee, F. (1988) *England's Boxing Heroes* Bloomsbury

Mullan, H. (1990) *Heroes and Hard Men: Story of Britain's World Boxing Champions* Hutchinson

Mullan, H. (1992) *Boxing Companion* W.H. Smith

Mullan, A. & Mee, B. (2008) *The Ultimate Encyclopaedia of Boxing* Carlton Books Ltd

Myler, P. (1999) *Boxing Greats: Inside the Ring with the Hundred Best Boxers* Robson Books Ltd

Odd, G.E. (ed) (1949) *Ring Battles of the Century* Nicholson & Watson

Odd, G.E. (1974) *Boxing: Cruisers to Mighty Atoms (Great Moments in Sport)* Pelham Books

JOURNALS/NEWSPAPERS

All Sports Weekly
Athletic News
Boxing
Boxing, Racing and Football (Incorporating 'Dog Racing')
Boxing and Racing
Daily Chronicle
Daily Herald
Daily Express
Daily Journal
Daily Mail
Daily Mirror
Daily News
Daily Sketch
Daily Telegraph
Daily Worker
East End News
East London Advertiser
Evening News
Graphic
Illustrated Sporting and Dramatic News
Newham Recorder
News of the World
The Evening Standard
The Field
The People
The Times
The Sporting Life
The Sporting Life and Sportsman
The Sportsman
The Standard
The Star

The Sunday Express
Topical Times
Sporting Chronicle
Stratford Express
Sunday Mirror
Sunday Pictorial
Sports Times
Westminster Gazette

WEBSITES

www.teddybaldock.co.uk

Boxrec Boxing Encyclopaedia

The History of Pre-War Boxing in Britain, www.prewarboxing.co.uk

Jackson, R. (19 January 2004) *Champ from the Orphanage* (Article from: www.superboxing.co.za)

Archives, etc.
British Library
British Library Newspapers
British Pathe
Guildhall Library
Numerous Boxing Programmes from 1920 to 1935

EPILOGUE

By Martin Sax

Since the publication of my grandfather's life story and subsequent book launch held in the West End of London, which, for my mother Pam and I remains a proud day and one that we shall certainly never forget, I have continued researching my grandfather's life in the hope of finding reports of unrecorded contests from my grandfather's early ring career. I have also created a website dedicated to his professional boxing career (www.teddybaldock.co.uk), set up a charity to assist people severely injured whilst competing in sport (The Teddy Baldock Sports Benevolent Fund) and am in the final stages of having his achievements commemorated in the form of a life size bronze statue being erected in Poplar, East London.

When asked to write the epilogue for this book, I decided to concentrate on my grandfather's second trip to America to face Panama Al Brown for the World bantamweight Championship, it could have been a career defining moment, but instead resulted in my grandfather returning to Britain, disillusioned and extremely disappointed, his chance of making his name in America and cementing his claim to the World Title had gone.

'To reach what you consider to be the very pinnacle of fame and then in a night discover that you are but one of a crowd is the most awful experience a pugilist, whether old or young, may have,' George Carpentier, World lightheavyweight Champion

Teddy's sensational collapse against Willie Smith had, without doubt cost him a lucrative contest with Bud Taylor, but had also taught him a cruel lesson, that he was not unbeatable. His uninterrupted success, the jumping from one victory to another, may have given him an exaggerated idea of his fighting worth.

If Baldock had beaten Smith the probability would have been an immediate visit by him to the United States. And he would have without doubt, gone to America with the feeling that he was invincible, instead of having been taught, as he was at the Albert Hall, that his ring education was far from complete. Hence it would be another two years before he would venture to America with the belief that he could defeat the great Panama Al Brown to become the undisputed bantamweight champion of the world.

As Teddy boarded the Leviathan for his second trip to America he turned to the waiting press reporters and declared, 'I shall train as well as I know how and I shall fight my very best and remember when I get into the ring that I am fighting as much for British boxing as for myself'.

Although Teddy's manager, Joe Morris and trainer Jack Lakey had sailed a few days previously on the Mauretania, his preparation for the championship match with Brown was not hampered. It was arranged that Jack Harris and Archie Sexton would travel with Baldock to assist with training and sparring, but perhaps the most important addition to the group was the ship's Physical Training Instructor, Packey O'Gatty. O'Gatty was an experienced bantamweight, his contest with Frank Burns at Boyle's Thirty Acres, Jersey City, on the undercard of the Heavyweight championship contest between Jack Dempsey and George Carpentier, was deemed to be the first sports radio broadcast in America. As number one contender, he had also challenged the great bantamweight champion Pete Herman for the title, but was knocked out in the first round.

O'Gatty took on the role as trainer with relish, he knew Al Brown and some of his fighting methods, so with Teddy's interests at heart, he put him through his paces on a daily basis, both in the gymnasium and in the ring that had been erected on the upper deck.

One of the ship's passengers who took a keen interest in the training sessions was Sir Thomas Lipton, he would often chat with Teddy about his fights in England and the proposed championship contest with Brown.

Teddy had enjoyed his transit to the US on the Leviathan and his training had gone well. Packey O'Gatty had been so impressed with the Englishman's ring-craft that he took time to write to his friend and boxing celebrity, none other than the legendary Jack Dempsey former heavyweight champion of the world. The first Teddy knew of this was when a letter addressed to him arrived at his Orangeburg training quarters. The letter started 'Packey O'Gatty has written to me saying what a clever kid you are, and if Packey says that you must be the real goods'. Dempsey went on to explain that he was busy film making in Los Angeles but intended to travel the 3,000 miles to New York to watch the contest with Brown and if possible, beforehand, visit Orangeburg to watch the young Londoner train.

There was a great crowd waiting to greet the British champion as he arrived in New York, but there was little time to waste on greeting his American admirers. Teddy had a short break in the city before travelling to Gus Wilson's Orangeburg training camp. The fresh air suited him and under the supervision of Wilson who had in the past handled such great fighters as Jack Dempsey, George Carpentier and Mickey Walker, it wasn't long before he was in the peak of condition and ready for the biggest fight of his career and the chance to make a name for himself in America.

This was reflected in a letter he wrote to Peggy Cummings, a close family friend to the Baldocks, it began;

Dear Mrs Cummings

Just a few lines from innocent little Teddy Baldock who is still thinking of East 4 although he's nearly 4,000 miles away. So sorry I couldn't come round to your place before I left but never mind will pop in as soon as I get back.

Had a pretty decent trip across after me missing the first boat.

Well Mr Cummings I have got the biggest task of my career and have taken a 100–1 chance in boxing my opponent in his own country, anyhow will do my best and really I am only out for what I can get as I don't intend to box all my life.

How's Peggy and Jack, alright I hope, honestly Mr Cummings I respect both very much, and I think Jack is one of the best and most unassuming chaps I ever met.

Tell Dee he could buy a car here for about fourpence with a "billiard" table thrown in.

Am training in a Wonderful spot 35 miles outside New York and by the time I fight shall be in Wonderful condition.

I don't suppose I shall stay here long as it is costing me £50 a week for myself and two sparring partners, things are terribly dear.

There's a heat wave on at present and every body is walking about in thin little white singlets so you can bet I am doing the same. Will send you a snap you'll laugh when you see it.

Mr Cummings let me know all the news or get Peggy to write and you can be sure of it being answered so with Kind Regards to all and my Best Respects to you.

Yours sincerely
Teddy Baldock

Teddy was just rounding off his training for the night and was beginning to count down the hours before he would be stepping out in front of the thirty thousand, capacity crowd at Ebbets Field Stadium, when he learned that the fight date had been rescheduled for 2 October. He was naturally disappointed and blamed Brown, 'Why did he go from Copenhagen to Paris? And why did he stay in Paris as he did? Of course he had no time to train. He came to America knowing that he had only to say the word and the fight would be postponed'.

Baldock was keyed up and irritable as most fighters are before a contest, his diet, roadwork and sparring had all been carefully planned so that he would be at the peak of physical condition for 17 September. 'To all intents and purposes the failure of Al Brown to sail for America from Europe on the appointed date has meant that I have been forced to begin training all over again, and for the most important match of my life'.

Teddy was only too aware of what his prospects would be if he were to beat Brown. Jess McMahon, his American promoter had already prepared a very ambitious and lucrative programme, including a match with Kid Chocolate, but it was all dependant on the result of this next contest.

Joe Morris engaged the services of an American featherweight, Willie McMichael, to assist Baldock in his training. Jack Sharkey, who would become the World heavyweight champion in 1932 and Iowa heavyweight 'Tuffy' Griffiths, also provided the Poplar youth with a number of rounds of useful sparring, although both naturally pulled their punches during the sessions in the open air ring.

Although disappointed about the postponement, Teddy was positive and still confident of beating Brown, but his quest for a World title crumbled when the Panamanian's manager demanded a second postponement, claiming that his fighter was suffering from neuritis (Inflammation of a nerve, characterized by pain and loss of reflexes). Joe Morris was unwilling to agree to the fight being delayed by another two weeks and booked a return passage on the Mauretania.

Baldock was devastated, 'I'm as unhappy about my affairs as any boxer could be, for I have been deprived of what I consider is my right to the World's Championship, and I shall not forget it. I blame Brown'.

It had already been rumoured in the British press that the fight might not take place. Only a few days after Teddy had departed England for America, Al Brown was telling reporters in Paris that he was willing to fight Baldock or any other man at the weight but a bantamweight World title match in New York on 17 September would not be possible. He justified these comments by stating that after defending his title in Copenhagen against Knud Larsen he was entitled to six months rest before defending the title again. As Baldock rightly pointed out, the contest with Larsen was in fact made well above the bantamweight limit, so his title could not have been at stake. This gave little credence to the Panamanian's argument.

Teddy was totally disillusioned with the American fight scene, but his mood was lifted a couple of days before he boarded the Maurentania. The English heavyweight Phil Scott was facing the Argentine, Vittorio Campolo and the Baldock camp had been invited to join Sir Thomas Lipton as guests at ringside, along with Jimmy Wilde, Jack kid Berg and Archie Sexton. During Teddy's preparation for the Brown contest, Campolo had taken up quarters at the Orangeburg training camp so the Londoner decided to pay particular attention to his tactics and training methods. He noticed that he lacked a decent left hand and possessed little in the way of defence, although exhibited a devastating right.

Teddy compiled a game plan and knew that if his English compatriot stuck to it, he would have a good chance of beating the Argentine. During a training session, he took the opportunity of talking to Scott about the contest and advised him on how he should fight Campolo.

From the opening bell, Scott started the round nervously and was driven into the ropes by Campolo, Arthur Donovan, the referee separated the pair but the Argentine immediately charged in and caught Scott with a vicious right, he was hurt, but weathered the storm. The only consolation for the British contingent at ringside was that Phil had survived the first round. His confidence returned in the second and he went on to win a decisive points victory. In Teddy's words, 'I have never seen a boxer given such a thorough lesson as was Campolo.'

Before leaving America, Teddy, his manager Joe Morris, Mr Charles Donmall, secretary of the British Boxing Board of Control and the American promoter, Jess MacMahon had a long conference, at the end of which a contract was signed, by which Baldock agreed to return to America to fight Kid Chocolate, at featherweight, between 15 November and 18 December. Each Boxer would deposit £500, Chocolate with the British Boxing Board of Control and Baldock with the New York State Athletic Commission, the fight to be held at the New York Colliseum. Because of the complexities of the sport and how a fighter's future can be determined by the result of his next contest, the fight with Chocolate never took place. Kid Chocolate went on to become World junior lightweight champion and World featherweight champion (only recognised by the New York State Athletic Commission). His final accolade was being voted in as a member of the International Boxing Hall Of Fame.

Teddy Baldock did finally meet Al Brown at Olympia on 20 May, 1931 at Olympia. He was already in the twilight of his career and was stopped for the first time, as the press reported, 'The Baldock we saw last night was not the Teddy Baldock of a year or so ago. He was apprehensive from the start, he was much slower of movement than formerly, and there was none of that pouncing aggressiveness that first brought the Londoner to prominence.'

Could my grandfather have beaten Al Brown if they had met at Ebbets Field Stadium, New York in 1929? Who knows, it would certainly have been a hard task, but no result in the sport of boxing can be predetermined. Sometimes a fighter's success and destiny is dependent on what stage he is at in his career and the same can be said for his opponent. My grandfather was probably just past his best, after his gruelling contest with Alf Kid Pattenden. However it may have been the perfect time to face Brown, his fight against Knud Larsen had been made above the bantamweight limit and he was certainly not in the peak of condition after the Atlantic crossing. Whatever the result, I doubt whether it would have influenced the latter stages of his life; it would however have added another interesting chapter to the life of The Pride of Poplar.